Charles Schwab

Charles Schwab

How One Company Beat Wall Street and Reinvented the Brokerage Industry

John Kador

John Wiley & Sons

Published by John Wiley & Sons, Inc., Hoboken, New Jersey.
Published simultaneously in Canada.

For general information on our other products and services, or technical support, please contact our Customer Care Department within the United States at
800-762-2974, outside the United States at 317-572-3993 or fax 317-572-4002.

Wiley also publishes its books in a variety of electronic formats. Some content
that appears in print may not be available in electronic books.

Library of Congress Cataloging-in-Publication Data:
Kador, John.
    Charles Schwab : how one company beat wall street and
  reinvented the brokerage industry / John Kador.
      p. cm.
   ISBN 0-471-22407-3 (hc : alk. paper)
    1. Charles Schwab Corporation—History. 2. Stockbrokers—
New York (State)—New York—History. 3. Schwab, Charles.
I. Title.
HG4928.5 .K336 2002
332.6′2—dc21   2002010446

Printed in the United States of America

10 9 8 7 6 5 4 3 2 1

To the men and women of the Schwab family
whose fierce loyalty to Chuck is surpassed
only by their commitment to the truth

First, they ignore you.
Then they laugh at you.
Then they fight you.
Then you win.

Mahatma Gandhi

CONTENTS

Introduction   1

Part One   Leveling the Playing Field   11

Chapter 1   May Day   13
Chapter 2   Opening Investment   27
Chapter 3   Building the Brand   47
Chapter 4   Innovation   63
Chapter 5   Branchland   75
Chapter 6   Advice and Advisors   98

Part Two   Profiles in Crisis   111

Chapter 7   Forsaken IPO   113
Chapter 8   Birthright   123
Chapter 9   Market Crash   144
Chapter 10   Margin Call   160
Chapter 11   Earthquake   171
Chapter 12   OneSource   182
Chapter 13   Heart Attack   191
Chapter 14   eSchwab   209

Part Three   Custodian of Uneasy Dreams   225

Chapter 15   Balance of Power   227
Chapter 16   Schwab Mythology   242

Chapter 17   Unfinished Business   251
Epilogue   Schwab Account   269

Appendix 1   Charles Schwab & Co. Timeline   273
Appendix 2   Charles R. Schwab's Employment
              Agreement   279
Source Notes   293
Bibliography   307
Index   313

ACKNOWLEDGMENTS

I t is a paradox that those who most deserve acknowledgment have the least need for it. I am literally indebted to more people than I can name. In the case of this book, a number of people who have been monumentally helpful have asked for no acknowledgment at all. To everyone who decided to help me with no other expectation than I would weave their individual experiences anonymously into the tapestry of this account, I offer my heartfelt thanks. I wish circumstances permitted you to be named individually.

I am also proud to acknowledge the following former Schwab employees who generously shared their stories, answered my incessant questions, and agreed to be quoted on the record: Ambre Abbott, Sheri Anderson, Rhet Andrews, Niel Armstrong, Mark Barmann, Dan Bass, Alison Bomar, Bruce Cardinal, Dennis Clark, Mark Collier, Barbara Daniels, Alan Diener, Ed Ferland, Roger Franklin, Jim Fuller, John Gambs, Bill Gillis, John Granholm, Marc Greendorfer, Robert Grosskopf, Genene Hamel, Ward Harris, Barbara Heinrich, Anne Hennegar, Christine Herbert, Sean Howard, Mark King, Bill Klipp, Ron Kloth, Ron Lay, Kathy Levinson, Jim Losi, Lisa Mak, Timothy McCarthy, Casey McClintock, Joseph McComb, Melinda Meahan, Madalyn Mitchell, Lauri Moss, Peter Moss, Dan Neumann, Phillip Parkerson, Bill Pearson, Earlene Perry, Chip Roame, Kevin Rogers, Robert Rosseau, Harvey Rowen, Bob Ruggieri, Tom Seip, Daniel

Sheehan, Jim Skinner, Larry Stupski, Tom Taggart, Robert Tantalo, Blodwen Tarter, Barry Uhl, Thomas Voltz, Kevin Wheeler, Jim Wiggett, Michelle Wolpe, Sherman Yee, Mansoor Zakaria. My thanks go, also, to the few former Schwab employees who asked that their only acknowledgment be the satisfaction of knowing they were a resource to the author.

I am indebted to a number of professionals who took time from their busy schedules to educate me about various aspects of the securities industry in which Schwab and its executives continue to play such a key part. I am pleased to acknowledge: Devanie Anderson, Tony Bianco, Moira Johnston Block, John Bowen, Daniel Burke, Tim Butler, Amy Butte, Mark Calvey, Dale Carlson, Benjamin Cole, Joe Cutcliffe, Harold Evensky, Jon Friedman, Jamie Dimon, Andrew Gluck, Warren Hellman, Ken Greenberg, Sam Jaffe, Sheldon Jacobs, Andrew Kahr, John Keefe, Lee Korins, Carolyn Leighton, Bob Levy, Dan Livingston, Leo Melamed, Scott MacKillop, John McGuinn, Mike McGreevy, Stephen McLin, Guy Moszkowski, Paul Merriman, Deborah Naish, Terry Pearce, Lori Perlstadt, Richard Repetto, Terry Savage, Pamela Sayad, Lewis Schiff, Amey Stone, Taylor McMaster, Lynn Upshaw, Alan Weber, Barry Young.

It is my pleasure to thank my agent, Susan Barry of the Swayne Agency, for helping me at every stage of this project, and Jeanne Glasser of John Wiley & Sons for providing a firm guiding hand.

Every writer, if he or she is lucky, gets the benefit of family members who provide more support than his or her desperate attempts at acknowledgement can repay. So it is in my case. I can only note here the patience and understanding demonstrated by my wife, Anna Beth Payne, my children, Daniel and Rachel, my brothers, Peter and Robert, and my parents Julius and Marianne, all of whom gave various chapters the benefit of their wisdom.

John Kador
jkador@jkador.com

Charles Schwab

In the beginning when investors were at the mercy of stock-brokers, financial self-determination, like airplane travel, was reserved for the well-off. Then Charles Schwab beat Wall Street and reinvented the brokerage industry. Now Charles Schwab & Co., Inc. continues to liberate the world of personal finance and we are all, rich and poor, better off for it.

This book narrates the evolution of Charles Schwab & Co. from a pure discount brokerage through four wrenching up-heavals. But while upheaval can be instructive and, when it happens to others, even entertaining, it is not the main focus of the story. The true subject is Schwab's organizational elasticity and how it is able to reinvent itself around a fixed set of core values. This value-based strategy has allowed Schwab to evolve within its industry. Many companies spout off about values. In reality, Schwab is one of a handful of companies that has actually capitalized on this approach.

Charles Schwab & Co. is the epitome of the anti-Enron company. In three decades, Schwab has emerged as one of the most inspired and inspiring financial services organizations in history. Thanks primarily to the values and leadership of its founder, Charles R. Schwab, the company has evolved a distinctive values-driven management mindset that encourages the company to put the interests of its customers first. This priority allows the company to question its most cherished assumptions

1

and thereby avoid the arrogance that hardens the arteries of other companies that are occasionally kissed by success.

Like all values, Schwab's values are easy to list but are more difficult to honor in practice, and lately they have come to conflict with other values. Emerging as an alternative against the excesses of the traditional securities brokerage industry, Schwab developed a transcendent set of goals to which individual egos could be willingly subordinated. All Schwab employees sign on to the value of serving the average, individual investor by conformity to a few non-negotiable values:

SCHWAB'S TRANSCENDENT VALUES

Core Value	*Implication*
No conflict of interest	Schwab people will be paid salaries instead of sales commissions.
No advice	Schwab customers are sophisticated traders. Schwab will not recommend individual securities.
No sales	Schwab will not push individual products. It will avoid proprietary products. "Call us because no Schwab sales person will ever call you."
Customers first	Empowering. Working from the customer in, rather than existing processes out. Identify what customers want and only then determine if you can supply the requirement at a profit.

From the very beginning, Charles Schwab has put himself squarely in the bulls-eye of this journey. His name is on the building. His face adorns the ads. Customers may do business with any of the thousands of Schwab people around the world, but Chuck—please, not Charles—is their broker.

What is in the company's DNA that has allowed it to succeed in so many harsh environments? What permitted a discount brokerage to give up $9 million in fees to offer the No-Annual-Fee IRA just because it seemed right? What made it think success would derive from slashing prices by 60 percent to enter the uncertain world of electronic trading? What made it think the Web would be a friend and not a foe? The company pivots freely around a set of standards that emerge out of its values. Everything else can change, but these standards endure:

Create a Cause, Not a Business. "We are custodians of our customers' financial dreams." Think about that. When was the last time you saw a business take itself that seriously? It shows. Schwab people act as if they are curing cancer.

It's easier to find the courage to abandon the practices that have been making you rich when everyone shares a transcendent purpose. The values serve as a safety net for the high-wire act. Sharing a cause provides cover for anyone poised to discard a familiar but tattered business model for a lustrous but untested business proposition. Schwab welcomes questions elsewhere considered subversive: *Who are we serving by this decision? Will my skills and my relationships be as valuable in this new world as they were in the old? How much will I be asked to unlearn?*

These are genuine, heartfelt questions that can't be answered in advance. The courage to leave some of oneself behind and strike off for parts unknown comes not from some banal assurance that change is good but from a devotion to a wholly worthwhile cause.

The Power of Culture, Done Right. Lots of companies pay lip service to a culture of ethics and values. Schwab people actually live it, for they know that a corporate vision may come and go, but the values stay put. In a world that blurs the distinctions between customers and suppliers and competitors and partners, values are the only thing that defines where Schwab, the company, starts and where it ends. Everything else can recede—the products, the services, the industry itself—but an abiding culture can serve as the custodian of dreams for the team.

Welcome Upheaval. Everybody talks about the power of new ideas, until a new idea actually requires them to change their behavior. Then stability suddenly looks attractive. How on earth did Schwab find the chutzpah to migrate its business to the Web, knowing that the move would force it to cut by more than half the prices on its bread-and-butter service? By adhering to its culture of core values. People up and down the organization who agreed on little else agreed on the value of putting the customer first. How would your company react to a similar proposition? Typical is how Merrill Lynch confronted the same problem: It denied. And then after it denied, it debated. And after it debated, it fiddled at the margins of the problem until Schwab took over. How did Schwab avoid months, perhaps years, of savage debate? What can Schwab teach us about welcoming the specter of cannibalization?

Success Is a By-Product of Something More Important. Schwab executives understand that you don't aim at success. For success, like happiness, cannot be pursued; it must ensue, and it only does so as the unintended side effect of a company's commitment to a cause. Serving customers fairly and honorably is that cause. Products and services at Schwab are developed because customers indicate a need for them. Only then does the company try to figure out if it can deliver the product or service at a profit. Grant Tinker, former head of NBC, was asked how he planned to make the network number one. His answer applies to Schwab: "First we will be best, and then we will be first."

Schwab has made its share of mistakes, and this book documents many of them. But it would be a bigger mistake to regard these reports as an attack on the company's integrity. That remains remarkably constant. It's probably true that Schwab makes fewer mistakes than other companies of its size. The quick pace of its decision-making process, ironically, works to minimize the number of significant mistakes. When a company is guided by a simple set of well-known principles, it compresses the cycle for making decisions, recognizing mistakes, and correcting them. Paying steady attention to integrity is the force that guarantees consistent performance.

Yes, there is a moralistic streak about the company that some consider off-putting. To be sure, Schwab grew out of the founder's righteous indignation over the corruption and cynicism of the brokerage industry and its systematic swindling of the average investor. As a consequence, the story the company tells about itself is not just that it is more efficient than its competitors. No, Schwab people believe that Schwab is on a mission to provide investors with the most useful and ethical brokerage services in the world. It is not just better operationally, it is better morally. Schwab, in this estimation, represents virtue. The downside is that this attitude reinforces a toxic "us versus them" consciousness that takes its toll on employees at all levels of the organization.

Schwab is on a crusade. Schwab people are not just running a brokerage. They pursue virtue. It's a cause that grounds the effort in goodness. It provides a feeling of belonging, a sense of purpose, and a catalyst for action. People will work hard for money, but will give their lives for meaning. Henry James described the task of working for a cause in which you truly believe: "We work in the dark—and we do what we can—we give what we have. Our doubt is our passion and our passion is our task." So it is at Schwab. Even a big setback, and 2001–2002 represented a huge period of doubt for the company, can't dim the manifest personal pride that Schwab people, current and former employees alike, have in what they accomplished. This is their story.

Schwab has reinvented itself three times. It is currently in the midst of its fourth transformation. "Leveling the Playing Field," Part One of this book, describes the original version of the company and the men and women who helped build it.

Schwab version 1.0 was the pure discount brokerage made possible by the deregulation of brokerage commissions on May

1, 1975, a date known in the history of the securities industry as "May Day." Chapter 1, "May Day," describes the cynical and corrupt securities industry from which Schwab emerged. Then in 1975, when he was 38 years old, Chuck (as he prefers to be called) awoke one day to realize that May Day created the conditions to start a brokerage for people like himself: savvy traders who neither needed nor wanted advice. It would be a brokerage for the rest of us.

Chapter 2, "Opening Investment," looks at the life and career of Chuck Schwab, the founder of the company, and how his moral vision inspired the firm's moral authority. Chapter 3, "Building the Brand," considers the early struggles and triumphs of the company as it systematically constructed its reputation.

Schwab has always been a technology-driven company. Chapter 4, "Innovation," describes Schwab's commitment to an innovation meritocracy in which great ideas win out, no matter where they come from. Schwab is a rule-breaker. From day one it has trespassed on respected boundaries. Discount brokerages, everyone knew, were supposed to do away with frills like branches so they could offer lower commissions. So what did Schwab do? It built an international network of branches—430 at this writing. "Branchland," Chapter 5, examines the history and culture of Schwab's branch and call center facilities.

For most of its first decade in business, Schwab focused on executing transactions efficiently. Trading commissions comprised most of the company's revenues into the 1990s. This situation was less than desirable because the cyclicality of trading volumes made growth unpredictable. The company needed new sources of revenue. At the same time, the customers Schwab served were beginning to change. Thanks partly to Schwab's services, they were wealthier and their portfolios were becoming too complex for them to manage. They needed advice and they asked Schwab to provide it. Now Schwab's aversion to advice came into apparent conflict with its commitment to giving customers what they wanted. Chapter 6, "Advice and Advisors," tells how Schwab challenged one of its most deeply held beliefs and started creating advice offerings that were true to its values.

Schwab version 2.0 emerged in the 1980s as it transformed itself into an asset gatherer. As the business model shifted from transaction fees to the benefits of having millions and then billions of customer dollars under management, Schwab diversified its product offerings with mutual funds and institutional services. It became intentional in serving growing numbers of independent financial advisors. It launched radical products such as the instantly successful Mutual Fund OneSource program that persuaded mutual fund investors to hold their fund positions at Schwab.

Over the years, a number of accidents, catastrophes, and misfortunes have threatened to ruin Schwab. Some of these calamities were of its own making; others were acts of Nature. All created a crisis that by fortune or skill Schwab managed to navigate. In each case, the company emerged stronger, wiser, and more in charge of its destiny. Part Two of this book, "Profiles in Crisis," chronicles eight of these episodes. Chapter 7, "Forsaken IPO," recounts an ill-advised initial public offering that a not-ready-for-prime-time Schwab mounted and then quickly withdrew. Chapter 8, "Birthright," tells the story of how a company desperate for funds and legitimacy agreed to sell its birthright to the largest bank in California. A cultural mismatch from the beginning, Schwab nevertheless maintained its integrity as it struggled to reclaim its independence. The celebrations following its independence and a successful IPO were short-lived, however, because of the events described in Chapter 9, "Market Crash." On October 19, 1987, Black Monday, the stock market tumbled, creating havoc throughout the industry and testing Schwab's ability to weather the downturn.

Continuing Schwab's tales of woe, Chapter 10, "Margin Call," tells the incredible story of how Schwab allowed one Hong Kong customer to expose the company to over $120 million in liabilities. The fast action and intrigue that Schwab applied to recover most of the money it was owed saved the company. As a result, the company beefed up its risk management disciplines and made sure such a thing would never happen again. Chapter 11, "Earthquake," describes an act of nature, the San Francisco

Loma Prieta earthquake of October 17, 1989. Schwab people pulled together in ways large and small to protect the company, restart its computers, and to be ready to serve very nervous customers the next morning. The company's reputation for dependability was enshrined that day. While not strictly speaking a crisis, the Mutual Fund OneSource program described in Chapter 12 represented the company taking a huge gamble as it gave up an existing revenue stream in exchange for the uncertain rewards of giving more account control to the customer.

Chapter 13, "Heart Attack," tells the story of a company coming unglued at the very height of its success. Under the vision and leadership of Charles Schwab as implemented by president Lawrence Stupski, the company was poised to meet its loftiest growth objectives. Then on January 10, 1992, Larry Stupski, a leader revered by all, had a heart attack. He was 46 years old and considered indestructible. Stupski survived, but the company would never be the same. The company recalibrated its leadership. The consequences of that event reverberate throughout Schwab to this day.

Schwab version 3.0 illustrates Schwab's struggle to seamlessly integrate the Web-based services it developed in the mid-1990s with the established company. Chapter 14, "eSchwab," tells the story of how the company took an unprecedented leap into the unknown and became a Net company. By fits and starts, the company figured out how to use its Web offering to cannibalize the company's bread and butter services. This is the story of how accepting a little pain now is better than enduring a lot of pain later. It was nothing less than eating your own young and there was nothing painless about it. Here, Schwab's celebrated "Clicks and Mortar" strategy first took shape.

Part Three, "Custodian of Uneasy Dreams," considers the company under the leadership of co-CEO David Pottruck. Schwab in the current period faces formidable obstacles from both external competitors and internal contradictions.

Schwab version 4.0 makes the company look more than ever like the full-service brokerage firms it used to scorn. Chapter 15, "Balance of Power," examines how David Pottruck is an ideal leader for Schwab as it enters the twenty-first century. It also criticizes the co-CEO structure that the company has adopted since 1997. The chapter reports on how the company pursues affluent investors, including its 2000 acquisition of U.S. Trust. But with this newest reinvention, Schwab faces a huge risk to the franchise that has become so successful. Average investors feel abandoned. Employees feel betrayed by the increased focus on advice-giving and sales.

Every company demands its share of myth and legend, but for a company less than 30 years old, Schwab is off-the-scale in these departments. What is it about Schwab that encourages myth making? Trying to determine the literal truth of certain Schwab stories is pointless. Myths are things that never happened, but are always true. But if we don't search for ways to become aware of the myths that are unfolding in our lives, we run the risk of being controlled by them. Chapter 16, "Schwab Mythology," attempts to deconstruct the mythology of Schwab to discern the lessons they offer about work and passion.

The last chapter, "Unfinished Business," concludes by looking squarely at some areas where Schwab has underperformed. International markets, for instance. Why has Schwab failed so utterly to find any traction for its brand in overseas markets? The chapter scrutinizes some management practices that concern investors and analysts. Foremost among these is Schwab's succession policy. It doesn't seem to have one, and that worries everyone with a stake in the company's future. "There always comes a moment in time when a door opens and lets in the future," the novelist Graham Greene wrote. Such a door now confronts Schwab. The question is whose hand will turn the knob?

The brokerage industry faces a crisis of confidence. For investors, the brokerage industry is no longer a trusted partner. Investors are abandoning the financial markets, devastated by the revelations that daily rock the industry: two-faced stock analysts who tout company stocks to the public while trashing them in private; greedy executives who pad their own pockets; regulators who act more like lapdogs for corporate interests than watchdogs for the public interest; auditors who willfully or negligently allow it to happen and then hide behind their shredders. In its latest marketing campaign—"It has never been a better time for Charles Schwab"—the company acknowledges that it must face the dark side of an industry out of control. To its credit, under the moral authority of its founder, Schwab is taking strong leadership to restore the confidence of investors.

Chuck Schwab continues to revitalize what he finds inadequate. Let's go to him with notebook in hand. He remains our teacher.

Author's note, a word about names. To avoid the inevitable confusion that reigns when discussing any eponymous company, "Chuck," the name he prefers, refers to Charles R. Schwab the individual. "Schwab" and "Charles Schwab" refer to the company he founded.

PART ONE

Leveling the Playing Field

May Day

May 1, 1975

May Day—the day when fixed brokerage commissions were abolished—marked a crossroads for the U.S. securities industry and created the conditions for the birth of Charles Schwab & Co. Most brokerage firms responded to deregulation by cutting their commissions rates for institutional investors and raising them for the average investor. Schwab chose a different course.

Every story organizes the collision of random events into an opportunity for learning. So it has been from time immemorial. Every story points to a beginning before which there was chaos. "Once upon a time" the most memorable stories begin, demanding that the storyteller assign a marker to separate the now from then, the light from the dark. So it is with the Schwab story.

A number of dates will serve. Shall we start with 1937, the year not only of Chuck Schwab's birth, but a reasonable marker

for the end of the worst of the Great Depression and the start of
the economic expansion that created, after World War II, the
prosperous middle class that would fuel the company that
Schwab was to found?

Maybe a better date is 1963. It's the midpoint of the era we
now call the Go-Go Years, a period when the stock market
threw off the predictability of the 1950s and danced the Hullabaloo. For the first time, trading stocks became sexy and young
brokers could grow facial hair and show their faces at the Chee-
tah and other discothèques. Advisory investment newsletters
were the rage in those Go-Go Years, and, not to disappoint,
Chuck launched *Investment Indicator.*

At its height, the newsletter had 3,000 subscribers, each paying $84 per year for the privilege. If you do the math, the newslet-
ter kicked off maybe a quarter of a million dollars per year in
gross revenues, which was not bad considering that the median
annual household income in 1965 was $6,597. But not bad was
not nearly good enough. Chuck realized you can't get rich selling advice through a subscription newsletter. Even then, perhaps, Chuck had a problem dispensing advice to others.

Chuck wanted to be a player. Motivated by the combined desire for professional respect and personal wealth, Chuck aspired
to join the new breed of mutual fund portfolio managers. The
superstars of this elite circle were consistently outperforming
the market averages, racking up gains of 30–40 percent for their
investors. Everybody loved them and Chuck wanted to be a su-
perstar, too. That's why he created one of the first no-load mutual funds. He called the fund Investment Indicators and it soon
became the largest mutual fund in California, with $20 million
in assets. Alas, as we shall see in Chapter 2, Chuck's excellent
adventure in mutual funds crashed and burned, as did much of
what he took on in the early years.

In 1971, Chuck established First Commander Corporation,
his first brokerage. From the start he had an inherent problem
with the way the brokerage industry compensates its stockbrokers. Here are the facts he had to contend with: Stockbrokers are
nothing more than salespeople. They are compensated based

on commissions. Commissions are a benefit only to the brokers and their firms. It follows that commissions are a detriment to the customer. Brokers earn commissions only when they persuade a customer to make a trade. That would be bad enough but it gets worse. Customers think they can rely on brokers for advice. That's a clear conflict of interest. To aggravate the matter further, brokerage firms have a commission structure that rewards brokers for selling the riskiest investments. The riskier the investment, the higher the broker's commission, and the greater the incentive for the broker to adjust his advice. That's why Arthur Levitt, the former chairman of the Securities and Exchange Commission made these departing remarks: "Let's begin with the first step for a lot of investors: selecting a broker. The very first question that a person should ask his or her broker is, 'How do you get paid?'"

Chuck considered all the commissions, front-end loads, margin interest, markups, fees and other "impairments of capital" as conspiracies against the public. He swore eternal hostility to every form of swindle of investors. No wonder First Commander Corporation didn't make it. Being a traditional stockbroker required selling as well as giving advice, and Chuck was constitutionally averse to both. Chuck decided to regroup. He bought out his partners and tried his hand in a variety of deals, many of which were presented to him by his obliging uncle, William Schwab. Maybe the better date to start the story, then, is 1973, when Chuck renamed the company Charles Schwab & Co., Inc., and floundered around for a while, waiting for an opportunity to present itself.

That opportunity came on May 1, 1975, and on this date we can reliably pin the beginnings of the Schwab Story.

It's difficult from this vantage point to grasp the arrogance of Wall Street traders before May Day, the name assigned to the day when, after 183 years of price fixing, the New York Stock Exchange (NYSE) was forced to give up a system of fixed brokerage commissions.

How audacious. Here was an industry celebrating the purest expression of free market enterprise and competition in the world, but embracing for itself government-sanctioned regulation. Ever since it was founded in 1792, the public face of the NYSE extolled the virtues of competition and the American Dream, where any kid can grow up to be the chairman of the board or, lacking that, the president of the United States.

Now the industry acted as if the reformers had proposed Karl Marx as the president of the New York Stock Exchange. The most sober industry spokesmen warned that American free enterprise would all but collapse if competition were allowed to be the arbiter of trading commissions. SEC hearings were filled with testimony such as, "May Day is a great holiday in Russia. And Russia has said there is no need to fight democracy; it will burn itself out. Well, Commissioners, you have the candle and matches, and it will be a short fuse."

No group in the United States—with the possible exception of major league baseball—enjoyed such a privileged position to organize its members into an association with the power to maintain a marketplace for their exclusive use, to fix prices to be charged in the market, to restrict entry to that market, and to boycott competing markets.

Behind the apple-pie veneer of good old American free enterprise, the NYSE represented just another cynical conspiracy against the public. Except this cartel—for that's what it was—managed to thrive for 183 years, reaping untold riches on its beneficiaries. The group of New York brokers who secretly met in what must have been the original smoke-filled hotel room contrived a monopoly to fix commissions and to keep all the trading business for itself. For almost the entire history of the country, these essential terms remained unchanged. Commission rates went up, of course, but they were always nonnegotiable. Take it or leave it. But if you decided to leave it, you were confronted by Rule 390, the sweetest provision of all. Rule 390 dictated that all stocks listed on the New York Stock Exchange could be bought and sold only through a member firm.

At first, the government had neither the mechanism nor the will to do much about it. Thus the NYSE prospered, and its monopoly acquired the respectable veneer of tradition. And it didn't help that, in the wake of the Depression, Congress gave the federal government's imprimatur to the tradition of fixed trading commissions. The Securities Acts of 1933 and 1934, which in addition to requiring brokerages to be licensed by the SEC, officially sanctioned the NYSE's price fixing for its member firms—a practice that effectively set commissions rates for the entire industry. "In short," says Los Angeles-based financial writer Benjamin Mark Cole, "if you wanted to buy or sell stock, you had to do it through a licensed brokerage. And they all charged the same rate. End of story."

The money, as the song in the musical *Evita* puts it, came pouring in. Over the next few decades, the exchange established formulas based on the number of shares and the dollar size of the trade. The NYSE traders grew rich on the commissions. The price fixing practically ensured that every NYSE member firm, regardless of skill or merit, made money. In a typical year, such as 1967, Cole reported, only one of the NYSE's 330 member firms was reported to have sustained a net loss, and even that case was less than clear. The prevailing attitude among regulators was that, like banks, brokerages should not be allowed to fail.

There were two big problems with the pre-May Day state of affairs. First, customers, especially retail customers, were being raped. The NYSE member firms were essentially charging the same commission to a retail customer trading 25 shares of IBM as it did for an insurance company trading 10,000 shares. There was no relationship between commissions and true costs of executing trades. A second problem was that innovation suffered. With everyone fat and happy and virtually guaranteed profits, there was little incentive for the NYSE wire houses to automate, introduce new products, or improve customer service.

Soon after May 1, 1975, you could hear the howling from full-commission brokers as their customers defected to the discount brokers. Many years later, when Schwab lowered trades to $29.95, *Fortune* magazine reporter Katrina Booker overheard a Merrill Lynch broker's side of a telephone conversation with a customer. These are the Merrill Lynch broker's exact words, as reported by Booker. For fun, I took a guess at what the other side of the conversation must have been like. The exchange might have gone something like this:

MERRILL LYNCH BROKER: I can't believe this. Suddenly you've got $29.95 trades, and you're empowered.

MERRILL LYNCH CUSTOMER: Look, I know what I want to buy. I don't need to pay for research. Why should I pay more than I have to?

BROKER: Okay, fine. You want to trade on the Internet? Fine. Go right ahead. You have to do what's right for you. Just don't expect much service from me.

CUSTOMER: We go way back. Why are you taking that tone?

BROKER: Why? Because I get goose eggs! I don't get paid, okay? So don't expect me to give you any more ideas.

CUSTOMER: When was the last time you gave me an idea? I know what I want.

BROKER: I have given you ideas. Okay. Maybe I haven't been as good about that as I could have. Starting today, that is going to change.

CUSTOMER: Listen, you guys have got to wake up. Why should I pay you $250 when I can get the same trade for $29.95? It's a new game out there. Get with the program, or I'm history.

BROKER: Look, I'm sorry. I didn't mean to piss you off. Hey, you want to go to the Mets game tomorrow? I've got tickets.

Here we get a glimpse of the old-boy networking and schmoozing that cemented the high commissions in place for so many years. Booze, ball games, yacht outings, and dinners lubricated the relationship between brokers and their customers. Entertainment, more than investment research, often proved to be the traditional stockbroker's fiercest weapon. A pair of seats on the 50-yard line combined with an occasional stock tip could beat cheap trades any day. But brokers soon learned that investors are fickle: most will go where they can execute trades for less.

The fat commissions had fed an excessive lifestyle that was frequently lampooned by jokes and New Yorker cartoons. Chuck begins his first book, *How to Be Your Own Stockbroker*, by telling a broker yacht story:

> I'm reminded of an eager-beaver stock salesman I knew in Florida who took a prospect to the harbor at Palm Beach. As they surveyed the various luxury craft floating before them, the salesman pointed out all the yachts owned by successful brokers.
>
> "But where are the customers' yachts?" the prospect innocently whispered.

Furious at losing customers, the brokers fought for their cartel. To protect its sweet monopoly, the brokerage industry built high walls securing it against any public interest reformists. Trade groups like the Securities Industry Association opened offices in the nation's capital to monitor legislation and make sure no one in authority considered the ill-conceived arrangements made in the desperate days of the Depression. Campaign contributions flowed to Washington, primarily to Republican candidates, who paid lip service to the music of deregulation and unfettered competition but didn't want to rock the yachts of the traders on which they were frequently entertained.

Reformers in the Kennedy administration started pressing the Justice Department and the SEC to challenge the issue of brokerage trading rate deregulation. The industry's lobbyists made lunch meat out of these efforts. The Street partied hard with the election of Richard M. Nixon in 1968. They thought their sinecure was secure with the White House in industry-friendly Republican hands. And it would have been except for two entirely predictable vices of those who have more than they deserve: greed and paranoia.

The NYSE member firms thought they had a sweet deal, but the monopoly carried within it the seeds of the system's destruction.

Bulls make money, bears make money, pigs get slaughtered. So goes the Wall Street truism, and so it was that greed, over-reaching and craven, killed the closest license to print money allowed by law. What happened is that the biggest mutual funds got sick of paying huge commissions and started demanding discounts. Instead of giving it to them, the brokers started to cheat each other by allowing "end-around" trading in which institutional trades bypassed the floor of the NYSE. Brokerages helped create an unofficial "third market" channel and began cutting deals on trading commissions, awarding "give-ups" or discounts to its largest customers. The NYSE and the brokerage industry also tried to outlaw such discounts and any erosion of the fixed commissions this alternative channel created, but they couldn't get the SEC to go along.

That didn't stop the brokers from trying. In 1973, the exchange actually asked the SEC for a commission rate increase of 10 to 15 percent. The napalm scent of deregulation was in the air, but the brokers, blinded by their greed, could smell nothing more than their own self-importance. Amazingly, the SEC approved the rate increase, but only on the condition that the exchange agree to phase in deregulated commissions, a process to be completed no later than April 30, 1975.

And that's where the paranoia comes in. The paranoia belonged to a corrupt and suspicious President Nixon, who was by 1973 so overwhelmed by his Watergate problems, that he had no energy to protect his pals on Wall Street. He was beyond the help of political contributions. In 1971, minions of Nixon were caught attempting to bug the offices of the Democratic National Committee in the Watergate apartment complex not far from the White House. The investigation of this burglary and Nixon's attempt to obstruct justice brought on his downfall. On August 8, 1974, President Nixon resigned in disgrace. An emboldened Congress, now controlled by Democrats intoxicated by the heady rush of reform, drafted legislation to outlaw fixed brokerage commissions.

Warnings of calamity issued from the full-commission brokers, who feared that the traditional means by which business was done would be destroyed. Investment advisor Peter Bernstein wrote, "All the known parameters of the stock market are bursting apart."

He was right. The world of investing was being turned upside down. Acknowledging the battle was lost, the NYSE agreed to a one-year transition period culminating in the end, effective May 1, 1975, of fixed commissions forever.

Geography is destiny. The promised upheaval of May Day created one of the conditions necessary for Chuck to succeed. The other condition was satisfied by the accident of the company taking root in California, and not just anywhere in California, but in northern California. It is hard to think of a locale more hospitable to a start-up like Schwab than San Francisco.

Schwab benefited from its San Francisco location in three main ways. First, it was almost as far geographically from Wall Street as you can get and still be in the contiguous United States. Had Schwab tried to establish the company in New York City, the air would have been sucked out of the company before it began. More likely, Schwab would never have considered starting a discount brokerage in the first place. The not-invented-here mentality of the established brokerages would have torpedoed Schwab's chances for raising money or attracting talent. "Wall Street has a crippling pack mentality," says John Gambs, who was deputy treasurer of Merrill Lynch when Schwab recruited him to be the discount brokerage's first Chief Financial Officer. "It's an extremely inbred and small community. I could never do any work on the commuter train ride home because the guy next to me was from Goldman or Hutton."

But the second reason supporting San Francisco as the inevitable location for a company like Schwab is that California in general, and the Bay Area in particular, attracted misfits and rebels. Everyone was new in California; most of the population settled there starting in the 1950s. California was particularly appealing to people who didn't fit in elsewhere: radicals, free thinkers, subversives, experimenters, and people favoring alternate lifestyles that were elsewhere considered immoral or in point of fact criminal. Credentials were considered an East Coast hang-up. Dress codes were as casually disregarded in California as every other code.

New York was text-centered. California nourished images in a way that Wall Street could not fathom. Chuck quickly understood that image is what it's all about. It's no accident that Hollywood, the crucible of image, is in California. The result? Chuck's face, larger than life, on ads, billboards, and TV. The executives at Merrill Lynch and EF Hutton were aghast at Chuck's photograph on Schwab ads. The prevailing attitude among financial executives cultivated by Yale and Dartmouth was that businessmen are allowed only two opportunities to get their photographs in the newspaper: marriage and death—but only one of each.

The third reason—although it wouldn't be obvious for 20 years—was due to the happy accident that Schwab would soon fall under the spell of the world-changing magic that was being created 30 minutes to the south. Silicon Valley in a few years was to become the greatest engine of wealth generation the world has ever seen. The Silicon Valley companies started paying their engineers in a new form of compensation—stock options. Within a few years, thousands of employees clutching stock options would be walking around. They couldn't take their options to the bank. So they made a beeline for the nearest stockbroker. Frequently, that was Schwab.

Imagine a human resources manager getting stock options. Kevin Wheeler, who would later become Schwab's Senior Vice President for Staffing and Workforce Development, was a young human resources manager at National Semiconductor in 1982 when he walked into Schwab's Silver Creek, California branch to open an account and sell his options. What Wheeler remembers most is the warm, fuzzy feeling that his finances were in capable hands. The Schwab staff knew exactly what to say and what to do. "They took something mysterious and a little threatening and made it easy," Wheeler says. Although Wheeler left Schwab in 2000, that original account is still active.

Chuck, a native Californian himself, grew up embracing many of the values that made California so attractive. He was one of the first employers to open his doors to people who traditional financial services companies would not touch. No college degree? No problem. Freaky appearance? No problem. Gay, lesbian, bisexual, or transgendered? Not an issue. The only thing that mattered: Do you have integrity and could you do the job? That's what Chuck cared about. As a matter of fact, Chuck was even a little bit ahead of other California firms in his tolerance for inclusivity in hiring. Maybe it was his own sense of being different. In any case, Chuck's untested business model became quickly appealing to a number of people who were not being hired elsewhere.

Fortunately for Chuck, Wall Street's attention rarely extended past the borough of Manhattan. This geographic myopia played a critical part in Chuck's ability to build his business before the Boys of Wall Street had the first clue that their clock was getting cleaned.

The full-service brokerages were fighting for more than their fat-cat commissions. They had an army of securities analysts to protect. Merrill Lynch alone had more than 8,000 of them. At this point in their development, analysts were generally anonymous drones who churned out reports on companies or industries, making earnings forecasts, and recommending which stocks investors should buy or sell. If investors ever complained about the high commissions and asked where the value-added was, the brokerages pointed to all those fat reports.

Trouble is, the investment reports are sometimes worse than worthless, and Chuck knew it from first-hand experience. He got to see the analysts work up close and personal and it turned his stomach. For one thing, the securities analysts are almost always compromised by the fact that the brokerages they work for have advisory roles with the companies the analysts cover. The pressures to cross the line from simply assessing stocks to promoting them becomes overwhelming. At one point there was said to be a "Chinese Wall" separating the analysis from the advising, and maybe the wall at one time kept the interests from conflicting, but by the 1980s, the wall was breached.

As securities analysts turned into little more than cheerleaders for stocks, the value of fundamental analysis deteriorated. In a world where there should by all rights be approximately as many "sell" recommendations as there are "buy" recommendations, what is the actual record of securities analysts? According to data put together by Zaks Investment Research, of 33,000 buy, sell, and hold recommendations made by brokerage analysts in 1999, only 125 were unalloyed sells. That means that just 0.3 percent of recommendations were sells. In the wake of the Enron meltdown, humor columnist Dave Barry lampooned the analysts who covered the stock: "Enron stock was rated as 'Can't Miss' until it became clear that the company was in desperate trouble, at which point analysts lowered the rating to 'Sure Thing.' Only when Enron went completely under did a few bold analysts demote its stock to the lowest possible Wall Street analyst rating, 'Hot Buy.'"

Why, Chuck asked, should investors be asked to pay for such fundamentally dishonest "analysis"? But perhaps the recommendations of securities analysts, as cynical as they are, might nevertheless guide investors to better performance in the stock market. Alas, they don't. Every study concludes that analyst earnings forecasts are consistently overoptimistic and their "buy" recommendations have consistently underperformed the market. In other words, investors would do better by randomly picking stocks.

But the full-service brokerages weren't stupid. They could sense a new day coming and struggled mightily against the inertia of 200 years of fixed rates and predictable revenues. Negotiated rates had everyone jumpy. Three thousand miles from New York City, Chuck worried that the major players on the Street would drop their rates and render his little company irrelevant. There was evidence that the Big Boys might do just that.

Executives at Bear Stearns, for example, went off for a weekend retreat to plan a pricing strategy. They came back and announced to the world that at the opening on May 1, 1975, they would offer an 18 percent discount. But greed is the hardest habit to break. "I don't know where they came up with that figure," recalls E. John Rosenwald, Jr., a Bear Stearns manager at the retreat, "but I'll tell you, it lasted all of 60 seconds." Eventually, the major brokers did drop prices . . . but only for their large institutional clients who had the clout to demand discounts. Most analysts looked to see what Merrill Lynch, the 800-pound gorilla of the Street, would do. It was the company with the most to lose. Would Merrill Lynch, the largest wire house—a major brokerage doing business on a national basis—ratify the laws of competition and lower rates? If it did, what difference would Schwab's pitiful handful of trades make?

Many years later, Schwab legend would rewrite history a bit. Chuck, the story went, opened the *Wall Street Journal* dated May 1, 1975, to discover that far from lowering rates, Merrill Lynch was actually raising rates by 10 percent. Jubilation in Schwab's offices was said to ensue. Here, let's be clear, we are in the realm of myth—something that never really existed but is nevertheless true. Merrill Lynch did raise rates, by 3 percent, but that's hardly the point. Had it dropped rates even marginally, Schwab's untested discount business would never have found traction among investors. Nor should it have been surprising to anyone that Merrill didn't. It was understood that brokerages would have no choice but to lower rates for their large institutional clients. But it was also common knowledge that brokerages could not serve most of their retail clients at a profit even at full commissions. There was no way they would lower retail commissions without a fight.

In the month after May Day, the *New York Times* reported that most brokers had cut their fees 25 to 35 percent, while some were offering reductions as steep as 50 to 60 percent. Those cuts however, were reserved for large-volume, large-order clients—mutual funds and institutions. As a rule, the big guys wound up paying about half the rates that the little guys paid. The little guys actually ended up paying more after May Day than they did before. To people outside the industry—a group that included much of the U.S. Congress—it looked suspiciously as if the small were subsidizing the large (though, in fact, the large trades were, on a per-share basis, cheaper to execute).

In the end, what probably doomed the ancient regime was the lugubrious spectacle of an industry paying unstinting lip service to free enterprise and competition, but embracing for itself government-sanctioned regulated rates. How could Wall Streeters plead for protection from the very values they extolled? As their sinecure collapsed, they thought it could be business as usual. They wouldn't know what hit them. Wall Street was about to be Schwabbed.

Opening Investment

1937–1975

In some ways Chuck is an improbable revolutionary. With his benign smile, silver hair, and (until recently) designer glasses, Chuck appears as a fat-cat banker straight out of central casting. But few executives have so radically changed the relationship millions of ordinary people have with their money.

California optimism runs deep in Chuck Schwab. Given the cards he was dealt, there's nothing inevitable about his unrelenting confidence in the future and the inherent decency of people. Many people born in 1937 internalized the humiliation and anxiety of the Depression, leading to lives of quiet desperation and aversion to risk. While the family's economic circumstances were middle class moving to prosperous, Chuck wasn't pampered. He also grew up with a learning disability—dyslexia—that wasn't even named when he was born and, in any case, wasn't diagnosed until more than 30 years later when he sought medical advice for his son who had the same condition. In these circumstances, Chuck could have been forgiven for being more grasping and petty. Instead he was generous, happy-go-lucky, and heedless of risk, willing to work harder than anyone else, with an instinctive preference for blaming himself before he blamed others. Most people he met liked him at once. The people who met him through his TV commercial and ads liked him just as much.

Although he is the personification of the company and his smiling face is seen by millions in TV commercials and has registered countless impressions in newspapers, magazines, and brochures, Chuck is by nature very private and even shy. That's what everyone who first meets him says. That and that he's . . . well, smaller than they thought he was. They drop their voices to a whisper and seem embarrassed to say it. Appearing on TV does that. Celebrity makes you larger than life and, as Hollywood stars have come to know, exacts a terrible price. At first, celebrity fills the world with smiles and opportunity. It opens doors. Later, it closes them. The greater the celebrity, the greater the restriction on one's options. Every actor struggles with the role that made him famous. It is no different for Chuck.

For a man who has lived in the public eye for as long as he has, the details of the early years of Charles R. Schwab are encumbered with more than the predictable veneer of myth and legend. Chuck is an intensely private person and has always been reluctant to talk about the details of his youth and early career. For example, what is Chuck's middle name? More than fifty of his closest associates smiled when they heard this question. None of them knew. Nor would the company confirm that it's Robert, the name of Chuck's father. In the same vein, his associates know that Chuck was born in 1937. But what's the date? Even those who remember celebrating Chuck's birthday recall that it was never attached to a particular day they could put on their calendars. It was like a floating holiday, much like an option, a celebration Chuck had the right but not the obligation to observe. Even today, Chuck guards this information with some vigilance. Check all the references such as *Who's Who in America* or *Who's Who in Business* and only the year of his birth is given.

Chuck's birthday, confirmed by Schwab corporate communications, is July 29. Chuck turned 65 on July 29, 2002.

By virtue of his face on all the ads, he is an accessible yet remote figure, a combination ideal for spawning legend. The myth making was quite unintentional but completely predictable. Any corporate culture in which a firm's values are an embodiment of its founder tends to outperform on the myth scale. Add to the mix a somewhat disengaged and remote leader who lends both his name and image to the cause, and you have a nutritious broth for cultivating a variety of narratives, some more authentic than others.

Chuck's early days were spent in Sacramento, the dreary state capital, where his father, Robert Schwab, worked as an attorney. The family later moved to the nearby community of Woodland. During World War II, Chuck's father served as district attorney of Yolo County, retiring from public service in 1946. "Although my father's life seemed to be interesting and rewarding, I was never interested in becoming a lawyer," Chuck wrote in his first book, *How to Be Your Own Stockbroker*, published when he was 47. Perhaps he saw the volume of reading his father brought home every night. Even then Chuck must have known that any reading-intensive career would elude him.

Ah, but with numbers, he shined. His father dabbled in the stock market and the son eventually became fascinated with the cycles and patterns of investing. Only later would he come to know the burdens of cyclicality. In the beginning, Chuck's interests ran to buying and selling, marketing and business. From his earliest days, it is certain, Chuck had an entrepreneurial streak.

When Chuck was twelve, the family moved to Santa Barbara, the quintessential Northern California city, even in 1949 a hotbed of progressive intellectualism, free-thinking bohemians, experimentation, tolerance for alternative lifestyles, and a general distrust of authority. Although he was by nature a conservative type, favoring English muffins over granola, a willingness to be a fellow traveler with people with alternative lifestyles would serve Chuck well. When he created a business that everyone in power told him couldn't succeed, he not only proved them wrong, he proved them wrong by staffing it with people no one else in the financial services industry would touch.

The privilege in the Schwab family did not keep Chuck from applying himself and doing the nastiest work for a buck. Here the stories Chuck tells begin to smack of legend. First is the walnut story. Chuck describes how, at age eleven or so, he scoured the woods for English walnuts, sacked them, and sold them for $5 per 100-pound sack. "Some other kids thought I was a little crazy, spending my free time rooting though the twigs and leaves," he recalls. His status as a maverick, willing to risk the scorn of the elites—in this case, the popular kids in school—was being refined.

A number of the management practices that Schwab holds dear are neatly illustrated by this story. Besides the teasing from his friends, Chuck had to overcome rejection ("Although plenty of people didn't want to buy, I quickly learned that if I kept at it and plowed right through the rejections, I would eventually get somebody to buy my wares"). Chuck learned that reward is in direct proportion to effort ("If I wanted to accumulate extra spending money, I had to pick up *extra* walnuts"). And Chuck learned to be sensitive to product segmentation ("If I wasted my effort on the cheaper but more plentiful [black] walnuts, I'd earn that much less").

Within a year, he had abandoned the nut business as too commoditized. He watched what people consumed and decided that chickens offered an entrepreneur considerable opportunities. First, the business model was self-sustaining. With a little care, chickens created more chickens. The business also combined a product (eggs and fertilizer) with a service (plucking fryers for market). By the time Chuck was thirteen, more than twenty-five chickens were doing his bidding. In business school, Chuck would joke that before he could shave, he was the chief executive of a vertically integrated business model that leveraged every aspect of chicken farming. "I sold the eggs; I learned to kill and pluck fryers for market; and I developed a list of clients for my own chicken fertilizer," he says.

The chicken story sparked more opportunity for durable lessons in management. He considered business cyclicality (". . . you have to move through plenty of bad times if you hope to reach the good"). For the first time, Chuck enlisted partners and learned about teamwork and how to discriminate between solid performers and flakes. Chuck's enterprise was seemingly organized on a profit-sharing model ("A couple of friends usually helped out, and I allowed them to share in the profits"). If so, this was an early experiment in compensating associates. Chuck doesn't say if he tried motivating his friends with commissions, but in later years, he would make a bold statement by paying his brokers a salary so as to eliminate any incentive for them to sell customers something that might not be in their interests to buy. The salary structure of Schwab customer reps would become a huge differentiator for Chuck.

Eventually he decided to move on. Chuck doesn't miss a beat in wringing some sage business lessons from his exiting the chicken business. ("There is a time to hold and a time to sell. Adult investors today far too often stick with a stock, fund, or other investment that they know is bad, because they became too fond of a company.") In his book Chuck writes of "liquidating my chicken business." Does anyone really want to know more about that? There can be such a thing as too much research.

The business lessons that would make Chuck a billionaire were already evident. He quickly grasped that it's much easier to find out what customers want and then figure out how to provide it than to develop a product and hope to find a market for it. His intuitive approach started with looking for the demand. Then he figured out how to meet the demand. Only then did he put energy into considering whether he could make money supplying it. In later years, after he got his M.B.A. from Stanford, Chuck would adopt business-speak: He rationalized the business only after he identified the opportunity. Here we have another of the patterns that would guide the business that would make him successful. Schwab, unlike every other financial services company, would give customers what they wanted—quick and cheap stock trades—not try to push whatever it was they had on hand on unsuspecting customers. In M.B.A. lingo, Schwab preferred a "pull" value proposition as opposed to a "push" business model.

The appeal of chickens for an adolescent is limited. The fourteen-year-old Chuck had discovered an activity that filled him with wonder and that he wanted to practice every waking hour. Golf became his vocation and avocation. Girls were interesting, but nothing gave him the satisfaction of control and accomplishment as thirty-six holes of golf on a beautiful California day. Caddying represented much more of an earning opportunity than chickens, and it didn't hurt that in general the hygiene of golfers exceeded that of chickens.

Golf had and continues to play a huge role in Chuck's life. Back then, Chuck was a fine caddy and he became the favorite of many righteous-tipping golfers. His earnings as a caddy provided him with a decent income, some of which he invested in the stock market. More important, the exposure to expert golfers helped Chuck improve his own game. He became a formidable golfer in his own right and his high school golf team elected him captain. Academics in high school were a struggle so Chuck relished the competence and leadership he showed on the links. Chuck's performance as a golfer, in turn, helped open the door to Stanford University, a school that was prepared to relax some of its academic requirements for a student athlete who could advance the Stanford golf team.

School was always torture for Chuck. Like many dyslexics, he was tempted to blame himself for being slower than everyone else. To his credit, he resisted the temptation. "I never perceived of myself as stupid; I can't explain why," he says. "I just thought that if I worked harder, maybe something would happen." His parents seemed to ignore his difficulties entirely, while the "wonderful but strict" nuns who taught at the parochial elementary school he attended were more interested in discipline than figuring out why Chuck's reading was so labored. It was a knack for schmoozing and his confident, sunny personality that helped him bluff his way through those early years.

High school represented the culmination of a lifelong struggle with the written word. To master his reading assignments, Chuck plowed through Classic Illustrated comic book versions of *Ivanhoe* and *A Tale of Two Cities.* "I bluffed my way through much of it, I'm sure," he recalled for the Stanford University alumni magazine many years later, "Fortunately, I have a pretty 'up' personality, and that helped me all the way through. I tried hard and I had pretty good communication skills, so I could persuade my teachers that I was a pretty good kid."

As a college freshman, he was completely buried, flunking both French and freshman English before finding refuge in economics. Reading still comes hard. Chuck confesses that he has attempted to read the novel *Shogun* six or seven times. "When I read, I can feel myself converting the written code into sounds [with my mouth] before I can process it," he explains. "Fast readers don't go through all that." Later, everyone at Schwab would learn that Chuck couldn't handle any reading. Even a list of bullet points taxed him, as Jim Wiggett, long-time head of human resources, discovered. He had given Chuck a list to use as an aid in addressing a group of HR professionals. After struggling with the first bullet point, Chuck looked up at the group and said, "I'm sorry, Jim, I'm going to do this a different way." Chuck then told stories and spoke from his heart and people loved him.

Primed by his great golf game and strong math and science scores, Chuck got into Stanford, taking a room in Wilbur Hall. He wasn't prepared for the difficulties he now faced. It was about academic performance, as evidenced by written expression, and all his sunny glad-handing was for naught. "English was 'a disaster,'" he recalls with a shudder, and French was akin to medieval torture. "To sit down with a blank piece of paper and write was the most traumatic thing that had ever faced me in life," he says. "I had ideas in my head, but I could not get the stuff down. It was a crushing time."

As Charles Schwab & Co. became an oversize enterprise, Chuck became more adept at compensating for his dyslexia. He relied heavily on dictation and, later, on computer technology. He didn't understand the root of his difficulties until his youngest son, Charles Schwab, Jr., (called "Sandy"), then eight, started experiencing learning difficulties that looked to Chuck suspiciously like his own. A frustrating series of testing ensued. By the time Sandy was diagnosed with dyslexia, he was already two grade levels behind in reading. "It was a bewildering time," Chuck's wife, Helen, recalled in a 1995 *Los Angeles Times* interview. "It's scary when you think there's something that can be done for your child but you don't know what it is, and there isn't one place for you to go to for help."

To provide that central place for the latest resources on dyslexia, Chuck and Helen founded the Schwab Foundation for Learning in 1988. The foundation supports a nonprofit agency to provide guidance for parents and teachers of children with all kinds of learning "differences" (a term Chuck prefers over "disabilities"), from persistent difficulties in reading and math to attention deficit disorders. Like Schwab's brokerage offices, the foundation gives people easy-to-understand information and resources to help them make their own decisions.

Chuck's colleagues quickly learned. If you wanted something from Chuck, go see him. Don't send a memo. Don't create a written presentation. Just go see him and talk to him. A simple graph or a chart might help, but you really don't need it. Just tell him what you intend to do. And then do it. Without a paper trail to fall back on, personal integrity and absolute follow-through on commitments became priorities in determining success at Schwab.

After struggling through Stanford and graduating with a degree in economics in 1959, Chuck gravitated to the securities industry. In those years, the normal career path for a young person in this industry was to become a junior stockbroker. That is if you were a man. Women were largely excluded, but if they made sufficient pests of themselves they were allowed to become assistants to stockbrokers. Their responsibilities under this system were limited to fetching coffee, typing, and being the objects of merciless sexual harassment.

But Chuck knew that cold calling people to get them to buy stocks (for stockbrokers are merely salesmen who sell securities) was definitely not for him. Chuck's facile mind ran to the analysis of equities, funds, and the companies behind them, the tracking of patterns, and taming the creative anarchy of the business cycles. By the early 1960s, the securities business was becoming more professionalized and Schwab was led to understand that a business degree would serve him well. So back to Stanford Business School he went for an M.B.A.

As Chuck looked to the end of his M.B.A. program, California was the place to be. It had recently assumed the status of the most populous state in America, it was the cultural trendsetter for the country, and it was awash with wealth. Annual income in 1961 topped $61 billion. California financial wizards, high perhaps on more than cultural innovation, were designing ingenious varieties of boutique investments and mutual funds to cater to every taste. Hedge funds, limited investment partnerships, private placements, and, of course, a seemingly endless variety of mutual funds. Soon individual investors would be turned on to liquid yield options notes, collateralized bond obligations, commodities options, and derivatives. It was a long way from buying certificates of deposit. Chuck was dazzled by the headiness of it all and wondered if customers really wanted those products. "What if I could figure out what customers wanted and provide that . . . ?" he started thinking.

Even before he got his M.B.A., Chuck had started working part-time for Foster Investment Services in Palo Alto. "I was the guy with the slide rule," Chuck told Moira Johnston for her book *Roller Coaster*, a history of the Bank of America. But Chuck's involvement with the Bank of America is still two decades in the future. For now, Chuck's responsibilities were clear: He was to create, register, and market anything that would compel investors to mail or wire cash to Foster Investment Services. Everyone in the country, it seemed, was pushing the envelope of the regulations that defined the boundaries of banks and securities companies. But nowhere were the boundaries being more challenged than in California. By age twenty-three, Chuck was a

Foster vice president and was, by his own account, "very hot stuff."

Following the path of executives who thought they were just a little bit hotter than they really were, Chuck partnered up with two men. Desmond Mitchell was an Australian who had made a small fortune in Canada. John Morse was an associate Chuck first met at Stanford. The new firm of Mitchell, Morse & Schwab (Mitchell got top billing because he came up with most of the cash) moved to San Rafael, north of the Golden Gate Bridge, and started business right as the Cuban missile crisis became hotter than all three put together. Undaunted, they launched a variety of funds and, in January 1963, began publishing an eight-page investment newsletter called *Investment Indicators*. At its high point the newsletter had 3,000 subscribers at $84 per year.

The team chemistry was not quite right (Mitchell ran the show). Chuck felt overworked and underappreciated, which is a deadly combination for a man with a high need for control and status. It didn't help that growth was painfully slow. Chuck's vision for scale was unbounded. Profits always took a secondary role to growth. Give me the growth, Chuck felt, and profits would ensue. The firm of Mitchell, Morse & Schwab was proving entirely too "me, too." Already Chuck was weary of incremental change.

Although he could not name it—naming things would never be his forte—Chuck was one of the first executives to favor discontinuous change over incremental change. All over the nation, people were considering the nature of change. In physics, they called it chaos theory. For mathematicians, it was catastrophe theory. Chuck understood on some level that success in the financial services industry (a term that hadn't yet been coined) could no longer be guaranteed by gradual, continuous change. He saw a new world roaring in from the horizon. The industry was entering an era of rapid and highly discontinuous change that Charles Handy would call the Age of Unreason. In a world of unpredictable, discontinuous change, all the established *rules* are vulnerable. In the next few years, Chuck struggled to implement a discontinuous, upside-down style of learning and thinking.

But first came a period of struggle. In mythological terms, it was his time in the dark wood where the way was hidden. Chuck, like all heroes, would have to find his own path out. Over a span of 8 years, Chuck struggled to make Mitchell, Morse & Schwab work. Some days looked better than others. Leveraging the success of the newsletter, the firm launched one of the first no-load mutual funds in the country. The Investment Indicators fund was soon the largest mutual fund in California, with some $20 million in assets.

In those early years, Chuck had yet to learn that he was an excellent leader but an indifferent manager. Maybe it was his learning disability, or maybe it was a personal limitation, but Chuck had no interest in administrative details. This failing would get him into hot water over and over again until he realized that he needed to hire strong administrative types to save him from himself. Early evidence of Chuck's obliviousness to detail appeared quickly. Chuck was placing ads for the Investment Indicators fund in publications around the country. Investors all over the country sent in their money. Unforgivably, the company never bothered to register its securities with the states and, predictably, the State of Texas called Chuck to task. Chuck faced an administrative crisis that in short order swamped the company. Chuck was willing to register, but the Texas regulators dug in their heels. Before it would allow Chuck's firm to register, the company would have to offer rescission to all existing Texas shareholders in Investment Indicators. You can hear the anger in Chuck's account:

> That's an ugly word, *rescission*. It means we'd have to give Texas investors the unlimited right to cancel all their transactions. In short, we would have had to refund their money, plus 6 percent interest, *at the price they had paid originally*. In other words, all the risk would be on us and

none on our investors, a sure-fire deal for the investor as long as the fund can stay in business. Unfortunately, staying in business then became our main problem.

Like many deep thinkers, Chuck responded with exasperation to people he termed petty bureaucrats. One of the attributes of Northern California culture was an unwillingness to abide by rules created elsewhere. Negotiations might have developed a solution, but Chuck felt cornered and then he did something he would regret. He called his lawyers. Big mistake. Chuck's fund might have survived a negotiated refund to the thousand or so Texas investors. But getting into an interstate pissing contest with a state whose most cherished bureaucrats fought to the death at the Alamo was, well, throwing good money after bad.

Chuck lost everything. The lawsuit brought the whole matter to the attention of the Securities and Exchange Commission (SEC). If Chuck thought "rescission" was an ugly term, what did he make of "undisclosed contingent liability"? The SEC came down on Chuck with the impact of a sand wedge. Chuck's firm was quickly blocked from selling the fund, not just in the Lone Star State, but elsewhere. Chuck blamed the regulators, but in more recent years, he has come to realize that the problem stemmed from his own hubris. By 1972, the fund, the company, everything Chuck had built was a nightmare from which he was trying to awake. Chuck was 35 years old. His reputation was tattered and he was $100,000 in debt. Moreover, the turmoil took its toll on his personal life. His marriage to his first wife, Susan, ended in divorce. His relationship with his three children— Charles, Jr. (Sandy), Carrie, and Virginia—was strained. With his second wife, Helen, Chuck would have two more children, Michael and Helen.

His extracurricular ventures fared no better. Time after time, Chuck's entrepreneurial instincts proved wide of the mark, as if validating John Kenneth Galbraith's observation that, "If all else fails, immortality can always be assured by spectacular error." Was it possible that a failing brokerage didn't provide enough satisfaction for him? No problem. Chuck invested in a wild-animal drive-through park called Congoland, USA. Chuck, his secretary, and a handful of friends invested with enthusiasm. It was a total write-off.

Music became a defining part of the San Francisco culture in the early 1970s, and Chuck wanted a piece of it. This was a guy who played golf and listened to Pat Boone records. Where he got the confidence that he could stage a Woodstock-like 3-day concert no one will know, but for Music Expo 1972, a musical extravaganza held in San Francisco's Cow Palace convention center, he spectacularly misjudged contemporary musical tastes. While The Doors, Canned Heat, and Jefferson Airplane were playing for Bill Graham at the Fillmore West, Chuck offered a mix of the Roger Wagner Chorale, Chuck Berry, and a variety of jazz and country acts. If the show—for which Chuck was both general and limited partner—was a hit, Chuck figured, Music Expo would go national.

He lost his team's investment of $80,000 and another $80,000 besides. "Guess who had to absorb the whole thing?" Chuck told *Inc.* reporter Lisa Sheeran in a 1985 article. Once again Chuck was left holding the bag when his associates bailed. But this episode reveals an important quality. Chuck generally pays himself last and he generally sticks around to clean up the mess. From his earliest years, Chuck has demonstrated a commitment for treating three constituents right: He treats his investors well, his employees better, and his customers best of all.

One person, though, still believed in him. That was his Uncle Bill. William Schwab was the most influential person in Chuck's life, with the exception of his father. Bill Schwab ran Commander Corporation, a Sacramento-based company with interests in oil, timber, or whatever caught his fancy. Early on, Uncle Bill sensed in Chuck an astute business mind and invited his nephew to serve on the board of directors and occasionally hired him to serve as a consultant on various projects. Now, even as Investment Indicators was going down in flames, Uncle Bill popped up again. He put up $100,000, allowing Chuck and four new partners to start a second investment company, which they named First Commander Corporation.

A fine name, but the firm had no products, no business model, no strategy, no business, and no prospects of any. Within the year a disgusted Uncle Bill sold his interest to Chuck and his partners, agreeing to take their notes in payment. Less than a year later, the four partners had bailed, turning over their stock in exchange for Chuck assuming all the liabilities. Chuck was in charge again, unencumbered by anything but debt. Against all odds, he felt optimistic that something would go his way. What gave this spectacularly unsuccessful entrepreneur confidence? What serenity allowed him to know that while he was responsible for past defeats, he was never limited by them?

Chuck changed the name of the company to reflect the new reality of Chuck at the center. Back in San Francisco, Charles Schwab & Co. was in business. Now its owner just waited and occasionally did some heavy lifting for Uncle Bill. But basically he waited for something to come along. It was early 1974 and change was in the air. Something, he sensed, would come his way. Enter Hugo Quackenbush, a Stanford buddy from Santa Barbara who hero-worshipped Chuck and watched with wonder as his hero failed at everything he tried. Quackenbush was by now in the financial services business himself, working as an institutional portfolio manager for Scudder, Stevens & Clark, and something he heard made him think of Chuck. Trading commissions were going to be deregulated. The retail market for trading stocks was going to be big because average individual investors would not be welcome at the Merrill Lynches and EF Huttons. Something called discount brokerages would emerge to fill the need. "Chuck, there's room for a new kind of business," Quackenbush said. "Why not turn your new company into a new type of business, the discount brokerage?"

The discount brokerage. Chuck didn't need to be convinced. The elegance of the idea appealed to him at once. He liked the novelty of it; he was forever resisting the tyranny of precedent, the limits of small minds muttering, "but this is how we've always done it." Here was a ground-floor opportunity wide open for an entrepreneur with imagination who would make his own rules. There was something at once familiar and electrifying about it. Chuck knew the brokerage business but it was the discount part of the term that really electrified him.

Entrepreneurs like Microsoft founder Bill Gates got rich by building value-added businesses. Microsoft started with a bare-bones operating system and added options at a furious pace for more profit until we now have, in the words of Scott McNealy of Sun Microsystems, the "hairball" called Windows XP. Chuck, by contrast, got rich through value-subtracted services. He started with a full-service brokerage and subtracted options for smaller chunks of new value until he had a bare-bones operation. It was a reverse form of versioning. Chuck took the full-commission brokerage, but instead of aggregating services, he started unbundling. Gone were the armies of costly stock pickers and investment bankers to provide advice and investment services. Gone were the prima donna and self-serving stockbrokers. Gone, in the beginning at least, was the need for branch offices and high-priced downtown real estate.

It was one of the first instances of creative deconstruction. It was one of those moments of clarity that come once per lifetime to every prepared entrepreneur. He would transform his company into a discount brokerage.

He hated to sell, so his firm wouldn't sell. Customers would call him, expecting only that he execute stock trades efficiently and economically. Schwab brokers would never dispense advice. His firm would unbundle the trade transaction from investment advice and other services, charging dirt-cheap rates for the former and dispensing with the latter. No more sleazy brokers snookering widows into buying the risky investment du jour. The customer's interests would reign supreme. The part of the brokerage business that Chuck hated the most was the cold calling, the constant dialing for dollars that stockbrokers must do. Here, at last, was a way to eliminate outbound calling. In Chuck's business model, average customers would pick up the phone and call him to initiate a trade. Why? Because it was so easy. The populist in him liked the idea of being the broker to the little guy. What's more he knew he had the marketing skills to get the word out and that the cost advantage he reaped would bring tears to the eyes of the elites on Wall Street. Of course, Wall Street had no clue what Schwab was up to and Chuck didn't want it any other way.

Chuck drew a line in the sand. Who are we to give advice? Schwab customers know their investing requirements better than we ever could, Chuck insisted. We are about executing trades for the average, individual investor. In years hence, Schwab customer reps would be fired for crossing this line. To remove all incentives for selling anything, Chuck's brokerage would eschew the inherent conflicts of interest in which commission stockbrokers put their own interests above those of the investors. Schwab brokers would be paid a salary. In his brokerage, customers would be empowered to act in their own interests so that they would return again and again, not opportunistically exploited for the often dubious investments that commissioned brokers at full-service brokerages were ordered to sell.

Thus was the creed of Chuck revealed. Henceforth, Chuck's mantra—no advice, no conflict, no sales person will ever call—imbued the organization from top to bottom. About everything else Schwab people could legitimately argue. But this was dogma! Chuck Schwab believed—and still believes to this day—that he was helping lead a revolution that empowered the little guy, the individual investor. The company's mission statement: to provide the most useful and ethical financial services in the world. Global religions have been founded on less.

Chuck used the one-year pilot period of deregulated commissions to fine-tune his business. Starting in April 1974, brokerages could charge whatever commission they liked for trades of $2,000 or less. Perfect! This level of trading represented the sweet spot of Chuck's business. Putting his marketing expertise to work, Chuck took out small ads in the *Wall Street Journal* introducing Charles Schwab & Co. to the world. The no-nonsense ads went to the heart of the matter: commission discounts up to 80 percent off the fixed rates people were used to paying. The ads listed a toll-free telephone number, a service that AT&T had only recently commercialized, for investors to call. Chuck didn't have to wait long. People began calling and sending checks almost immediately. Not enough to attract the attention of anyone on Wall Street, but enough to send a thrill down Chuck's spine. Maybe, just maybe, he was finally riding a horse that had a shot, and that's all he needed, just a shot.

Chuck's vision of his business anticipated the Internet dot-com craze by a quarter of a century. Above all, he wanted market share and scale. A little bit of a lot seemed to Chuck much more impressive than a lot more of a little. If he succeeded in bulking up the company, Chuck knew, profits would take care of themselves. He knew this in the same way that Chuck knew a lot of things, but if you asked him for evidence he would just laugh. This was on faith. Shortly after Bill Pearson joined the company as its operations guy, when Schwab had fewer than twenty-five people on board, he was at a meeting with Chuck and Rich Arnold, Schwab's chief deal maker. It was his first glimpse into how important Chuck regarded growth. Arnold re-created the conversation for a Schwab video:

RICH ARNOLD: How big do you want the firm to get?

CHUCK SCHWAB: Big!

ARNOLD: How big? Is there any size at which you would begin to feel that it was more than you can manage?

CHUCK: No.

ARNOLD: Well, let me ask you this: Would you rather have $100 million in revenues and 10 percent profit, or $50 million in revenues and 25 percent profit?

CHUCK: I'll take the growth every time.

ARNOLD: What about profits?

CHUCK: You give me the growth now and the profits will come later.

Pearson's head was spinning because he knew it would be up to him and his team to support Chuck's ambitions.

By the following May, all brokerages would be obliged by the SEC to deregulate commissions. But Chuck wanted to jump in early. Charles Schwab & Co. became one of the first of the discount brokerages. The timing was not ideal. The stock market was falling in the mid-1970s, a barometer of the dangerous inflation that would soon buffet the country. But while many of the new middle-class investors who entered the market in the Go-Go years got burned and stopped trading, Schwab became attractive to inveterate investors who traded regardless of the direction of the market. News about Schwab's low commissions gradually spread across the country.

Chuck and Hugo further spread the gospel by appearing on virtually every radio or television program that would have them. Hitting the road, the college buddies from Stanford talked up every business editor about the values of self-directed investing, conflict-of-interest-free trading, and low commissions. Something about the way that Chuck handled himself must have been powerful. Why else would people in Peoria, Illinois send their money to this guy in California they never heard of? Quackenbush saw it, too. People liked Chuck. They trusted his open face. They resonated to his vision of giving a break to the little investor. Hugo Quackenbush resolved to brand the company around Chuck's trustworthy persona.

Slowly the company took off. That first month, the company registered an average of 4 trades per day. By the summer of 1974, it was 85 trades per day; 6 months later, 250 per day, and the slope of the curve seemed to have no upward limit. Chuck was slowly on his way.

Not everyone in those early days knew what a discount brokerage was. Anne Hennegar, a Schwab registered representative, recalls the following conversation with a customer who was unclear on the concept:

CUSTOMER: What is the price of IBM?

HENNEGAR [reading the quote off the Quotron]: 55 ⅜.

CUSTOMER [outraged]: 55 ⅜? What kind of discount is that? I can get the same price from Merrill Lynch!

Sophisticated customers were another issue. Right after Schwab started offering discounted trades, Patricia Spaugh, another registered rep, received a call from an experienced options trader who asked her what Schwab would charge for a specific options trade. Spaugh gave him a figure, which she recalls as $34. "He sputtered he couldn't believe it and slammed the phone down," she says. A few minutes later he called Spaugh again and repeated the same question. She gave him the same answer. Again he slammed the phone down. A half hour later the same customer walked in the front door of the branch. He was accompanied by two men. "These are my attorneys," he addressed Spaugh. "I want you to tell me in front of these witnesses what you are going to charge me." He said. "Then he pulled out a confirmation slip from another brokerage that charged him $175 for an options order for which we were charging $34." Clearly Chuck had a lot of educating to do.

During his initial job interview with Chuck, Charles "Chip" Roame was fascinated with the materials on Chuck's desk and office walls. "He was comparing Schwab's monthly statements with the statements of competing brokerage firms. Statements were pasted all over the walls. He was cussing about how much more friendly the Schwab statement should be. 'Why can't we give our customers a simple pie chart of the asset allocations?' he asked. Later I realized that the statements he was criticizing were his own. This was not just an academic question. He really wanted a friendlier statement for himself." Roame played a key strategic role in Schwab's mutual funds and financial advisor businesses. He is currently managing principal of Tiburon Strategic Advisors, a market research, strategic consulting, and venture consulting firm based in Tiburon, California.

So the race was on, but the finish line was still a year off and 3,000 miles away. What would Wall Street do? Until Chuck saw what the established brokerages would do on May Day, it would still be a toss-up. Chuck understood that while the race does not always go to the swift, nor the battle necessarily to the strong, that's the way to bet. To many handicappers, the odds-on favorite to benefit from May Day was Merrill Lynch. If the big boys lowered their commissions, there'd be no price advantage for Schwab to exploit and he'd be back to carrying water for Uncle Bill.

But Chuck, for the first time in his patchwork history as an entrepreneur, was dipping his toe into liquid gold. Nor did he have anything to fear from the established brokers. No one ever went broke underestimating the greed and shortsightedness of Wall Street.

Building the Brand

1975–1980

Thanks primarily to the values and leadership of its founder, Schwab has evolved a distinctive management mind-set that encourages the company to question its most cherished assumptions and thereby avoid the arrogance that hardens the arteries of other companies that are occasionally kissed by success.

"Thank you for calling Charles Schwab & Company. This is Chuck Schwab. May I help you?"

Some customers during the busiest trading periods during those early years must surely have been taken aback to hear the founder of the company on the other end of the line. Within a few years, Charles Schwab & Co. had become the largest discount broker in the country and Schwab's face was increasingly recognizable. In 1977, Chuck became the first person to have his photograph in the *Wall Street Journal*. The company committed to a daily ad in a choice location on the inside back page. The

Wall Street Boys laughed at this upstart. For them, having your photo in the newspaper was just not the way it was done.

But that was Chuck. He resisted the idea of using his image, but ads with his face pulled much better. And as for answering phones, that was Chuck, too. Whatever needed doing—answering phones, stuffing envelopes, sweeping the floor—Chuck was right there. After you've processed chicken fertilizer, there's no aspect of office work, however mundane, that is not downright delightful. When the phone calls came fast and furious, no one had to ask Chuck to lend a hand.

A device that resembled a vehicular traffic light signaled Chuck and other executives down from their offices to join the troops on the phones. The device had three light bulbs of different colors. When the green light was on, that meant that the company's customer service representatives were staying ahead of incoming calls. When the yellow light came on, that meant that the company was operating at capacity and that some callers had to wait on hold. When the red light came on, Chuck—and every other executive who had a Series 7 broker's trading license—dropped whatever they were doing and ran downstairs to take calls. The customers came first. Everything else, including managing the back office operations, came second.

It was utter chaos from the beginning. Despite his M.B.A., Chuck was woefully unprepared for the challenges of managing a rapidly growing brokerage. Like all transaction-driven businesses, brokerages require huge investments in what the industry calls operations. The back office is where the paperwork—and in those days stock transactions were entirely based on passing paper tickets and stock certificates around—was recorded, executed, reconciled, balanced, and audited for quality. Nor did the press of business allow managers to devote much time to issues of organizational governance, infrastructure, and strategic planning. Chuck might have remembered an old adage from his M.B.A. days: "The urgent drives out the important." But Chuck had no time for management theory. The phone was ringing and Chuck rolled up his sleeves.

Schwab alumni recall those first days as the most heady of their careers. With the founder beside them, they battled an avalanche of orders, serving customers with integrity, making the business up as they went along. The orders just kept coming in, more and more every day. It was like Marine boot camp. Something you hated as you went through it, but subsequently regarded as a time when real character was cemented. The people who lived through those first days came away with an abiding loyalty to Schwab, the company, and a deep affection approaching love for Schwab, the man. These attitudes were forged in a crisis atmosphere and the coworkers would rise to the occasion for the many crises the company would subsequently confront.

Schwab lore has it that those first days after May Day were so chaotic because of the incessant calls from investors wanting to trade stocks and options. Their memories of chaos are no doubt accurate. But the cause of the chaos was less the volume of customers demanding service than Schwab's slapdash business practices. If that sounds too harsh, one must remember that Chuck is just not wired as a detail guy. He has the vision thing, but every manager who ever worked for him uses the same terms. Not detail-oriented. Avoids conflict. Tactically tone deaf. Detail-averse. And those are the compliments. Schwab was the least rigorous of the financial services companies, for which the SEC occasionally slapped Chuck's wrist. The company had to endure many crises to develop a mature governance structure, validating the theory that life is attracted to order but uses messes to get there.

What was it like to work for Schwab during its first year of operation? Melinda Meahan, a temporarily derailed music major, dropped out after two years of college to find a direction for her life. Without a degree or experience, no employer would take a chance on her. But Schwab did. Her report:

> I started at Schwab in March 1976, on the 24th floor of 120 Montgomery Street. There were about 70 of us in the company then, including five people in the Sacramento branch. I started in the order room, typing confirmations for open orders and options. Later I coded completed trades for billing. I loved how down-to-earth Chuck was, what an ethical company he ran, and how

much the company supported my development. When things got really busy, Chuck would come to the order room and get on the telephone like everyone else. Chuck encouraged everyone in the company, and that includes clerical people like I was, to get a license to be a registered representative. If we passed the test, the company reimbursed us for the cost. The man who hired me was Peter Moss. We both took the same commuter train, and for a few weeks he spent all that time teaching me about the stock market and the industry.

Outside the front desk there was a waiting area where a number of customers would congregate each day, watching the Bunker Ramo machine as it printed stock quotes. Many of these customers listed their occupation as "unemployed." They were the day traders of the period and some of them made a pretty good living. Chuck would often talk to them. He even hired one of the more successful traders, a man named Ken Dong, and he did a good job for us until he quit because he could make a better living doing day trades. There was nothing plush about the offices. We worked on plywood tables. You could tell that we were growing because of the different colored carpets. We tore down interior walls but we kept the original carpets and you could see where the walls used to be. Chuck ran a pretty loose outfit except for one thing. He didn't tolerate any funny business or unethical behavior. Integrity was critical. If you violated one of the compliance rules or did something illegal, you were out of there, no questions asked, even if we were super busy and needed every person we could get.

Bill Pearson had seen some ugly back offices, but nothing in his 14-year career managing data processing system and brokerage operations prepared him for what he saw when he poked around in the cellar of Chuck Schwab's fledgling brokerage at 120 Montgomery Street. "There was a total lack of operational control," he recalls. This was the new wave of brokerage? To Pearson it looked like the Keystone Kops opened a brokerage. "There was paper everywhere," he laughs. "People were running around. I opened a desk drawer and found bank statements that hadn't been opened, much less reconciled. I found backlogs of exceptions and errors. If there were controls, I didn't see any. I saw someone taking reconciliations home in a shopping bag. I learned that she called in sick the next day. One thing that did impress me was that Chuck was in it up to his armpits. He was certainly not sitting in his office."

Maybe that's where Chuck should have been, instead of running around in the basement. Pearson had, of course, heard the phrase, "How can we drain the swamp when we're up to our ass in alligators?" but never had he seen it acted out. "Chuck, you have some basic problems," Pearson remembers telling his prospective boss. It was July 1, 1975, just one quarter after May Day. Chuck just nodded helplessly and asked if Pearson wanted the chance to clean up the mess. Chuck's first recruiting question is usually, "Do you want to work here?" Pearson blinked. He had driven in a yellow Volkswagen Bug from Dallas to San Francisco to be with his girlfriend. He had experience in brokerage operations. What he didn't have was either a college degree or an appointment. No matter. He had walked into the Montgomery Street office and now he had a job.

Pearson considered the offer of $1,500 per month, even in 1975 not a lot of money in San Francisco. But he was among the endless wave of young, smart people looking for something. Mostly it was not about money—where else but in California could you say that?—so he took the job on the spot. Many of the systems Pearson developed are still in use more than 25 years later, something he would have laughed off as utterly improbable had anyone raised the possibility. Pearson would become Schwab's first chief operating officer (COO). He would become one of a handful of people in Schwab's history to have the privilege and frustration of reporting to Chuck.

In its 28-year history, the company has had only three people besides Chuck operating in the COO role. Pearson was the first. In every important way, Pearson was ideally suited for his job. Born in Lubbock, Texas, Pearson knew about the brokerage industry. His grandmother worked for Fenner & Beane starting in 1923. Fenner & Bean later merged with a New York firm to create Merrill Lynch, Pierce, Fenner & Beane, for which his mother worked in the Dallas office. Pearson got his start in 1961 at the Dallas broker Rauscher Pierce. By the time he waltzed into Chuck's basement, Pearson had 14 years of broker-specific operational experience plus all the SEC licenses.

Pearson got himself a ringside seat for the most daunting and exciting job of his career. The job burned him out just before the company really made it. He left about $300 million on the table when he suddenly walked away from Schwab 10 years later. But insiders know that it was Pearson's technical acumen and his willingness to play bad cop to Chuck's good cop that pulled the company out of an administrative morass from which it could not have recovered.

He did the best he could with the manual, paper-based systems underpinning the business, but Pearson knew that computers were the only answer. Chuck also understood that in a transaction-oriented business such as discount brokering, computer technology promised more efficiency and lower operating costs. In 1978, Chuck deputized Pearson to develop or find a computer system capable of doing what no other brokerage was then capable of: giving a broker the ability to take a buy or sell order, edit it on a computer screen, and then submit the order for processing . . . all without generating paper.

Paper. The bane of Wall Street. Every stock brokerage was awash in it, drowning in it. Armies of clerks and runners were responsible for the care and feeding of paper. Trade orders. Stock certificates. Confirmations. Invoices. Every transaction generated a paper trail that had to be managed. Regulators spent their careers promulgating rules and standards about the handling and storage of documents. During trading hours, Wall Street would be filled with runners carrying trays of confirmations from the brokerages to the clearing houses. Every season, a brokerage would be embarrassed because a runner tripped and the winds took the documents he was carrying to the four corners of lower Manhattan.

"Paper was killing us," notes Pearson. The company used a three-track conveyer belt to move the equities and options orders around the office. At the nodes sat early staffers such as Mike Baldwin, who handled equities, and Patricia Spaugh, who took care of options. Here was the drill: They would take a call, write up a paper ticket, tear off a copy, and send it to the back office where others would execute the order, write the price at which it had been executed, and then send it back. When it got busy, the volume of paper often jammed the conveyer belt. To recover the jammed order tickets and inject some levity into a tiresome process, the staff called on a device affectionately called the Rammer Duck to unclog the pipeline. The Rammer Duck was a cardboard cutout of a duck (some insisted it was a penguin) mounted on a weighted base. The laughter that periodically emanated from the back room indicated another visit from the Rammer Duck.

Of course, Pearson was not so naïve to think that computers could do away with paper altogether. Periodically over the next 30 years, the computer industry would proclaim the advent of the "paperless" office, but Pearson was a realist. He knew that there'd be paperless offices when there were paperless bathrooms. No, for now he simply wanted to automate the customer-facing part of the transaction. Of course, there was nothing simple about it. What Pearson took on had never been done at any other brokerage. Again, Schwab's position as an upstart far from tradition-bound Wall Street gave it breathing room.

One of the strands of Chuck's success is his appreciation for what business he's in. Paradoxically, Chuck would often say, it's not the brokerage business. Depending on what hat he was wearing at the moment, Chuck would say that he's either in the direct response business or the technology business. "Chuck understood that he was a direct marketer supporting a business that just happened to be brokerage," says Jim Fuller, one of Chuck's earliest lieutenants. "But he could have been just as successful selling Ginsu knives. Schwab's competitors were preoccupied with the brokerage business and that's why Chuck was so successful."

The association between Schwab and technology got its start in 1979 when Schwab risked $500,000—100 percent of its revenues that year—on a turnkey back-office settlement system, becoming the first discount broker to bring automation in-house. "People warned him he'd have all those weird technical people working for him," says Dawn Lepore, Schwab's chief information officer at the time. "But as the low-cost broker, he felt we had to have control of the technology." Pearson located a Milwaukee software company that had something close to what Schwab needed. Chuck hired the company to modify the program to Pearson's specifications. Then Schwab needed a mainframe computer to run the software. When many companies were buying computer processing power on a time-share basis or leasing computers, Chuck made the decision to buy a used IBM 360 Model 150 mainframe computer. All things being equal, Chuck preferred to own rather than rent.

Schwab soon had the first online order entry system in the brokerage business. It was called BETA—short for Brokerage Execution and Transaction Analysis. Schwab brokers now had computer terminals in front of them when they took orders. For the first time in the securities industry, brokers could handle on a computer screen everything required to buy and sell securities. The benefits proved astounding. Each Schwab broker could now handle more transactions. The system provided instant execution of orders. The software offered sophisticated controls that promoted quality. For example, if a customer wanted to sell stock, the system automatically checked to see if the stock was in the customer's account. It checked for open orders and did some rudimentary margin calculations. It electronically swept cash in customer accounts into money market funds. Not only did costs plummet, but Schwab's cancel and rebill rate—a measure of the accuracy of trade executions—dropped from an average of 4 percent to 0.1 percent. With the system increasingly automated, Schwab could offer 24-hour service. As the system grew in sophistication, customers were encouraged to bypass the customer reps altogether and access the system directly through the telephone and then, much later, through personal computers. Perhaps most important, the computer system generated extensive customer data that the company could mine to discover trends and patterns.

Almost overnight, Schwab order takers could handle twice as much volume, at less cost, with greater accuracy than any broker in the business. It was all so heady and so new that the brokerages on Wall Street for the first time took real notice of this upstart. They didn't like what they saw and put up every roadblock they could think of. For example, the New York Stock Exchange (NYSE) saw its chance to challenge Schwab precisely on BETA's greatest innovation: no paper order tickets. A NYSE reviewing team cited the rule requiring all NYSE member organizations to save paper tickets for 7 years. Where, the NYSE asked, were the storage rooms for safekeeping the tickets? They were going to go by the book. No paper tickets, no certification for BETA.

But two can play the by-the-rules game. "The NYSE rules required only that member firms *save* paper tickets," Pearson insisted. "Show me the rule that requires NYSE member firms to *write* paper tickets." There was no such rule. The NYSE threw in the towel. The BETA system gave Schwab a preferred position to exploit the trading volumes generated by the bull market of the early 1980s. Within 2 years, every other brokerage had developed similar systems, but Schwab's early technological lead would always give it a strategic advantage.

It was by no means smooth sailing. The company often took a step back to move two steps forward. As Schwab's marketing kicked in, orders rose to more than 2,000 per day, stressing the small back-office staff past all reason. Yes, the money started rolling in, but success always comes at a price. In this case it was the need to keep a certain amount of cash in the bank. The SEC requires all brokerages to maintain precisely regulated levels of capital. Brokerages are required by law to settle the trades they execute on behalf of their customers. If a customer defaults, the brokerages are obliged to settle the account. Mostly it's not an issue because 80 percent of Schwab's customers had sufficient cash in their accounts or, if not, paid up within the required 5 days. The remaining customers bought stock on margin. These customers put up some of the cash—typically half—of the value of the stock they ordered Schwab to buy or sell for them. The other half customers borrowed from Schwab and the resulting margin interest they paid was a significant contributor to the company's revenue stream. Schwab needed to maintain sufficient reserves to (1) have capital to lend to margin borrowers who required it and (2) to cover the possibility that some margin borrowers might default. The more margin debt balances Schwab carried, the higher the SEC's minimum net capital amount Schwab had to have. It was a constant struggle to keep the capital in the bank when there were so many opportunities to grow the business. Every month was a moment of truth as Schwab filed the required SEC FOCUS (Financial and Operational Combined Uniform Securities) report attesting that it had the capital on hand.

The constant hunt for capital took its toll on the company and its founder, both professional and personally. It was desperation for capital that, 5 years later, drove Chuck to sell Charles Schwab & Co. to Bank of America, a move that he immediately regretted. Meanwhile, Chuck did whatever he could to meet the minimum net capital requirements, even mortgaging his residence on a number of occasions, much to the consternation of his second wife. Helen, the daughter of a wealthy Texas oil family, was not used to what seemed like a hand-to-mouth existence.

The brokerage often did best when Chuck got out of the way of the day-to-day stuff and kicked himself upstairs. The best leaders know their limitations and when to step back and let others take charge. Abraham Lincoln perfected this brand of leadership. In 1832 Lincoln raised a company of soldiers to fight in the Black Hawk War. As the organizer, he automatically became the commander of the company. Trouble is, Lincoln knew absolutely nothing about soldiering or military tactics. He had trouble remembering the names of the simplest drills. The moment of truth for Lincoln came when he was marching the company across a series of fields and he needed to guide them through a narrow gate to the next field. But what was the command for creating a single file? "I could not for the life of me remember the proper command for getting my company endwise [into single file]. So I gave the command: "This company is dismissed for two minutes when it will fall in again on the other side of this gate." Chuck's ego made it very easy for him to trust that his managers knew their way. Because he was a good judge of talent, they generally did.

The company was quickly taking shape, at once defining the best practices of a discount brokerage and violating accepted truisms of the securities industry. The "No advice" rule was perhaps the main differentiator between Schwab and its full-service (or as Chuck would insist, "full-commission") brethren. His antipathy to advice giving and the conflicts of interest it created were genuine, but Chuck also did the math. He knew it was impossible to employ well-trained full-service brokers working for commissions while offering discounted trades to customers. As a result, Chuck hired glorified telephone order takers and paid them a salary of about $10,000 per year. To be fair, Chuck paid himself only $24,000 in 1977.

Another axiom that bit the dust was the assumption that "Stocks are sold, not bought." The precept that most investors rarely came easily to a decision to buy or sell a stock or bond was the first lesson pounded into every broker. Investors, brokers were taught, had to be sold, had to be closed, whatever sales tactics, fair or foul, it took. It was called dialing for dollars and everyone reading this book, no doubt, knows the experience from the receiving end. Schwab's ranks are filled with refugees from traditional brokers because they hated the constant cold calling and the casual morality of the brokerages.

Schwab demolished that axiom. Of course stocks are bought. Customers picked up the phone every day and called Schwab to buy and sell stocks. No one held a gun to their heads. Good times or bad, there are inveterate investors who need to trade and a critical and growing mass of these investors gravitated to Schwab. Meanwhile, Schwab order takers waited for the phones to ring. They had strict orders to be helpful and efficient but to draw the line at advice. They could offer limited information ("Many investors are considering mutual funds") and explain definitions ("An index mutual fund is a fund that is designed to match the performance, neither underperforming nor overperforming, of the overall market"). But crossing the line into advice would get them fired.

These so-called self-directed investors who flocked to Schwab rarely needed or wanted advice and Chuck was glad to accommodate them. Once they called, the investors became "customers" and Schwab soon had more than 300,000 of them. But Chuck was clear that brokers were not to pester them with sales calls. Did he miss opportunities? Probably. But the upside was that Schwab attracted a base of relatively loyal customers who responded enthusiastically to the company's sales policy, so memorably reduced to the headline of one of its first ads: "Call us because no sales person will ever call you."

Schwab had transformed what everyone assumed was a "push" business into a "pull" business. The implications were staggering. The discount brokerage helped reverse the power relationship between investors and brokers, buyers and sellers. "Suddenly, the impressive-looking offices, the reassuring-sounding brokers—even the thick research reports—weren't as important to customers as they used to be. In the brave new world of competitive rates, what increasingly began to matter most was price. Why pay Merrill Lynch $350 to $400 to execute a trade when a discount broker would perform the task for just $36?" writes Benjamin Mark Cole, author of *The Pied Pipers of Wall Street: How Analysts Sell You Down the River*. Customers were shaking off the bonds of powerlessness that held them captive to their brokers.

Despite its initial successes, the company had enormous obstacles to overcome. Some of the obstacles were internal. The more complex the bookkeeping became, the more the back office struggled to keep pace. Staying ahead of the company's capital requirements every month proved grueling. Chuck's desire for more growth, more customers, more branches—and the capital to fund it—was insatiable. "We hated to see Chuck go away on vacation because we knew that he always came back with ideas for great new products and services. But to develop them took capital," Pearson says.

There were constant reminders that the company had a lot to learn. Strategic planning in those early years was often a joke. In 1977, Peter Moss, who had joined Schwab as controller in May 1975, proposed that the company set up a telephone call center in Reno, Nevada. By centralizing telephone order takers in a region with lower wage rates than San Francisco, Moss argued, the company would realize operational efficiencies and save money on both the inbound 800 telephone numbers and payroll. But Moss's projections for business were overoptimistic and especially at night—it did not yet offer 24-hour access—the company found itself with excess capacity. Not to worry, Moss told Chuck. There are lots of telemarketers using 800 numbers that would buy Schwab's excess capacity. The good news was many of them wanted the lines at night when they were sitting idle. The bad news was that these companies turned out to be the kind of fly-by-night record companies that filled the television airwaves in the dead hours with come-ons for Elvis Presley collections. The deal was inked in the summer of 1977 and Chuck felt relief that some of the bleeding had stopped. But on August 7, 1977, the world awoke to the news from Memphis that The King was dead. Hello Heartbreak Hotel. Suddenly the phone lines were so overwhelmed with weeping fans wanting to buy Elvis records that for several days Schwab customers couldn't get through. "Such was life at Charles Schwab & Co.," notes Joseph Nocera, author of *A Piece of the Action: How the Middle Class Joined the Money Class.*

Not all of the Schwab troubles were its fault. The big brokerage houses and commercial banks hated Schwab and threw up every obstacle they could. "The major firms employed the rankest discrimination against us," Chuck recalls. When Schwab attempted to negotiate a lease for a branch office, other brokerages in the same building would threaten to move out. "They might have the plum position in an office building, on the ground floor or mezzanine, but like spoiled kids they would threaten to break their leases if we were allowed a puny thousand square feet way up on the twentieth or thirtieth floor."

Schwab's competitors were quick to report the new discount broker for rules violations, real or perceived. As a result, the NYSE, the Pacific Stock Exchange, and the SEC routinely called Chuck and his executives in for various inquiries. Of course, it didn't help the firm that a certain amount of us-versus-them arrogance had already infiltrated the Schwab culture.

One day a regulator from the SEC called asking some questions about operations. The call was taken by David Taylor, a vice president who had the self-importance that comes from having three college degrees. "By what authority are you requesting this information?" the vice president haughtily demanded. He soon got his answer. "Have Mr. Schwab in our Los Angeles offices tomorrow morning!" Chuck was not happy as he and Pearson presented themselves to the SEC the following morning. "The SEC represented restraint, control," Pearson says, "everything Schwab hated." Thankfully, the company actually was in decent shape by then. "But they could have confiscated our records if they didn't believe us. We were that close to not being a firm anymore," Pearson adds.

The regulatory agencies nickel-and-dimed the company for various infractions. In September 1975, the Philadelphia Stock Exchange slapped the company with a $5,000 fine and censured Chuck for failure to maintain up-to-date books and records, an acknowledgment that Schwab's back office could not keep up with the heavy influx of new accounts. Two years later, the National Association of Securities Dealers fined Schwab $500 for a technical violation of a minor SEC rule having to do with excess margin securities. Chuck dutifully paid the fines and both matters were settled.

The young company had to battle on every front. The SEC challenged Chuck with the know-your-customer rule. Like most of Wall Street's rules, it gave the impression it was a consumer-friendly policy. In this case, the idea was that brokers should know something about the circumstances and tolerance for risk of the investors they served so they would not give out inappropriate advice. If a broker discovered that his client was a retired person dependent on dividend income, for example, he was expected to recommend a portfolio of only appropriately conservative investments. A broker could suggest more aggressive investments for a younger investor who indicated more of a desire for equity growth. Advice was supposed to be measured. In practice, the know-your-customer rule was used by brokers mainly to know if customers could pay for their trades. It was routinely and even wantonly violated, as brokers had a financial interest in pushing the most aggressive investments, the widows and orphans be damned.

But now the regulators called Chuck to task because discount brokers didn't make any attempt to understand the customers' financial requirements. Chuck's response was that the rule didn't apply to discounters because discount brokers knew nothing about their customers' financial situations. "You couldn't be accused of giving out inappropriate advice if you gave out no advice at all. Schwab's no-advice policy, besides being cost-effective, kept him on the right side of the law," Nocera observes.

By the end of the 1970s, Schwab, like the entire nation, had weathered monumental changes. Inflation, the scariest word in economics, had steadily risen during President Jimmy Carter's inept administration. From the vantage point of the twenty-first century, it is easy to recognize that Jimmy Carter has been a much better former president than a sitting president. When Gerald Ford stepped down in 1976, the Consumer Price Index (CPI) was 4.9 percent. Two years later, the CPI was 9 percent. By the time the new decade kicked in, it was 13.3 percent. High inflation combined with the humiliation of the Iran hostage crisis meant that Jimmy Carter's chances for re-election were approximately zero. The country prepared for the era of Ronald Reagan.

Schwab, like every other financial services company, was profoundly buffeted by the changes in consumer behavior prompted by unforgiving inflation. The biggest change to float Schwab's boat was that the country shifted from a nation of savers to a nation of investors. Savings make absolutely no sense when inflation is raging. Throughout the late 1970s, consumers started withdrawing their savings (the average passbook account had $10,000, according to a survey sponsored by Stanford Research Institute) and moving them into money market funds.

Schwab was a net beneficiary of an inflationary cycle that fueled a tremendous transfer of wealth from savings accounts into investments of all types. It was well positioned to benefit from the nation's new interest in investments that promised good returns. Soon it would have the Schwab One Account, a money market-type account, as well as wildly successful mutual fund products. By the end of the 1970s, Schwab was the largest discount broker in the world. It had revenues of $14.5 million, 520 employees (145 of whom were registered employees), 90,000 customer accounts, and 19 branches.

Chuck himself was becoming, for the first time in his richly checkered business career, a respected executive, a familiar face to any reader of the *Wall Street Journal*, a celebrity in his home town, and if not yet the multibillionaire he would soon become, he was well on his way. He and Helen had acquired a luxurious home in one of the Bay Area peninsula's most fashionable neighborhoods. Soon to follow were a Montana ranch where Chuck could indulge his fervor for duck hunting, a condominium on the Big Island of Hawaii, and a ski chalet in Park City, Utah. And then there was the golf, which he pursued with passion and precision all over the world. He collected prestigious club memberships—San Francisco Golf Club, the Menlo Circus Club, Pacific Union, Olympic, and Castle Pines in Denver—the way other executives collected putters. The corporate jet would come later, but for now he was chauffeured in his Cadillac Brougham. He joined boards, both corporate (The Gap) and civic (the San Francisco Museum). To his credit, Chuck never let any of this go to his head. He retained his populist appeal and employees loved him more than ever.

Schwab has never let itself become ensnared in any one business model. Rather, Schwab has always defined itself in terms of its evolving competencies as informed by its cause. The company's durable core value is to be the most ethical financial services company in the world. The main competency is technology. Now, with some money in the bank, Schwab embarked on a string of technology-oriented experiments that ensured Schwab its dominant position in the industry and streamlined its eventual success on the Internet.

4 Innovation

1980–1988

Call them Schwab's product development years. It was 1980–1988, the Ronald Reagan era. A new morning for Schwab as well as America. Discount brokerage as a business and Schwab's leadership of the industry was increasingly respected. For the first time, the company was profitable. Now it put much of those profits to work building technology infrastructure and gaining experience in developing, integrating, and marketing products.

Clutching his newly issued Bank of America ATM card, Chuck took an uneasy look at the ATM station that had just been installed on the second floor of the Schwab building. Chuck hesitated. As the largest individual shareholder in Bank of America, he was concerned that if something went wrong, he would bring down the bank's statewide ATM network or worse. Finally, he put his card in, entered his PIN, and withdrew $20. Somehow, the bank survived.

While a bit of a technophobe, Chuck has always had deep confidence in technology. Early in the company's history, he assembled a team of technologists and gave them extraordinary autonomy to innovate, expecting them only to focus their efforts on the customer. One Schwab executive, paraphrasing Chuck, put it this way: "Our basic philosophy is to ask, 'Who's getting screwed, where and why?' Let's go out and solve that problem." This kind of commitment makes every customer problem an innovation opportunity. While other parts of the financial services industry seem to look on customer ignorance as a profit center, Schwab assumes the customers it serves are intelligent and rational.

When Schwab started taking baby steps to Net dominance, the Internet was a fugitive shadow of what it would grow to be. Down the peninsula from where Schwab was building its upstart discount brokerage, a small group of academics and government spooks were slowly laying out the protocols that would in 15 years explode as the Internet. For now, the company began building the technical and product development disciplines it would need. Soon, the forces would converge, making Schwab arguably the world's most successful Internet company.

Schwab set up Schwab Technology Services as a stand-alone unit to explore a variety of technological initiatives. "We are running this division as an entrepreneurial start-up," Chuck told William F. Gillis, recruited from Mattel Electronics to be president of the unit. "I want you to develop products and services to help individual investors make better investment decisions," Chuck told Gillis, one of the few African-American executives in the company's history. The technology group would have its own, separate facility and the resources to pursue interesting work. Many companies were setting up their technology units as autonomous divisions in recognition of the fact that technology people did better work when liberated from corporate bureaucracy. Initially, the company believed that Schwab Technologies might develop transaction-based services and products that could also be marketed to other financial services companies.

The work at 315 Mission Street anticipated the dot-com days of the future. The young technologists considered themselves entrepreneurs in a start-up. They worked at all hours, twenty-five people in a big room, pursuing their projects. They knew that their work was serving Schwab, but on a day-to-day basis Schwab Technologies felt like an independent company. Still, they shared much of Chuck's outlook. "Our enemy was the full-commission broker," says Bruce Cardinal, a Stanford under-graduate with an M.B.A. from Wharton who came on as director of electronic information products. "We brought in customers and asked them, 'If you could have whatever you wanted, what would it be?'"

To Mansoor Zakaria, number two at Schwab Technologies, Chuck was more specific: "We want to serve the customer; not to invent technology. Love the customer, be willing to challenge the conventional wisdom, and think about the future." With that Schwab pretty much left the group alone to develop transaction-based systems for the company and the brokerage industry.

Chuck's timing, as always, was excellent. Schwab Technologies had everything in place to rival the other start-ups of the period: Apple, Microsoft, Oracle, and dozens of other start-ups were figuring out how to use computer technology. A number of people came to Schwab Technologies for help with their own enterprises. In fact, if just one decision had been different, Charles Schwab & Co. might today be a subsidiary of Schwab Technologies. In March 1983, an entrepreneur named Bill Porter suggested that Schwab Technologies handle the transactions for a system he intended to brand as TradePlus. His rationale was to avoid investing in expensive infrastructure and the revenue Schwab obtained from TradePlus would defray some of the costs it would incur in designing an online transaction processing environment. Gillis decided that he didn't have the resources to develop products that Chuck wanted and to design systems for others. So when Bill Porter demonstrated the world's first online trade on July 11, 1983, some other company's system was under the covers. Within a few years, Bill Porter had re-named his company. TradePlus became E*Trade.

Gillis realized that the initial charter to develop transaction-based products missed the mark. "We wanted to serve the customer as completely as we could. How could we electronically create everything an individual customer needed to have to be a smart investor?" he says. That meant delivering research, company reports, news, stock quotes, and even financial management tools so that customers could handle multiple portfolios on line. Implicit in this challenge was the requirement that technology not only improve service for customers but reduce costs for Schwab. Schwab Technologies decided to deconstruct the process of buying and selling stocks. The case of providing customers with stock quotes is an exemplar.

Schwab considered how giving the customers what they want is not always the same as giving the customers what they need. Consider free stock quotes. Customers wanted to dial an 800 number and listen to a broker read quotes off a terminal. Schwab, of course, provided stock quotes at no cost. But while it's true that customers were not charged for the service, it was far from free. The infrastructure supporting stock quotes imposed a huge cost: pricey access to the quote feeds from each of the exchanges, which were delivered on leased telephone lines into an expensive leased terminal, so that the quote could be read by a salaried broker, who provided it to the customer over an 800 telephone number, also paid for by Schwab.

Schwab was racing Fidelity Investments to provide the world's first automated stock quote system. Here, Schwab's customer focus paid off. While Fidelity insisted on developing its own systems ("no one can do it as well as we can"), Chuck pushed for speed ("the customers don't give a damn about where the technology comes from"). Because Schwab Technologies bought and customized critical parts of the system and formed valuable alliances with other highly respected companies, Schwab beat Fidelity by 8 months, a lead it has never relinquished.

After a year of development, SchwabQuotes was ready. For Gillis, the best part of his job was show and tell. Chuck would become giddy with excitement as he tried out the products. "He was a great test case," says Cardinal. "If we could make it work for Chuck, we knew the average customer would not have trouble getting it." SchwabQuotes allowed customers with a Touch-Tone phone to retrieve not only real-time stock quotes but also breaking company and industry news. Best of all, it was automated. Digitized voice technology, brand new at the time, was used to deliver the information. Because the service was localized in key cities, most customers accessed the service by dialing a local call, slashing the company's telecommunications expenses. The company negotiated new rates with the exchanges and the Dow Jones News Service, which transmitted a special feed for news straight to Schwab's database. In some cases, Schwab customers received breaking news before anyone else.

Chuck was stunned and became emotional during the days before the release of SchwabQuotes in 1985, Gillis says. "Schwab-Quotes particularly pleased Chuck because it not only served customers in a more complete way but it reduced costs and conferred status on the company." Gillis remembers how exhilarated Chuck was on the day he welcomed executives of Dow Jones to San Francisco to sign the contract setting up the strategic partnership that enabled SchwabQuotes. "Five years ago," Chuck confided to Gillis, "Dow Jones would not have returned my telephone call. Now here they are in my office."

On February 25, 1985, the company announced Schwab-Quotes and a number of other products at a black-tie event featuring Nobel Prize recipient Dr. Milton Friedman as the keynote speaker. It was by far the grandest public event in the company's history. Chuck noted that the event came 10 years after May Day. "I know that if I called a news conference 10 years ago, I know I would have been the only person in the room," Chuck said, clearly basking in the attention.

Gillis was a supremely talented manager. In the software development industry where most projects are late and over budget, Gillis delivered the goods. Gillis could have written his own ticket at Schwab. But he made a classic mistake to which technologists are prone: He overstated and in doing so he violated a key piece of Schwab culture. In response to a question, Gillis announced that Schwab expected to sell 50,000 SchwabQuotes subscriptions. Chuck was aghast. Schwab people simply didn't make such projections. Gillis's wildly overstated forecast—only about 5,000 subscribers signed up—ended one of the most promising careers at Schwab.

SchwabQuotes did not meet Gillis's projections, but it gave the company valuable lessons about pricing, customer segmentation, product integration, and marketing. Success had to wait for the next iteration of the system. Renamed TeleBroker, the system became fully interactive, allowing customers to not only receive quotes but to make trades. By 1995, TeleBroker was handling 80 million calls and 10 million trades, 75 percent of the total calls Schwab fielded that year. If TeleBroker transactions had been considered an independent brokerage service, it would have been the third largest discount broker in the world. To service this telephone-based application, Schwab invested $20 million in four regional customer service telephone centers. Before Schwab had call centers, the telephone numbers for branches were published in the telephone directory and appeared on customer statements. Now the branch phone numbers disappeared. Instead, virtually all calls were routed to the call centers, which handled customers' requests 24 hours a day. Pooling efficiencies resulted in nearly all customer calls being answered within three rings and hold times of less than one minute.

The speech synthesis enabling SchwabQuotes has morphed into a versatile speech recognition application, allowing TeleBroker to respond to voice commands. Schwab learned by watching which customers used the system. For example, it found that many non-English-speaking customers preferred TeleBroker because the Touch-Tone quote system didn't require strong English skills. This observation prompted the company to provide segmented language-specific services to Schwab's Spanish- and Chinese-speaking customers.

The Equalizer, an investor software package that allowed customers with PCs to leverage much of the power of the Schwab database, actualized the Schwab value of self-reliance. Was there ever a more appropriate name for such a product? "What drove us was the idea that we were doing something right by equalizing the playing field for the little guy," Zakaria says. "The Equalizer came out of our challenging the fundamental assumption driving the securities business: the belief that stocks are sold and not bought. Everyone thought brokerage was a quintessential push commodity," he says. Schwab Technologies decided to test that theory and see what happens if it could give average investors all the information they needed to make intelligent investment decisions.

Not every Schwab product made it. In 1983, pagers and wireless technology were in their infancy. Investors had identified a need to have more immediate access to stock prices. In response, Schwab developed the PocketTerm (short for pocket terminal), a first generation pager capable of receiving stock quotes over an FM radio frequency. The product was ahead of its time in some ways (the paging network was too limited) and misguided in others (it was not interactive enough), but it paved the way for other efforts. It's not surprising that, like technologists everywhere, the Schwab developers reached for the newest platforms and sometimes couldn't pull a rabbit out. "That's the price of admission to the 'bleeding edge' of technology," Gillis says. Dial-up computer services soon made SchwabLine, a device that downloaded market data over a phone line and printed it out on adding machine paper, irrelevant.

Like other companies, Schwab toyed with other business models. In 1984, it entered the packaged software business by launching a personal financial management product called "Financial Independence." An ambitious stand-alone financial package that provided services such as tax preparation and loan analysis, Financial Independence was designed to let customers manage their personal finances on the PC. It failed for a number of reasons, the lack of an integrated check register being unforgivable. It didn't help that it was delivered on eleven floppy disks, making installation an ordeal. But mainly the product didn't share a good fit with Schwab's core competency. In *Clicks and Mortar*, co-CEO David Pottruck called Financial Independence "a little ahead of its time," and unceremoniously killed the product. In fact, the system was hard to use and hopelessly ill-fitted for Schwab's customer demographics. Schwab never stayed the course long enough to learn the lessons of Computer Associates

International when it launched a similar product called "Simply Money": the costs of supporting consumer products are exorbitant. The key concept learned: Redirect focus on the customer and, above all, keep it simple.

The big benefit to Schwab of all this innovation was not so much the products that were developed but the product development disciplines it cultivated. "Product development is a muscle an organization can count on only if it exercises it every day," says Larry Stupski, president of the company at the time. Nor can a company be opportunistic about product development. Unless a company deals with issues such as pricing, distribution, integration, channel conflict, and customer ownership, it cannot be prepared to jump on emerging opportunities. "We learned critical lessons about what to charge for and what to give away, segmenting the customer, and building for customer loyalty. When the Internet took off, the lessons we learned during this period provided a clear model for what we would do," Stupski says.

The work as well as the independence of Schwab Technology Services was coming to an end. By 1987, Pottruck had convinced Chuck and Stupski that Schwab had but one business—brokerage—and the technology division should be folded into the company's Information Services Division to create as seamless a value proposition as possible. To the Schwab Technologies techies, it felt like a betrayal. There had been talk of spinning off Schwab Technology Services as a separate company, perhaps even issuing its own initial public offering (IPO). To the techies, Pottruck's decision felt like an enormous setback and most of them departed.

From a corporate standpoint, it was exactly the right thing to do. Customers are not well served by technology that is not integrated into the business. In the end, the Schwab development effort fell victim to the cluelessness of some of the technology bigots on the team. They forgot that every effort must serve a real business need. Instead, they loved the idea that they were the rebel innovators, off the grid with respect to the realities that constrained other parts of the business. "Success," Zakaria says, "comes from discarded teams, not anointed ones." Maybe, but they would have to be successful elsewhere. Zakaria, Gillis, Cardinal, and most of the others on the excellent Schwab Technologies team disbanded, many moving on to found successful companies of their own where presumably they also had to struggle with the issue of integrating technology with business.

Schwab had fallen victim to the "disconnect" between technologists and businesspeople described in *TechnoVision* by Charles Wang, chairman of Computer Associates International. "The disconnect," Wang writes, "is the conflict, pervasive yet unnatural, that has misaligned the objectives of executives and impairs or prevents organizations from obtaining a cost-effective return on their investment in IT." Pottruck saw it firsthand at Citibank, his first job after getting his M.B.A. from Penn State, when he took a data processing assignment. The classic symptoms of the disconnect require businesspeople to lock technologists out of the conversation and technologists to conclude that businesspeople "just don't get it." The result is silence, missed deadlines, cost overruns, and systems that come up short in critical ways.

When Pottruck arrived at Schwab, he was determined to repair the disconnect wherever he found it. He understood that it has almost nothing to do with computers. It is a management problem for the chief executive. He laid out his vision in *Clicks and Mortar*: "The first principles of generating engagement, partnership, and passion are the same for technologists as for everyone else: Get them behind the vision of serving customers, and make sure that everyone is conversant with and aligned with the values of the company. When that alignment and understanding is in place, then both businessperson and technologist will be open to using their respective skills toward the same end."

Although no one could see it clearly, Schwab was evolving from a strictly discount broker to a value-added company. The company began navigating the tensions that would later define its commitment to being a "high-tech, high-touch" provider. Pottruck pushed the company to think deeply about its core competency: Was it providing low-priced services using automated channels and other high-tech channels? Or was it providing spectacular personal services using a network of branches, call centers, and other "high-touch" vehicles. "We learned a lot about innovation during this period. As we began to ponder our choices in strategy, our research was telling us that customers wanted *both*—and so did we. We wanted the strong deep middle of our market, and the middle demands it all: great service, great products. And fair prices."

As only an outsider can, Pottruck began warning the company about the perils of becoming enmeshed in incumbency, the not-invented-here syndrome that stifles innovation. Even small, scrappy firms can become mired in unexamined assumptions and commitments to the status quo. But Schwab's value of looking out for the customer served as a check on some of these excesses. It took an uncompromising commitment to putting the customer first to dislodge the basic assumptions governing IRAs. When Congress passed the legislation enabling IRAs in 1982, no one thought that they would take off as fast as they did. The best estimate of the *New York Times* was that IRAs would attract $50 billion within 10 years. The actual figure was $725 billion. But despite evidence that IRAs represented a unique product, people in the banking industry insisted on treating them as if they were just another account. Because of that, every financial institution, including Schwab, charged customers a small annual fee (typically $25 to $50) to open and maintain one.

The proposal to eliminate the IRA fee came from a non-banker on the Schwab IRA team. Jeffrey Lyons, currently an executive vice president, appealed to Chuck's vision that if Schwab really stood for putting the customer first, and if the company wanted to accumulate assets from customers, then maybe Schwab should eliminate the fee. Lyon's logic was that the loss of the fee would be more than offset by profits driven by the incremental assets. Moreover, it would be a neat piece of marketing jujitsu, using Fidelity's fee collection strength against its competitor in the IRA space by eliminating Schwab's own fees. Plus, no small matter, Schwab practice would be more aligned with its central values.

John Bowen, founder of CEG Worldwide, had a ringside seat to the No-Fee IRA decision. He was on a Schwab customer advisory board participating in a brainstorming session in which Lyons's suggestion was being debated. Chuck asked about the impact of doing away with the IRA fee. The answer came back: $9 million per year. Chuck thought for a minute. "Let's discontinue the fee. It's a nuisance, and we'll get it back," Chuck said, according to Bowen. The juxtaposition of the phrases "It's a nuisance" and "$9 million" struck Bowen as remarkable. "For Schwab in those days a $9 million hit to the bottom line was significant. My estimation of Chuck went up that day," he says.

This is an example of how the power of corporate values is tested. The downside was concrete and immediate: $9 million in lost fee revenue per year. The upside was hypothetical, untested, and risky. There was no assurance that customers would respond by bringing their IRAs to Schwab. Moreover, having eliminated the fee, the company could not go back and reimpose it without looking greedy and inept.

As a value, "for the good of the customer" is aces. But good intentions must not be mistaken for analysis. "Don't let the power of intuition be an excuse for laziness in doing the analysis," Stupski told Lyons, insisting he do the research. The obvious question—how much in incremental assets would Schwab have to attract to balance the loss of $9 million in fees?—was not hard to calculate. But the rest of the problem defied easy analysis. "Markets that don't exist can't be analyzed," says Clayton Christensen in *The Innovator's Dilemma.* The more innovative the idea and the more disruptive it is to the status quo, the less of it there is to analyze. But just because it's difficult doesn't mean that the team presenting the idea gets a free pass. If they want to be taken seriously, they had better conduct the most concrete research possible, complete with targets. "Then we could look each other in the eye and ask, 'Do we think we can hit or exceed this number?' This type of analysis is not as scientific as we would like, but our reaction gives us some sense of the possibility," Pottruck says. For ideas that are as disruptive as the No-Fee IRA, this kind of intellectual honesty keeps the company nimble: Sound ideas get through the front door but are checked out before they take a seat in the main dining room.

The company trusted its analysis and took the plunge. It rolled out the Schwab No-Annual Fee IRA and it immediately exceeded the company's most optimistic projections. "This is a case where incumbency could have kept us from doing the right thing," Pottruck says. "There were executives in the firm, including me, who were not enthusiastic because of their own preconceptions, and we were dead wrong. The trap of incumbency can stifle the changing of systems, processes, or even shifting the fundamentals of an organization, when to do so would be the best course of action." The lessons learned from Schwab Technologies have inspired every initiative, technological and otherwise, that Schwab has taken since.

Branchland

1975–Present

Charles Schwab & Co. has 430 branch offices. In Schwab parlance, the people who work in the branches live in Branchland. It is by far the most important and least understood part of the company.

There is something counterintuitive about a discount brokerage having branches. Everything in the discount brokerage business model mitigates for maximum centralization of resources. Chuck knew that for the model to work, nonessential services would have to be streamlined and costs kept as low as possible. What could customers do in branches that they couldn't do more easily over the telephone? Branches, with their associated costs and management headaches were definitely an artifact of the dinosaur brokerages Chuck was determined to replace. In fact, Chuck had to be forced into the idea.

Chuck is not easily forced into courses of action against his better judgment. There was really only one person in the world that had that kind of influence. Chuck's Uncle Bill, who had bailed out in disgust a year earlier, was now back on the scene, his nostrils full of the scent of embryonic profit, his lips whistling to the tune of $300,000. Chuck, as always, needed the money to grow his business and to fund the capital requirements account. The company had recently run afoul of the Philadelphia Stock Exchange, which was restricting its trades for failing to comply with the Uniform Net Capital rule. The company had been turned down for credit by Crocker Bank and Bank of America— a sleight Chuck would soon avenge—so it was particularly hard up for an infusion of cash.

Uncle Bill had just one condition. He insisted that Chuck open a branch office. And the branch office would have to be located in, of all places, Sacramento. Chuck's jaw dropped. Branches didn't make any sense for a discount brokerage, he believed, but maybe, just maybe, a branch in, say, Los Angeles or a growing Sunbelt city such as Phoenix, would pay for itself. But Sacramento? The dreary capital of California? The last time Chuck had to deal with state government bureaucrats, he got badly burned. The bad taste of the Texas rescission order was still fresh in his mouth. Conservative bureaucrats were never going to be *investors*, Chuck argued, but savers.

Uncle Bill was unmoved. That was the condition attached to the cash. Bill never pretended to be a hands-off venture capitalist. But perhaps, Chuck now considered, his uncle—an astute businessman—sensed a revenue opportunity that eluded his less experienced nephew. No, as it turned out, the Sacramento branch would be little more than a sinecure for Uncle Bill's son-in-law, who would be branch manager. Blood, it appears, is thicker than money. Chuck didn't have a choice; he needed the funds. In September 1975, in a storefront across from a state office building, without any hope except that the branch would not be too much of a drain on the firm's perilous coffers, the first branch office of Charles Schwab & Co. opened for business.

No one, not even Uncle Bill, anticipated what happened next. Simply stated, the company saw an immediate and dramatic increase in activity. Customer inquiries jumped. Both the number of trades per day and new accounts spiked upward. "Hell, the numbers skyrocketed," recalls Jim Fuller, who, as head of marketing for the New York Stock Exchange, kept a close watch on the fledgling discounter in San Francisco before he joined up a few years later. "When Chuck looked closer, most of the new business seemed to come from Sacramento. Apparently the Sacramento branch was thriving," Fuller says.

But where was the foot traffic? If there were all these new Sacramento-based customers, no one could see them. Based on the numbers, one would have expected the small branch office to be overwhelmed, with customers lining up six deep to open accounts and make trades. Yet office traffic, while far from dead, did not seem as busy as the incremental business would imply. Chuck saw this pattern over and over again. Hugo Quackenbush opened Schwab's second branch in Century City. A few months later, Elliott D. Friedman, one of the most successful traders for First National Bank in Seattle, offered to put $500,000 into the business for the right to open a Seattle branch. Subsequent branches opened in Newport Beach, Virginia, and Phoenix, Arizona. By the time Chuck opened the firm's eighth branch in Denver, he decided to be a little more rigorous about the pre- and postbranch data analysis. Schwab had about 300 customers in the Denver area before the branch opened. In the next 12 months, the company picked up more than 1,700 new Denver accounts. Something was working, yet in each case business volume associated with that city increased, but foot traffic in the branches by no means reflected the volume upsurge that followed each opening.

Out of this mystery was born a powerful insight that would fuel the company's growth for the next decade: *People want to be perceptively close to their money.* The branches mattered; not to meet the customers' transactional requirements, but their most elemental psychological needs. Investors often felt gun-shy about sending their money off to a distant city. "Discount brokerages were a new animal and people didn't quite trust them," Fuller says. "We discovered that 80 percent of the customers in a branch came in once to open accounts, kick the tires, and then rarely came back. There was something reassuring about seeing a real office."

This insight explained the missing traffic in the offices. Many potential customers opened their accounts and, satisfied that they were dealing with a durable company, subsequently did their business by telephone. For routine transactions, there was little need to visit a branch. For other prospects, simply walking by the branch and peering inside was enough due diligence. They picked up the phone.

The question was settled. As a marketing tool, branches could not be beat. Branch offices, far from being a drain on the company, were engines of growth. *People want to be perceptively close to their money.* From the moment of that insight, Chuck made opening new branches a top priority for the company. In the first 5 years of the company's existence, it opened up eighteen branches, in the following order:

1975

September   Sacramento, CA

1976

July   Los Angeles (Century City)

1977

May   Seattle, WA
May   Newport Beach, VA
August   Phoenix, AZ
November   Dallas, TX

1978

July   Houston, TX
August   Denver, CO
September   Chicago, IL

October	San Diego, CA
October	Los Angeles (Downtown)
October	Kansas City, MO

1979

February	Ft. Lauderdale, FL
October	Washington, DC
October	Fairfax, VA

1980

January	Detroit, MI
January	Philadelphia, PA
April	Santa Barbara, CA

By 1980, the company was convinced that a branch network represented a durable competitive advantage for Schwab. Over the next two decades, it added an average of twenty branch offices per year (see the following list). Some branches in busy financial centers employed as many as fifty people and occupied prime downtown real estate. During the years it was owned by Bank of America, the company co-located brokerage facilities in bank branch offices. In recent years, Schwab experimented with one-person minibranches. Competitors such as E*Trade and Ameritrade now have a limited branch strategy, as well.

Number of Branches (cumulative)

1981	33
1982	52
1983	69
1984	89
1985	88

	Number of Branches *(cumulative)*
1986	96
1987	106
1988	111
1989	111
1990	130
1991	158
1992	175
1993	198
1994	208
1995	225
1996	235
1997	272
1998	291
1999	349
2000	384
2001	395
2002	430

The branches, combined with Chuck's image on the advertising, represented the major differentiation Schwab offered the market. It was a formidable combination. "The big question was, What would it take for a customer to leave his trusted investment advisor and go with Schwab?" asks Fuller. "The discount was great, but it wasn't enough. Chuck's face was trustworthy, but it wasn't enough." The presence of brick and mortar facilities proved to be decisive. "Together, the branches *combined* with the discount and Chuck's face proved to be the most effective magnet for new accounts," Fuller adds.

Fuller was working for Ronald Reagan's reelection campaign in 1979 when he first met Chuck. Fuller was on a business advisory panel that included heavyweights such as William Agee, chairman of Bendix Corporation and William Batten, chairman of the NYSE. William Casey, Reagan's campaign manager, insisted that the committee needed some younger corporate blood on the panel. Casey told Fuller to call the Young President's Organization (YPO), an association of CEOs under the age of forty. Chuck, a rising star in the YPO, quickly responded to Fuller's invitation and Fuller was instantly impressed with Chuck. Much to the derision of his colleagues at the NYSE, Jim Fuller joined Schwab in 1981. Why would anyone want to work for what the established brokers derisively called a "bucket shop"? The insults came fast and furious. "A broker working for Schwab is like a chef working for McDonalds," scolded a wag. But Fuller realized that big opportunity was available with this little firm. But before he joined up with Chuck, Fuller helped develop the wildly successful Schwab One Account.

Chuck immediately realized that a long-distance relationship with a broker is possible, but only if the relationships starts with and is sustained by human contact. Thus Schwab's branch strategy created a prime example of a "high tech–high touch" company, as defined by John Naisbitt in his 1990 book, *MegaTrends 2000*. Naisbitt predicted that as technology replaced humans in repetitive tasks, we would need new ways to effect human connection. The human connection came in the form of hundreds of Schwab branches over the next 20 years even as it rolled out innovation after innovation to make the branches redundant. This high tech–high touch concept would be emblazoned on every initiative of the company. By 2000, even with most people interacting with Schwab through the Web, about half of Schwab's retail net new assets came to it through the branch network. It remains true that people are just more comfortable starting their investing relationship in person, even if they later choose the telephone or Web as their primary method of transacting business.

Schwab enforces rigorous quality control and commonality of experience across branches. Just as McDonalds wants all of its restaurants to offer a familiar menu and predictable experience whether you are in Burbank or Burma, Schwab goes through significant effort to make every branch familiar and comfortable to Schwab customers who may drop in from out of town. For the first years, Schwab branches resembled banks, complete with counters and teller windows. More recently the emphasis in the branches has changed from order taking to asset gathering and advice giving. This transition has been difficult because it bumps up against the fundamentalism of the first generation of branch managers, a generation zealous in their attachment to original Schwab values.

It was in the branches, isolated from headquarters where people actually got a chance to test the myth of Schwab against the real thing. Here, Chuck's credos took on definite mythological persistence. Although Chuck tried to visit each branch once a year, to most people in the branches he remained a distant and larger-than-life figure. Moreover, the values Chuck represented—putting the customer's interests first, eschewing all sales efforts, and avoiding anything that smacked of giving the customer advice—resonated deeply with the people in Branchland.

Most of the people in the branches came to Schwab from other brokerages where they had been thoroughly disenchanted and disgusted by the practices they saw and how they were treated as employees. Schwab offered them a chance to come clean and for the first time to feel valued and rewarded. They gave their hearts and minds to Chuck and worked tirelessly for the mission. They weren't just traders. They were guardians of the customers' financial futures. They were missionaries for Chuck, fighting the good fight in the name of Schwab.

A successful branch network was great at creating loyal customers, but it had one downside. It promoted the development of a relationship between the customer and the local broker. That's one thing Chuck wanted to discourage. Chuck wanted to keep the relationship for himself. He wanted to be the broker, if only metaphorically, to every Schwab customer. Chuck knew what happens in traditional brokerages: When brokers leave to go to another firm, they typically take up to two-thirds of their customers with them. Chuck worked diligently to break that traditional linkage between brokers and customers. He did this in a number of ways: by distributing calls across the company, hiring people from outside the securities industry as much as possible, deemphasizing what would come to be known as customer relationship management, and, most conspicuously, forbidding soliciting.

From its early days, Schwab was the least relationship-oriented company imaginable. Chuck basically didn't want relationships. He wanted transactions. His motivation was part operational, part philosophical. On one level, Chuck understood that his self-directed customers wanted to escape the gravitational field of traditional brokers. So Schwab distributed customer inquiries across branches. Every time a customer called, he or she would speak to a different representative. Customers were not to be associated with individual brokers so no broker would lay claim to individual accounts. Schwab made brokers easily replaceable. He even rejected calling the people doing business with him as "clients." They were "customers" and would remain so for two more decades. The prime directive: There would be no selling. Schwab adopted a purely passive business model. About this Chuck was adamant.

Chuck drove his business by putting himself into the shoes of customers. As a result, he opposed the tactics that would become professionalized into customer relationship management. Chuck's view was that customers cannot be managed; they can only be served. If anything, it's the customers that managed a company. If the company did its job well and exceeded expectations, the customers would allow the company to continue to serve them.

This streamlined approach accrued a number of advantages to Schwab. For example, Schwab was the first brokerage to provide stock quotes 24 hours per day, a service so attractive one would think every brokerage would immediately follow suit. None did. Was Schwab technology that far ahead of the other brokers? No, the technology was trivial. It had everything to do with Schwab's emasculation of the brokers. Merrill Lynch couldn't do what Schwab did because its powerful brokers would go ballistic. If a customer wanted a quote, they were supposed to go through their brokers. That's what account control is all about. Schwab deliberately severed the kind of control to which other brokerages held customers hostage.

Of course, one downside of Chuck's loose customer relationship policy is that it made it easy for customers to move their accounts. Schwab needed a way to increase, in M.B.A.-speak, the barriers of migration or, in Web parlance, to make the accounts more "sticky." Chuck knew exactly what he wanted. It was called a Cash Management Account (CMA) and he wanted one for Schwab. To start, he called on Jim Fuller, who had recruited Chuck for Ronald Reagan's business advisory panel.

Jim Skinner is typical of the people who gravitated to Schwab and became successful in Branchland. Three days after graduating from Granite City (Illinois) High School in 1967, Skinner got a job as a margin clerk at Edward Jones, a traditional broker with headquarters in St. Louis. His career on the dark side then took him to Dean Witter in Miami and then Paine Webber in Boca Raton, Florida. By the time he made his way to Schwab in 1983, Skinner was totally demoralized. Without a college degree, Skinner's chances of becoming a manager at Paine Webber were nil. But what really hurt was how dirty he felt after a day of work.

"I wanted to get out of the business because it was so skuzzy," Skinner recalls. "Brokers forged customer orders every day. We recommended inferior products because it made us a few more bucks in commissions. When I brought these practices to the attention of the branch manager, I was ignored. It was not a healthy environment for people with any conscience." The point is not to pick on Paine Webber. As the following stories will show, all the traditional brokerages were about the same. The point is that not every broker was corrupt. Every brokerage had a small number of financial services professionals who put their desire to be able to look at themselves in the mirror each morning above their desire for money. Many of these people found a home at Schwab.

To Skinner, the differences between traditional brokerages and Schwab were stunning. "At Schwab, there was absolute and total focus on customer and doing the doing the right thing for the customer. To me, coming from a place where the only thing brokers cared about was making their numbers, whatever it took, it's hard to describe what a relief it was to work at Schwab," Skinner says. "The company was on a mission and we were changing the industry."

"The company took a chance on me," he says. "College degrees weren't important. The focus was on serving the customer, knowing the business, and staying true to the rules and regulations." Compliance was a huge issue at Schwab. Skinner helped open the Palm Beach, Florida branch, and later worked in branches in Ft. Lauderdale and Austin, Texas. He ended his career at the Phoenix call center.

For the first few months, Skinner almost didn't believe his good fortune. "Chuck came at us like a laser: Do right by the customer, do right by the customer. It took me a while to get it. If I wanted to waive a fee or penalty, I always got the message to do it. However, some of the brokers had a hard time following Chuck's prime directive of no advice. It wasn't just a myth that Chuck terminated brokers because they offered advice. "Chuck's promise is for real," he says, and the word about such decisions flew quickly between the branches.

Alice Wood didn't know what hit her. Nothing at the all-girls parochial college she attended prepared her for her introduction to the brokerage industry, first as a runner on the New York trading floors and then an institutional trading assistant at one of the most prestigious securities firms. Alice Wood is not her real name. The long-time Schwab employee asked that I not use her real name or identifying details. She joined Schwab in a western branch office in the early 1990s. Before joining Schwab, she was traumatized by the excesses of the securities industry that only later came to light: the relentless swindles endured by investors and the unrepentant and unrelenting sexism endured by women in the business. Her concerns to management were met with indifference or laughter at her naïveté. "I had to fight hard just to get permission to get a general securities license. I could never get past the gender discrimination. Even the few women managers told me to just put up with it," she says. Many years later, Wood walked away with a five-figure check as her share of a settlement the brokerage offered in acknowledgement of the abuse.

"Where's the corruption? Where's the sexual harassment?" That's what she asked herself after her first day at Schwab's Beverly Hills, California, branch in the early nineties. "I was so grateful to be with a company where I wasn't harassed every single day. Schwab *wanted* me to get the broker training that [the brokerage] said would be wasted on me. There were women in management. People believed in me. From then on, I knew this was the place for me."

Even now, it's hard for Wood to describe without crying the relief she felt that, at Schwab, there was a place for her in the financial services industry. Every difference impressed her and intensified her allegiance. "There was no conning customers at Schwab. If you didn't keep the customers' interests first, you were out," she says. Innovation was another difference. At her previous place of employment, she got in trouble because a group of sales assistants suggested an innovation. "At Schwab, I was rewarded for coming up with new ideas," she says. "In fact, if you didn't come up with at least one idea per quarter that didn't fundamentally improve things, my manager wondered why."

Another survivor of traditional brokers takes a structural view of the abuses of the industry. He came to Schwab from Dean Witter, and because he still does business with the company, asked to be unnamed. "There are people in the traditional brokerages that are as good and ethical as anyone at Schwab," he insists. "They do everything in their power to deliver for their customers. It's the structure that's at fault. Even ethical brokers can't be sure that people up the line are telling the truth or acting in the best interests of the firm's customers. It's almost impossible for an ethical individual broker to resist the pressure from above." By 1982, this Dean Witter broker discovered that many of his customers were defecting to discount brokers. He was not alone. Brokers all over the county were finding that their customers were happy to receive advice and analysis, but then transacted their trades at Schwab. Meanwhile, business as usual at Dean Witter was making it difficult. "The lack of ethics began to undermine my ability to work effectively."

Chuck's periodic visits to the branches were eagerly awaited. Every branch manager has a story. Mark King, who joined Schwab in 1983 at the Sunnyvale branch, remembers Chuck's visit for the official opening of the Orlando call center. King and his associates were waiting in the circular driveway for the limo they anticipated would deposit the founder. When a little Ford Escort pulled up and a slight man got out from behind the wheel, no one paid attention to him. Then King took a closer look.

"Chuck! What a surprise," King exclaimed, gesturing toward the Escort.

"This is all they had," Chuck explained sheepishly. He had flown in on his private jet and simply rented whatever car was available.

"I will never, ever get used to seeing my name on the side of a building," King remembers Chuck sighing as they walked up to join the festivities.

Schwab's four telephone call centers support one of the three main channels customers have for communicating with the company. The four call centers—a national call center in Phoenix supported by four base centers in Indianapolis, Denver, Phoenix, and Orlando—handle millions of calls every week as customers check quotes, determine balances, request a prospectus, or execute trades. Together, the call centers employ about 4,000 people.

An electronic voice link between brokers and investors, Schwab's call centers are vital to its business. Customers who call their local branch are switched through to one of the national call centers where much branchlike business can be handled by an investment specialist or, increasingly, by a telephone-based integrated voice response (IVR) system. Of course, customers can request to speak with an individual at the branch, but, as noted, Schwab discourages close local relationships. By freeing up branch reps from answering the phone, they have more time to discuss with investors such topics as financial planning, mutual fund strategies, or the pros and cons of various classes of investments.

When call volumes really became unbearably fast and furious, Schwab would declare "Market Storm" and the call centers would go into a frenzy. People worked all hours, sometimes as much as 20 hours per day. They grabbed a chair for a few hours of shut-eye and then got back on the phones. The sense of camaraderie was intense. The company did everything in its power to make life bearable. The cafeteria was open 24/7 and everything was free. A masseuse was available to give back rubs. Schwab retained a concierge service to assist employees with chores such as dry cleaning, car repairs, swimming pool maintenance, and anything that would take employees away from the phones.

With all those calls, call center reps might be forgiven for occasionally wishing that the customers would just stop calling. But such was the sense of ownership of the process that reps fought for every transaction. Every call center rep has a success story about helping a customer. Robert Grosskopf, at the Phoenix call center from 1991–1998, recalls a somewhat confused elderly customer from the Midwest who said that a salesman from a local bank had come by to pitch his brokerage services and she was afraid that she had been tricked into transferring her Schwab account. "She called me for help but she had no contact information," Grosskopf says. In the next hour, Grosskopf made a variety of calls. Using the Internet, he tracked down every branch office of the other bank and then called every branch, working from one side of the state to the other, until he hit the manager of the rep in question. "I put him on hold and conferenced in the customer, and I heard her tell him she did not want the Schwab account transferred. The account wasn't much more than $25,000, so it wasn't the money, but I hated to lose even a single account," he says.

Schwab is trying to shift as many transactions onto the Web, by far the most efficient of its three channels. When the company went online, there were some in the company who anticipated that the 4,000 employees in its call centers would eventually go away. This was great news because all of Schwab's call center agents are licensed stockbrokers, whose starting salaries can be $30,000 to $40,000 a year or more. The more of these broker's functions that can be shifted onto the Web, the bigger the payback. But, if anything, the need for people at the call centers increased, indicating that the channels are complimentary. Just as TV did not replace radio, the Web will not replace call centers. The technologies feed on each other.

They were somewhere over the Midwest. Fuller watched in astonishment as Andrew Kahr, sitting next to him, balanced a portable typewriter on the airplane tray and furiously filled six pages from edge to edge with the essential elements of the Cash Management Account (CMA). Both consultants with Stanford Research Institute, the team was struggling to give their client, Merrill Lynch, a financial product that would become the backbone for its asset gathering strategy. Merrill Lynch saw trillions of dollars sitting in savings accounts. It asked Fuller and Kahr to design a product attractive enough to convert people from savers to investors.

The names of the people who invented the wheel or paper are lost to history, but the financial industry prides itself on celebrating the names of the people who developed the ground-shaking products that changed the world. A. P. Giannini, for instance, who developed branch banking at Bank of America. Or Dee Hock, who gave the world the credit card. Or Andrew Kahr, the father of the CMA. Kahr was born in 1941, the son of very accomplished parents. From his father, a New York City psychiatrist, and his mother, an art historian, Kahr inherited a formidable intellect and ability to synthesize innovative financial products.

The CMA is a remarkable combination of brokerage and banking services, including a securities margin account, money market and checking accounts, and a Visa card. Kahr faced an intricate challenge because of the regulations tightly governing what activities brokerages, mutual fund companies, and banks could take on. The product that came out of Kahr's fevered imagination was a trespass on previously respected boundaries. First, the CMA looked like a stock account: It was anchored by a portfolio of stocks and bonds. But it also had the attributes of a money market product resembling the offerings of mutual fund companies such as Fidelity and Dreyfus. Like other money market instruments, the CMA paid interest on any cash the customer deposited. But it also regularly swept in dividends from stocks and other payouts, allowing customers to earn interest on money that otherwise would sit idle (and provide a nice revenue stream for the fund manager who would earn interest for its own account). Of course, since the CMA offered check-writing privileges, it trespassed on the province of banks. The coup de grace to the established order was that the CMA came with—incredibly!—a credit card. "The card alone was a remarkable creature," Nocera recounts. "It could serve as a debit card or a credit card depending on the circumstances: If the customer had enough cash in his money market accounts, funds would immediately be 'debited' to cover the charge. If he didn't, the charge would trigger a margin account—in effect, allowing the customer to borrow the money retroactively against the value of his stock portfolio."

Chuck wanted a branded CMA product. He asked Fuller, who in 1981 had left SRI for Schwab, for an introduction to Kahr. Kahr was happy to oblige and counts his assignment with Chuck as one of the more agreeable professional relationships of his career. Within short order, Chuck had a CMA product customized for Schwab. The Schwab One Account, as Chuck reluctantly allowed it to be called—for Hugo Quackenbush insisted that it be branded, like everything else, with Chuck's name—was a more advanced product than Merrill Lynch's in several important respects. Because Kahr reinterpreted some NYSE rules, the Schwab One Account did not have to invest in money market funds exclusively. As a result, it could pay investors any rate of interest that Schwab wanted.

The Schwab One Account was immediately profitable. Unlike Merrill Lynch, which required 10 years to make its CMA profitable, Schwab had less channel conflict. Its values were much more aligned to create win-win situations with customers and less driven to sweep every last cent off the table. It was less hung up, in other words, about giving up the easy money that investors had in their free credit balances. Schwab was still earning more interest than it was paying. And because the interest rate paid by a Schwab One Account was a few points higher than traditional savings accounts, many customers made their Schwab One Account their primary banking relationship. The assets rolled in. Schwab was beginning to create real relationships with its customers.

"Obituaries of branch networks are quite premature," says Tom Seip, former executive vice president of retail brokerage operations. "People tend to want to go around and pat their money on the head and visit it once in awhile, particularly when they're worried." Other industry players also see a future for branches. Merrill Lynch and Edward Jones are two brokerages rapidly building branches. Even the discount brokerages—E*Trade and Ameritrade—are taking a cue from Schwab and establishing branches.

Eventually, Schwab's branch strategy became mythologized and therefore no longer subject to debate. In 1998, Kevin Wheeler, former vice president for staffing and workforce development, questioned the value of branches. He ran headlong into the accepted wisdom that branches are good, end of story. "You can live on an idea only so long," Wheeler notes. "The cost-benefit is no longer there in most cases." Wheeler lobbied for the company to commission an analysis to study the question, but Chuck refused to even consider the issue. "The lore of the company is that branches are an indispensable part of Schwab's value proposition," Wheeler notes. No career at Schwab can thrive after questioning one of the founding myths, and Wheeler soon left the company. He is now president of Global Learning Resources, a consulting and training company in Fremont,

California, and serves as adjunct faculty at both San Jose State University and San Francisco State University. Wheeler's biggest regret is his inability to help transform Schwab University, the company's training center, into a world-class resource for developing managerial and executive talent. "Schwab University could have rivaled what Jack Welch created at General Electric," Wheeler says. "Instead it's more like a trade school than a university."

Beginning in the early 1990s, the branches began hearing disturbing noises from headquarters. The established order was no longer viable and the branches took the brunt of it. Chuck and Dave Pottruck at headquarters could point to the charts that proved how much customers really did want Schwab to provide advice and research. But the branches had a hard time believing it. Fundamentalists believe that at some distant point in the past, there existed a world of harmony and that it is their moral duty to reclaim those values. Chuck had done his job all too well. Branchland was filled with a critical mass of Schwab fundamentalists who resisted the new dictums.

The changes were gradual but disturbing. First, the compensation structure changed. Since the start of the company, Chuck had proclaimed the symmetry of having salaried instead of commission-based representatives. Only this type of structure, he held, gave investors a fair shake. And when the branches distributed year-end bonuses, as they usually did, the brokers rejoiced. They were happy with this arrangement because the compensation structure created an agreeable, collegial environment. Either everyone received a bonus, or no one did. If the branch made its numbers, the branch bonus was distributed to each member of the branch according to a published formula. The emphasis was on pulling together for the good of the customers and the good of the branch.

Yes, Chuck, agreed, but the company was too dependent on trading commissions. It needed a less cyclical source of revenue. The company needed more assets under management so it started rewarding asset gathering. Naturally, the compensation structure was modified. Now individual brokers would receive a modest salary plus a bonus if they met individual quotas. Oh, they called them targets, but no one was fooled. Each broker was assigned a number. If you didn't meet your quota after a couple of quarters, you were gone.

What former branch Schwabbies lament, though, is how the atmosphere in the branches immediately changed from one of cooperation to competition. Now it was no longer "you for me and me for you," it was "me for me." "The branches used to be helpful and friendly with people helping each other," Wood says. "Suddenly we were pitted against each other." It became critical, for instance, to get "credit" for customers who transferred assets. The last thing anyone wanted was for a customer to walk in unannounced and make a deposit because only the omnibus branch account would receive the credit. While reps were still not allowed to make cold sales calls, the number of warm sales (contacting people who had a relationship with Schwab) calls suddenly picked up in frequency. "It became an exercise in getting leads into the system. There were boards with rankings. We had a quota for new accounts," she says. For many people in the branches it was dialing for dollars again.

The incentives worked. Branches became frenzied engines of delivering new assets to headquarters. Schwab brokers became more sales-oriented. Instead of just taking the order, they became more proactive. Is there anything else I can help you with? Do you have accounts with other brokerages we can consolidate? I notice you have a lot of cash sitting in your account; let's put the cash to work for you. Do you have any insurance needs? "I often felt I was pushing the envelope on giving advice and crossing that line in the sand," says a former branch manager who was forced out for questioning the new incentives.

The lure was money. More money than the branches had ever seen. And Chuck was prepared to share the wealth with brokers who met their numbers. It wasn't easy, but if they could survive in the cutthroat world that many branches turned into, brokers could see more money than they ever imagined. Nick Carroway (not his real name), a Schwab rep from an Eastern branch, agreed to share his story if his identity was protected. Carroway joined Schwab in 1990 from a traditional brokerage. His base salary was $25,000 plus a bonus of $3,000, his share of the branch's profit-sharing arrangement. By the time he left Schwab in the late 1990s, his compensation had increased to over $75,000 per year. Carroway's base salary remained the same, but under Schwab's quarterly bonus system, he earned as much as $25,000 in some quarters. Of course, in other quarters he'd earn less. The bonuses were tied to Schwab stock, which fed the company's extremely generous 401(k) and employee stock ownership plan (ESOP). In some years, during the height of the Internet boom, Carroway's total compensation (on paper, at least) increased by a quarter of a million dollars. "The bonuses and the stock price were all we could think about," Carroway says. "All I thought about was cashing out and leaving the madness. The best interests of customers became of secondary importance to me." Carroway bailed out when Schwab stock was at its highest point and is now retired. "I hated to see what happened to the branches, even though it made me rich," he says.

For many branch employees, the turning point came during the rollout of the Welcome Representative program. Welcome Rep, as it was called, was a poorly conceived attempt to turn Branchland order takers into proactive, advice-giving asset gatherers. Before Schwab abandoned it, Welcome Rep turned many formerly harmonious branch offices into something resembling war zones. To understand how Welcome Rep shook things up, let's see the before and after experience of a customer walking into a Schwab branch:

Pre-Welcome Rep: The customer walks in and finds a number of Schwab branch people (mostly women) behind the counters. The customer goes to the representative that can serve him first, takes care of the transaction, and then leaves. The emphasis for the branch was on giving the customer the cleanest, quickest transaction and then moving to the next customer.

Welcome Rep: The customer walks in and finds a number of Schwab branch people (men and women) behind desks. Gone are the counters and other barriers. The transaction out of the way, the Welcome Rep launches into a checklist of items designed to identify customer assets not under Schwab custody and bring them into the fold. The Welcome Rep has a script to follow and a toolkit of graphs, portfolio assessments, and risk tolerance curves. The reps are encouraged to take baby steps in the direction of giving advice.

Welcome Rep certainly professionalized the branches, turning what were transaction-oriented order takers into more rigorous sales people. Welcome Reps were encouraged to develop expertise in specific disciplines such as retirement planning, fixed-income investing, or insurance. Some branch people thrived with the program, using the Welcome Rep templates to forge stronger relationships with their customers, a fact that eventually spelled the program's demise. There were other problems.

Schwab didn't anticipate some obvious customer traffic issues. As a customer walked in, which representative would serve him? It was the same problem that automobile dealerships face. There, the standard policy is for the salespeople to take turns approaching customers. But Schwab never thought that far ahead, so the reps closest to the entrance received a disproportionate share of the business. Worse, customers tended to approach the rep working closest to the entrance even if he or she was serving another customer. In response, the branches instituted a greeter system. Greeters were branch people whose job it was to escort visitors to the appropriate desk. But this job quickly became the most disliked in the branches.

Branches became nastily competitive. The emphasis on meeting the quotas pitted rep against rep and branch against branch for the coveted quarterly bonuses. People worked incessantly. Their relatively low base pay made the bonuses indispensable. Carroway and his colleagues worked every weekend, often till midnight. Taking a day off was out of the question. "The biggest fear was that you couldn't hack it," he says. Schwab normalized a workload that literally made employees sick. "Everyone hid their ulcers, headaches, bad backs, and family turmoil," he notes. Carroway himself developed an ulcer. "I saw some of my colleagues throw up blood and then go back to work."

The job became all consuming. "The perplexing thing was that the damage was all self-inflicted," Carroway insists. "No one was forcing us to work as hard as we did. We were doing it to ourselves." The pressure sometimes became overwhelming. Carroway remembers one Schwab broker shouting out, within earshot of customers, "I hate my job, I hate my job, I hate my job!" Another of his colleagues told the branch greeter not to bother him with customers unless they had a least $25,000 in their pocket. In the back office, thankfully out of sight of customers, two reps actually broke into a fist fight over who would get credit for a $1 million customer both claimed, according to Carroway. These were not behaviors Chuck wanted, of course, but they were entirely predictable given the incentives he established.

Eventually, the Welcome Rep program fell apart under the weight of its own contradictions. In addition to its other problems, the program succeeded in building personal relationships between Welcome Reps and individual customers. These were precisely the kind of relationships between individual brokers and individual customers that Chuck tried to avoid. By 2000, Chuck would be forced to capitulate on this point, as well. Welcome Rep was shelved, but the goals it was designed to pursue remained.

For Chuck and Pottruck, the issue was clear. The brokerage had a mandate to provide more advice, do more selling, create deeper relationships with customers, and become more competitive in aggregating the assets of wealthy investors. Some of the old values that motivated the existing branch managers were now obstacles. Between 1990 and 1995, a majority of the branch managers hired before 1990 were forced out and replaced by people who generally had no experience with the company's previous organizing principles. Many of the old Branchland hands hated to see what was happening to the company they loved and wrote impassioned letters to Chuck. Chuck and Pot-truck understood that the branch managers who made Schwab the leading discount broker in the world could not accompany the company on its bid to be a full-service brokerage for wealthy investors. The company was generous with them in terms of severance and appreciation, but wouldn't back off, and many of the branch employees who implemented the company's old values felt betrayed.

Advice and Advisors

1975–1995

In the beginning, advice was a dirty word. There was no way, Chuck insisted, for Schwab to give advice and not create conflicts of interest. Guess what? Chuck was right. But things change. Today, advice, far from a dirty word, is a huge profit center for Schwab. Some of Schwab's partners feel betrayed. It's a conflict Schwab can live with.

"**O**h, shit. This is not good," David Pottruck whispered as out walked 8 percent of the $50.6 billion in assets that Schwab Services for Investment Managers (SIM) then had under management. It was September 1992, and the investment managers were angry. They had asked for this meeting to tell Pottruck and the SIM team why they felt betrayed. The Schwab team had badly misjudged the mood of the investment managers and within 5 minutes the delegation had angrily left the room for an outside caucus.

It was a wake-up call for the company and evidence that Pottruck needed to extend his understanding of the issues beyond his retail experience. Pottruck pulled out his cell phone. "Cancel my meetings," he said, "it's going to be a long day." The investment managers filed back into the conference room at the San Francisco Sheraton Palace and took their seats.

John Bowen spoke first. "David, you told us Schwab would not give advice. You told us that Schwab would not cross the line in the sand between the do-it-yourself brokerage and the business of giving advice," he said. "We believe you crossed it."

There it was. A year earlier, John Coghlan, the executive in charge of services for investment managers, stood at the front of a room and with a colored marker drew a line on a whiteboard. On one side of the line was Schwab and its no-advice standard. On the other side were the independent investment managers whose business it was to give investors advice on a fee basis. "Our relationship with you is sacrosanct," Coghlan said. "This is the line we will never cross."

John Bowen, founder of CEG Worldwide, an advisor to independent investment advisors in New York, led the advisors. He had more than $2 billion of his customers' assets with Schwab. Widely regarded as the nation's leading authority on the independent financial advisory business, Bowen is the principal author of *The Prudent Investor's Guide to Beating the Market,* published in 1996, followed by *The Prudent Investor's Guide to Beating Wall Street at Its Own Game* in 1998. His first industry book, *Creating Equity: How to Build a Hugely Successful Asset Management Business,* was published in 1997. When Bowen talked, as they said of EF Hutton, people listened.

On Bowen's side of the table sat Scott MacKillop, Gene Dongieux, and Harold Evensky. At the time of the meeting, MacKillop was President of ADAM Investment Services, Inc., a pioneer in providing mutual fund managed account services to independent financial advisors. He had $1.25 billion in assets under management with Schwab. MacKillop is now president of Trivium Consulting in Evergreen Park, Colorado. Gene Donguiex is president and chief investment officer of Mercer Global Advisors, Santa Barbara, California. Harold Evensky is chairman of the Evensky Group and the author of *Wealth Management. Accounting Today* named him one of the profession's most influential people and he was awarded the Dow Jones Investment Advisor Portfolio Management Award for Lifetime Achievement. At the time, he had $24 million under management at Schwab.

Evensky picked up the discussion. He spoke of the unwritten contract between Schwab and the investment advisors. Did he misunderstand the relationship? Schwab was supposed to provide services to make the independent advisors successful. In return, the advisors would use Schwab as a custodian for the assets their customers entrusted to them. The deal was that Schwab would not compete with the advisors by giving advice. They were to be partners, not competitors. Now Schwab had announced plans to roll out a product that resembled a service that advisors provided. What's more, Schwab's fee for the service undercut the advisors. This "fund-of-funds" portfolio offered several mutual funds in one account, using an asset allocation model that is tailored to an investor's risk tolerance and goals. It looked very much like an advice-driven customized portfolio. "Dave, it looks to us that Schwab is saying one thing but doing another," Evensky said.

It wasn't the business decisions Schwab took in its own self-interest that riled Evensky, but rather its attitude. "Schwab wasn't doing anything the other brokerages weren't doing," he says. "But the other brokerages never told us they weren't going to do it. Nor did they insist they were doing it for my benefit." As Schwab moved from being a partner to the investment managers to a competitive provider, it was bound to step on toes. The same issue arose when Schwab acquired U.S. Trust in 2000. "It's absurd for me to get upset about it," Evensky says, "but say it like it is. I resented the implication they were doing it to help me."

In the beginning, Chuck enunciated the standards for Schwab. Not goals, but standards. Goals don't have a moral dimension. Moreover, goals can be attained, and then what? Schwab was to be built on standards of integrity and principle. That's the beauty of standards. It *stands up* and proclaims: Here's what we *stand for*, the ground we *stand on*; here's how we *stand apart* and *stand out*; and this is where we *stand together*. When Chuck started the firm out of a deep sense of personal outrage that the brokerage industry systematically exploited its customers, he vowed eternal hostility against three things: advice, commission-based sales, and sales calls. Those were to be Schwab's standards. Over the years, the company has had to redefine its commitment to each one.

And yet, and yet . . . customers wanted advice. Schwab employees were stuck in a classic bind: following Chuck's value of resisting advice or following Chuck's value of serving the customer. It was crazy making for the company. Which value was Schwab to honor?

Conflicts in values pop up frequently, in business as well as at home. Recently, I paid a visit to the home of a rather formal couple who instructed their teenage children to address adult guests by their surnames. This rule was enforced, the adults explained, to teach the teens to respect their elders. So I was greeted with rounds of "Mr. Kador, what kind of books do you write?" and "Mr. Kador, would you kindly pass the butter?" Now, I am much more informal and prefer that everyone, especially teens, call me by my first name. I had the rules of etiquette on my side— guests, after all, are entitled to be addressed in the manner they request—but I sensed the conflict that would ensue were I to voice my preference. My request to be addressed by my first name would put the children in conflict with the instructions of their parents that they address adults by surname. Schwab employees were very much in the position those children were. Which master were they to serve? For many years, daddy Chuck had told them the standard was, "out of respect" for the customers, *no advice.* Now the customers on whose behalf Schwab issued the standard said, *actually we do want advice.*

What does a company do when two values collide? It struggles. It disappoints one constituency or another. It makes mistakes. It challenges authority, whether it calls itself dogma or paternalism. And it eventually discovers that enduring values are never in permanent conflict. The admonition against advice couldn't be sustained not because it was wrong, but because it was too broad.

Not all advice is the same and not all advice is tarnished by conflict of interest, which was the real bugaboo all along.

It wasn't easy, especially in Branchland. For many years, "Thou shalt not give advice" was the company's most sacred commandment. "As I hired traders, I would focus more on people who had good customer service skills and less on people with previous market/advice-giving experience," says Rhet Andrews, who managed a number of Schwab branches in the early 1980s. "I found that people who had been advice givers had a real problem resisting offering advice. Since our trade confirmations were marked 'not solicited,' we needed to make sure we stuck with our promise."

Stories abounded about brokers getting fired for giving advice. Jim Skinner, manager of the Fort Lauderdale branch, fired a broker for crossing the line. "He was meeting with customers on his boat and it appeared that he was conducting himself in a very unSchwab-like way." Schwab was scrupulous about tape recording customer telephone transactions for just this purpose and an investigation confirmed that the broker was way over the line. "He came from a full-commission brokerage and he couldn't make the transition. Chuck's promise was for real," Skinner says.

Even Chuck's eldest son, Charles Schwab, Jr., who went by the name of Sandy, got pinched by the taboo. In the early 1990s, Chuck encouraged Sandy to try his hand at various areas of Schwab to better understand the organization and possibly take a leadership role in the company. One such role was a Schwab telephone representative at a call center. So off Sandy went to the Indianapolis call center to learn the ropes. He started by ghosting the ghost. Ghosts monitored samples of the calls coming in to ensure against compliance and training breakdowns. When a customer calls and hears the Schwab announcement, "This call may be monitored for training purposes," there's a decent chance customer service may actually be listening. Sandy was to monitor calls for a few days to better understand the issues. But Sandy was impetuous and couldn't help himself from jumping into the call and trying to "help" out. Frequently, the help took the form of giving advice. It wasn't helpful, it became disruptive, and that was the end of Sandy's call center career. Even Chuck's son was powerless against the no-advice admonition.

The whole thing started as a compliance issue. A Schwab compliance officer noticed a disturbing pattern. A number of customers had given other people limited powers of attorney over their accounts. That, by itself, wasn't disturbing. Generally the account holder shared a name with the person holding the power of attorney. It wasn't unusual for the child, grandchild, or relative to manage the account of an elderly parent or grandparent. No, what was disquieting was that some individuals had gained privileges by limited power of attorney over dozens, occasionally hundreds, of apparently unrelated customer accounts. What was going on?

After a few calls, it became clear that Schwab had been serving an entirely unknown set of customers. They were independent financial advisors that Schwab account holders had hired to provide the kinds of advice and hand-holding that Schwab refused to offer. The financial advisors managed the accounts on behalf of the customers they shared with Schwab, using Schwab services such as OneSource to get in and out of mutual funds. When he heard about this, Chuck immediately saw an opportunity. If Chuck understood anything, it was the cost of acquiring customers. Financial advisors represented a powerful way to acquire customers. From that day on, no longer would the firm simply target individual investors but would broaden its mission to serving financial advisors. In Internet terms, the financial advisors were "aggregators" and the entity they aggregated was "assets." The typical financial advisor controlled dozens or even hundreds of individual accounts.

Schwab had uncovered a new market as well as a marketing opportunity it could leverage. When a company is focused on ruthless execution for its retail customers, it can be forgiven for having tunnel vision and missing possibilities to serve the wholesale market. To its credit, Schwab didn't let its commitment to efficiency keep it from stumbling on a $235 billion business serving 5,800 fee-based investment managers in 2001.

These advisors simply used Schwab accounts, software, accounting, and brokerage execution to manage money for their clients. Unlike conventional brokers, who are employees, these financial advisors are free agents who set their own fees, carry their own overhead expenses, and manage their advisory services entirely without the command structure of traditional brokers. Operating as single-person offices or in small organizations, they could do battle with the massive marketing power of Merrill Lynch, Fidelity, Shearson, Smith Barney, and Prudential. They could become an army of guerrilla fiduciaries ready and willing to provide the one thing Schwab was not willing to provide for its customers . . . advice.

Business requirements changed. The customers that Schwab attracted in its first 10 years were, by and large, relatively sophisticated. But in the 1990s, customers flocked to Schwab who didn't know equities from mutual funds, let alone options. They voiced a mounting demand for more help and advice on where to put their money. "More and more of Schwab's customers are asking for help and advice," Coghlan, currently vice chairman of The Charles Schwab Corporation and enterprise president of Schwab Institutional, told the *Wall Street Journal.* "The market is filling with competitors who are willing to provide this help if Schwab does not."

Schwab had to deal with facts and trends. Its customers were aging. The average age of a Schwab customer is 47, versus 57 for the full-service brokerages, and the challenge is always to keep older, presumably more wealthy, customers in the fold. Customers who no longer wanted to go at it alone now asked Schwab for advice. It really was a paradox. The wealthier Schwab made its customers, the more they took their business elsewhere. As Schwab's no-advice standards helped self-directed investors beef up their portfolios, those same investors, increasingly overwhelmed by the task of managing their wealth, started leaving Schwab for the same full-commission firms whose practices

Chuck rejected in the first place. When Chuck saw that many of his customers were leaving for Merrill Lynch and Bear Stearns, he took a second look at the no-advice standard and decided that it had to be subordinated to the greater good of giving customers what they asked for.

Schwab took the opportunity to segment its customers into three categories: delegators, validators, and self-directed investors. Delegators are the bread and butter of full-commission brokers. They feel secure turning over their accounts to investment professionals. Validators are investors who want to listen to their broker's advice but also have their own ideas and occasionally want to run those decisions past a professional for feedback or fine-tuning. Self-directed investors are total do-it-yourselfers. "It's not easy for one brokerage to provide services to balance the needs of these constituencies, but if any firm can pull it off, Schwab can," says Dan Burke, director of brokerage services at Gomez Advisors. "When in doubt, Schwab always sides with the customer; which will help them as they conquer the advice beast."

Rather than turn customers away, Schwab slowly, indirectly moved into the advice business. Pottruck talked about reframing Schwab's mission to help "coach people on investing. When we talk about advice, we use the phrase 'expert advice that is objective, uncomplicated and not driven by commission.'" But the taboo against advice giving was so strong it made it impossible for Schwab to look at the issue square in the face. It squinted and, until recently, offered advice only by proxy.

In 1995, Schwab rolled out AdvisorSource, a program brilliantly conceived to give customers access to advice and thereby keep them in the fold without directly giving any advice at all. The program offered big carrots to the investment managers. For individuals who wanted a personal investment manager, AdvisorSource matched investors with a list of prequalified independent, fee-based financial advisors. If a Schwab client asks for a recommendation on an advisor, they receive several names from a select list of more than 600 advisors, all of whom have met

Schwab's standards of competence. The advisors, in return, park their client's assets at Schwab.

AdvisorSource is consistent with Schwab's other programs in that it offloads the costs to the partners, not the customers. Customers who have at least $100,000 under management pay the advisor's standard annual fee, roughly 1 percent of assets. The advisors then rebate Schwab 30 percent of the first year fees, 25 percent in the second year, and 20 percent in the third year. To protect its customers, Schwab carefully screens the investment managers. Managers participating in the program must have at least $25 million in assets under management and either 5 years experience and a college degree, 10 years experience, or a certified financial analyst designation. Schwab monitors its managers for personal bankruptcies, credit, licensing, national and state regulatory compliance, and filings with the Securities and Exchange Commission.

Each of the 600 independent advisors pays $2,000 a quarter for Schwab to refer potential clients their way. The quarterly fee doesn't even cover the cost of administering the program; the profit for Schwab is in building relationships with money managers and getting them to park more of their assets with Schwab. Customers looking for more advice than the standard asset allocation models passed out at Schwab's offices are given the names of local money managers, and often the branch will schedule the first appointment. Schwab had to experiment to find the right way to introduce its clients to financial advisors. The first attempt flopped. It started by offering customers a toll-free referral service. Customers received a faxed list of a number of financial planners from which to choose. That attempt failed because prospective clients rarely followed through. John Bowen was not surprised. "This isn't the sort of business where people feel comfortable choosing a name from a list." Today, advisors are affiliated with individual branches offices. Schwab reps work with customers on their requirements and follow up to facilitate the introductions. Some of the closings actually take place in Schwab branches.

One of the features that made Schwab attractive to financial advisors is SchwabLink. Introduced in 1991, SchwabLink allows financial advisors to leverage Schwab's computers to trade and manage customer accounts using software provided by Schwab. SchwabLink allows the advisor to offload all transaction record keeping and statement preparation duties to Schwab for a fee based on the number of transactions and the size of customer assets. This service was so successful that of all assets generated through fee-based advisors, 82 percent were managed using SchwabLink.

Schwab's concept of establishing SchwabLink as a platform from which to trade mutual funds transformed the business of investment managers. Advisors who attempted to work with no-load funds with clients with diversified portfolios had an impossible task. Even working with as little as four fund families created an enormous paper headache. "Before computers, it was totally unmanageable," says Harold Evensky. "Even after automation it was a nightmare. The practical result was that the burdens of record-keeping practically forced advisors to stay with a single family of mutual funds. The family was important because it was too difficult to manage accounts across families." With Schwab-Link, advisors won their emancipation from the fund families. "It led to development of the independent investment manager. It transformed us from working with packagers to being individual managers, making possible the core services of wealth management," Evensky says.

"Schwab's relationship with independent fee-based advisors allowed it to reach more customers and to provide them—albeit indirectly—with investment advice. These advisors have become a virtual sales force for Schwab," say Sanjeev Dewan and Haim Mendelson in their case report on Schwab for the Stanford University School of Business. It is this army of independent financial advisors, empowered by SchwabLink, that threaten both the fund families and the full-service brokerages. "We don't compete with the discounters," explains a Merrill Lynch vice president, "We do compete with Schwab. They have essentially built a Merrill Lynch by proxy."

Technology has leveled the playing field. The information and analytical tools available to individual investors is roughly equivalent to what investment professionals have at their disposal. Thanks to the Internet, trading and information have become commodities. So where's the value-added to working with an advisor? "Assurance," insists Tom Seip. "The future, and the money, is moving to advice and assurance. Financial advisors have no better than equal footing with their customers in terms of the information they can get. Their value-added will be assurance."

Schwab Services for Investment Managers, a division of Schwab Institutional little known to people who follow the retail side, provides trading support and discounted commissions to independent financial advisors. In 2001, 5,800 independent advisors had accounts totaling $235 billion in assets with Schwab. Schwab built a wonderfully symbiotic relationship with investment managers and then began to dismantle it. The investment managers resented it. "They wanted us to help them keep their business, but they wanted us to pay for the privilege," says Robert Veres, editor of *Inside Information*, a newsletter for financial advisors. "There was a dark suspicion among advisors that Schwab was making a land grab for their customers. They came as close as they could to insisting that we hand over all of our client accounts to them. So in essence they wanted us to dump service providers who compared well on the price, service, trade execution matrix and pay them a fee, all for the privilege of helping them stop losing their clients."

Pottruck handled the meeting beautifully. He apologized for not listening well enough and allowing the issue to come this far. He made it clear that they had his full attention for as long as it took. He listened carefully, taking copious notes. He acknowledged the advisors had valid points. He mirrored feelings. Some suggestions he committed to making immediately. The "fund of funds" rollout would be withdrawn. Other issues he took under advisement and promised answers by certain dates. And then he said what everyone was waiting for him to say.

"We did say there was a line and that we would not cross it," Pottruck told the group. "When we said it, we meant it. We probably shouldn't have said it because business requirements change and they have changed. I've learned my lesson abut committing to lines we will never cross. If we're going to help build our brand on being empathic, fair, and responsive, we need to take every opportunity to prove it. We accept that we will be held to a higher standard. Now I'd like the opportunity to tell you why we are doing what we are doing and why we think we can work with you."

It was a masterful performance. When Pottruck is on, no one in the world is as good. It was clear that everything was spontaneous. Everyone in the meeting appreciated the subtext of what Pottruck faced: Schwab's no-advice model is not sustainable because its customers will leave for brokerages that provide more hand-holding. "Our customers tell us they want certain kinds of advice and we're going to give it to them. I don't see us changing that. But I don't think this will be competitive with your business because we are serving different populations," Pottruck said, adding that the company had a responsibility to Schwab shareholders to optimize value. Not maximize, Pottruck suggested, but optimize. What's the difference? Optimum body temperature for humans is 98.6 degrees Fahrenheit. Maximum body temperature will kill you every time.

Shivers went up Dennis Clark's spine as he watched the mood of the room change under Pottruck's performance. He had a lot riding on the outcome of this meeting. Clark had organized it. As the marketing manager for Schwab Services for Investment Managers, it was Clark who first got wind of the grumbling. Now he faced a mutiny by the financial advisors who had come to rely on Schwab's unfortunate promises. Clark had tried and failed to get the company to take their objections seriously and now it had come to this: a summit. Clark represented a fresh, new generation of Schwab managers: sales-oriented and openly questioning of old assumptions. He is impossibly young looking. If you picture a grown-up, slightly more laid back Alex Keaton of *Family Ties*, you would not be far off. He was the type of kid who in high school created and tracked a model investment portfolio. Right after college, he got on a plane for the first time in his life and walked into a Dean Witter office in San Francisco. He looked no older than when he was in high school. "Where do I sign?" the Dean Witter manager asked, expecting to be handed a delivery. After Clark asked for a job, the manager said "Go sell something, anything, and then come back to see me." He got a job selling printing services and within three years he was a Dean

Witter stockbroker. In January 1989, Clark joined Schwab as a sales manager for Schwab Services. His job would be to promote the service to independent financial advisors.

As for Bowen, Evensky, MacKillop, and the other investment managers? They read Schwab the riot act and came away thinking that Pottruck got the message. Despite the friction, MacKillop continues to back Schwab, as do the others. "Even though we are nervous, the advisors can't find anything as good. Schwab continues to exert a stronger and stronger gravitational pull on advisors," he says. Adds a former Schwab employee who went to work for an independent investment advisor now tightly associated with the company, "Schwab has a mandate to make their offerings better for the clients they serve. Their services can't be beat. We were once going steady. Now we're sleeping together," he says. Sleeping together, but not yet married.

PART TWO

Profiles in Crisis

Forsaken IPO

May 9, 1980

What was Chuck thinking? His company was showing modest success and was by 1980 even profitable. But only in Chuck's dreams was his company ready for prime time. An early attempt to take the company public was met with scorn and ridicule by anyone who read the prospectus, and a humiliated company withdrew the initial public offering (IPO). Chuck became determined to make his company ready for the next opportunity.

A s the decade opened, Charles Schwab & Co. looked like a player. In 1980, it was the largest discount broker in the world. It had over 140,000 customers around the country, served by a network of 20 branch offices from coast to coast, staffed by more than 150 employees. The company was now a member of the NYSE. Chuck was being recognized on the streets of every significant financial center in the country. The company, finally, was profitable.

What more could Chuck want? As it turned out, a lot more. Chuck wanted to hold his head up in the company of financial industry superstars such as Fidelity's Ned Johnson, Citibank's Walter Wriston and John Reed, and even Merrill Lynch's Don Regan, the mention of whose name made Chuck shiver. Chuck wanted to be big, and not just as a discounter. The entire discount industry represented less than 10 percent of the brokerage business in America. He wanted respect. He wanted to swim in the adult pool, where the big money was. Chuck knew that he couldn't become an Olympic swimmer by kicking butt in the kiddie pool. He needed to make a big splash.

There was only one thing standing in the firm's way, Chuck believed: cash and more cash. Getting to this point in its development—the computers, the branches, acquiring the occasional competitor, the relentless advertising—consumed every cent his company generated. The company was often on the verge of being in violation of the SEC's capital requirements for brokerage firms—and the NYSE's requirements were twice those of the SEC. Helen was unhappy when Chuck had to mortgage their home yet again to bail the company out of one financial crisis or another, according to sources close to the family.

So it was that in May 1980, Chuck first publicly articulated the three letters that would stand for the easy riches of Wall Street: IPO. But that would be much later, when investors lined up for the chance to buy stock in companies selling dog food over the Net. In 1980, with the country in a minirecession, IPOs made investors skeptical.

For good reason, in Schwab's case. Chuck thought the company's big problem, and principal obstacle to growth was lack of capital. In fact, the company's big problem was Chuck's insatiable appetite for growth combined with his unwillingness to tease the growth into some semblance of order. Nor had he developed a subordinate strong enough to challenge him on the growth expectations that were throttling the organization. The company had no strategy to manage the growth except to hire more people, buy more computers, and open more branches.

Growth, uncontrolled and uncontrollable, was bringing the company to its knees. Chuck's unrelenting pursuit of growth as the only measure of the firm's success kept the company so unbalanced that it threatened to implode from the weight of its manifest destiny. Schwab people were true believers, working tirelessly to keep up with the constant phone orders, and as true believers, they welcomed an ordeal as vindication of their missionary status. The dedication of the Schwabbies could not have been more intense.

Out of this crisis atmosphere developed the pile-it-on, workaholism-as-a-norm environment that extends to the present day. Job definitions didn't exist. People pitched in as needed, pulling together, further cementing an intensely loyal family atmosphere. Out of this mix, enduring customer-driven values emerged. For example, the precept, "if you touch it, it's yours," was born. By this precept, if a customer inquiry came your way, it was your responsibility to handle it on a cradle-to-grave basis. Schwab people didn't just make trades, they were curing cancer.

People were making it up as they went along. Most of them were sharp, so the trades got executed and the statements went out on time and the branches were opened. But the cost in terms of duplication of effort and quality remained high. "There was never anything smooth about any of it," according to Nocera in *A Piece of the Action.* "Working for Schwab in those days usually meant leaving for home at the end of each working day feeling a little more behind than the day before. Schwab was a harried, frantic place. Mistakes piled up, long-range planning was nonexistent, and too many days were spent coping with the latest crisis."

Is this description reminiscent of a college campus during finals week? That's how it often seemed to Kathy Levinson, who joined the firm in 1980. "Many of us thought of Schwab as a substitute college we either couldn't afford or didn't have the discipline for. It was in some ways the coming out place that college is," she says. Schwab employees at the time enjoyed a freedom that present day employees do not, Levinson adds. The firm was new and untested. The Schwab brand did not yet inspire world-wide reverence. In other words, because it didn't have a lot to lose, the company could and did take real risks. "We were young and it wasn't like the business was a household name," she says. Later, when the company became a public company, with millions of customers, thousands of careers, and billions of dollars at stake, people would be a lot more conservative. But for the time, real risks were possible.

Kathy Levinson joined Schwab on the same day in February 1980 as did Larry Stupski. Her first job was as a registered customer service rep and she took positions of increasing responsibility in branch administration. In her 13-year career at Schwab, Levinson held increasingly senior positions and many people expected her to become president of the company after Stupski. Levinson was perhaps the most visible lesbian woman at Schwab and vocally applauded by both the gay and straight employees. When she abruptly announced her resignation in 1993—on the same day that another very visible gay executive resigned—many colleagues saw it as part of the company's lashing back against the perception of Schwab as a company that flaunts its gay culture. "It's okay to be gay at Schwab, but not too gay" says a former manager. In this view, Levinson was a victim of homophobia. But that view is not supported by a majority of the gay Schwab employees interviewed for this book. And Levinson herself dismisses it. The backdrop for her decision was Larry Stupski's heart attack in January, 1992, an event that prompted every employee to look inward. "One day I was on the commuter train and I realized I didn't have the passion to be at Schwab anymore," she says. "It had nothing to do with sexual politics."

Pottruck tried to talk her into staying, and dangled considerable money and stock if she did. "Dave," Levinson replied, "Maybe you can entice me to stay. But do you really want me here if I'm here just for the money?" Pottruck nodded knowingly. Levinson knew that Pottruck often confronted apparently unfocused executives by asking, "Are you really here or are you in transition? Are you excited? Do you have the drive? Or are you just going through the motions?" Pottruck respected Levinson's decision.

After retiring from Schwab in 1993, Levinson was recruited by rival E*Trade Group, Inc. As president and chief operating officer, she built E*Trade into a formidable competitor that beat Schwab to the World Wide Web and Internet trading. In 1999, she was named one of the "25 Top Unsung Heroes on the Net" by *Inter@active Week Online.* Her advocacy work on behalf of the gay community also intensified. Levinson was named the top executive in the "gfn.com Power 25" by *Gay Financial Network,* and one of the "OUT 100," the most influential gay men and lesbians of 1999, by *OUT Magazine.*

The place was falling apart and still Chuck insisted on issuing an IPO. That he actually thought the public would invest in his wreck of a company underscores the extent to which he drank his own Kool-Aid. More charitably, some of the people who were there believe to this day that Chuck was so aloof from day-to-day operations that he genuinely wasn't aware of the extent of the chaos. Perhaps, focused as he was on marketing, and indifferent to other aspects of the business, Chuck really didn't know—or worse, didn't care—that the company was slowly eating itself up. Others are convinced Chuck had to have known. Anonymous, often bitter, memos were flying back and forth, detailing the latest screw-up. The computer people posted daily reports on the errors and the system crashes. Even then the company was known for its "ready, fire, aim" approach. There was never enough resource to do anything right the first time, but time was always made to redo it. Perhaps Chuck's aversion to conflict kept him in denial. To be sure, it was a high conflict environment, according to Jim Fuller, one of Chuck's top lieutenants. "Maybe it was Chuck's generalized optimism. Chuck really believed that he could grow his way out of any difficulty."

The company released the prospectus on May 9, 1980. Chuck decided to issue 1.2 million shares of stock, at a price of $4 per share. If things worked out, the company would add $4.8 million, less expenses, to its drained coffers. Even in 1980, $4.8 million was not a lot of money, but it provides a clue to the scale Schwab found significant at the time. Schwab revenues for the preceding year were just $16.2 million, so the offering represented a significant increment of capital. The company stated the IPO would give it some relief from the constant demands of the uniform net capital rule. Net proceeds of the sale, the prospectus promised, would be used to reduce the short-term bank borrowings the company activated to finance loans made to customers who purchased securities under margin agreements and to cover the security settlement process.

The IPO arrived DOA. That's what the analysts said, and after some weeks of criticism, a humiliated and fuming Chuck withdrew the offering. For years afterward, Chuck and his executives groused that the IPO was torpedoed by malicious and small-minded underwriters, the same types that opposed the company in its early days. The company's us-against-them attitude was by now firmly entrenched. The record does not support this interpretation. It is true that the leading underwriters wanted nothing to do with bringing Schwab public. It is also true that the B-list underwriters valued the company significantly below the $4 Chuck anticipated. But the fault, dear friends, lay not in a Wall Street cabal or shameful underwriters, but in the facts on which rational investors are entitled to base their financial decisions. The beauty of a prospectus is that it lays out the record for all to see, so let's take a look at just what the investors saw.

Some companies attempt to bury the bad news in a few lines of dense boilerplate. Schwab was too high class for that. Instead, it put the bad news in page after page of clearly worded disclosure: the losses, the hurdles, the brutal competition, the failures, the "no assurances can be givens." But the most unforgivable statistic was the error rate. The prospectus revealed that in the 6 months ended March 31, 1980, Schwab had been obliged to use 10.5 percent, or $1.1 million, of total commission income of $10.4 million to cover bad debts and execution errors. The average error rate for NYSE member firms was just 1.4 percent.

A dejected Bill Pearson, architect of the Schwab computer system, took personal responsibility for the error rate. "I'm totally to blame for the aborted IPO," he wrote Chuck. "The IBM 360

computer I installed couldn't keep up with the growth. It generated the errors that became the lightning rod for intense criticism." Chuck wouldn't have any of it. When Pearson got overly
self-critical, Chuck reminded him to examine the watch on his
wrist. Pearson wore a gold Rolex that Chuck gave him to celebrate the activation of BETA in 1976. Engraved on the back was
a personal message from Chuck: "Thank you for loyalty and incredible ability."

The resulting furor among investors demonstrated how badly
Chuck had miscalculated. For all the stink the prospectus generated, the EPA should have required Schwab to file an environ-
mental impact statement. Only an intoxicating mix of hubris and
selective analysis could have given Chuck any confidence that
the Street would find Schwab ready for prime time. In fact, it
wasn't, and wouldn't be for another 7 years. The facts, revealed
for the first time, simply scared investors away. When the underwriters started backing away from the $4 per share price they
had initially represented and suggested that a more realistic estimate would be $2.75 per share, maybe, Chuck withdrew the
offering. It was a humiliating moment for the executive and his
entire team. The prospectus identified the Schwab management
team:

Charles R. Schwab	President, chief executive officer, chief financial officer, chairman of the board of directors
William L. Pearson	Executive vice president, director
Hugo W. Quackenbush	Senior vice president, director
William G. Bloodgood	Director
Barbara L. Ahmajan[*]	Corporate secretary, vice president—administration
Peter H. Moss	Vice president—planning and communications

[*] Later known as Barbara Wolfe.

Richard W. Arnold   Vice president—finance, assistant
                                 to the president

The ownership of the new company was structured to ensure that Chuck retained control of the company:

	Number of Shares Beneficially Owned	Percentage of Outstanding Shares
Charles R. and Helen O. Schwab	2,221,514	51.8%
William L. Pearson	384,999	9.0%
Barbara M. Schwab, Trustee	372,780	8.7%
Gold and Company, Trustee	357,499	8.3%
All executives and officers	2,378,007	55.4%

A footnote states: "Mr. and Mrs. Schwab may be deemed to be 'parents' of the Company as defined by the SEC." Another footnote offers that Hugo Quackenbush, one of the six executives and officers, owned 115,904 shares or 2.8 percent.

In the next few months, the business press gleefully dissected the prospectus. "In registering the deal with the SEC, Schwab & Co. lifted the lid off the discount business for the first time. The results were devastating," a typical report stated. Chuck went into damage control mode. He said that he withdrew the offering in response to an unexpected dip in the volume of stock trading. But that dog wouldn't hunt. *Business Week* quickly noted that stock volume—along with prices for the shares of other brokerages going public—was actually in good shape in the middle of 1980. "What is clear is that Schwab made several damaging miscalculations, not only in estimating how much he could receive for the stock, but also in not predicting the furor that would result when the firm's previously private books were opened up. 'At least you have to mark them down for naïveté,' says one full-service broker," the August 18, 1980 article reported.

As for the unpardonable error rate, Chuck attempted to pin the blame on growing pains related to the new computerized order processing system that broke down frequently under the heavy trading volumes of the first quarter of 1980. By doing so, did he notice he was contradicting himself with respect to the "unexpected dip in trading volume"? In fact, there was no dip, unexpected or otherwise, in trading volume. The error rate was a function of poorly trained people and lack of controls. The prospectus itself suggests that the back-office foul-ups were business as usual.

A financial journalist covering Schwab during that period took a peek under the covers and was amazed at what he saw. "The place is falling apart," read the notes a business journalist took immediately after a 1980 interview. "The company simply can't handle the growth, and the growth is modest." As a manager, Chuck was perceived as a lightweight; his image as a visionary elder statesman was still in the future. But at that time, he was being evaluated as a hands-on manager of a struggling operation. The subjective results were not attractive. "Schwab is a sort of male model, an empty suit, effective at presenting a very simple point of view, stubbornly simple minded, on the side of the angels, but has zero aptitude for operations. The first time a reporter shows a little skepticism, he gets thin-skinned," state the journalist's notes.

To be fair, the business press went overboard—as it always does—on the doom and gloom. "Many observers think the swift turnaround has dealt a severe blow to the industry, postponing for a long time—and possibly canceling—any hope it had for becoming a credible part of the financial market mainstream," *Business Week* wrote. But Chuck was unapologetic and his overarching goal was clear for all to see, despite his momentary setback: "In this business, unless you grow, you die."

It was a fiasco, yes, but the company recovered and emerged stronger from the setback. The management team realized that some radical changes were long overdue. A newly chastened Chuck finally accepted the limitations of his management skills and hired Larry Stupski, a gifted top executive who would be the catalyst that transformed Schwab into a true financial services powerhouse. By stepping back and doing what he is best at—advocating for customers, imagining new products, and championing inspired marketing—Chuck began a new assault on profits and respectability that would make Schwab the poster child for the most credible brokerage in the financial market mainstream.

And in some ways, the failed IPO worked out better financially, too. The company's cash needs were met by a last-minute private placement that raised $4 million in exchange for 20 percent of the company. This private infusion of capital gave the company some breathing room in more ways than one. Yes, the venture capital provided most of the cash the IPO was supposed to supply. But more significantly, by staying privately owned, Schwab avoided the relentless pursuit of quarterly results that hobbles many newly public companies from taking on the necessary but long-term objectives that result in real success.

With a capital crunch avoided, at least temporarily, Schwab gave Stupski the reins to impose some discipline on the company. This he did with remarkable ability and humanity. The company doubled in size over the next 2 years, giving Chuck the satisfaction that his goals for growth were on track. Stupski ordered a long-term forecast for the company. The forecast revealed some disturbing news. The $4 million from the private placement would last just 2 years before Schwab was out of cash again. Another IPO so soon was out of the question. There were only two options: Slow down the expansion and growth or hope someone else with deep pockets would come along.

Birthright

November 22, 1981–March 31, 1987

Bank of America represented wealth, prestige, and privilege, all of which Chuck coveted in equal measures. On November 22, 1981, Chuck Schwab temporarily relinquished his independence in exchange for $53 million and the unlocking of the gate to real establishment success. On that day, Charles Schwab & Co. became a wholly owned subsidiary of BankAmerica, the holding company which also owned Bank of America, and thereby forfeited an essential piece of itself.

Six years later, when the damage was reversed, jubilant employees wore buttons that read "Free at Last!" It would cost the company $190 million to extricate itself from Chuck's excellent adventure.

Illusion yields a hypnotic effect, but by itself it is unsustainable and, except in a movie, unsatisfying. In the film classic *Casablanca*, the hero, the independent saloon owner Rick, is quizzed by the police prefect, Renault:

RENAULT: What on Earth brought you to Casablanca?

RICK: My health. I came to Casablanca for the waters.

RENAULT: The waters? What waters? We're in the desert.

RICK: I was misinformed.

Later, when the relationship was falling apart and Chuck was more miserable than at any point in his life, he would echo Rick's sentiment. How could he have allowed himself to be talked into giving up his independence? How could he have tethered his company's destiny to what he now came to realize was a behemoth of an organization even more dysfunctional than his own? Privately (he was too much of a gentleman to vent in public), Chuck would emerge from the Bank of America boardroom aghast at the arrogance and incompetence. In the mirrorlike finish of the immense slab of mahogany that made up the table in the Bank of America boardroom where he now had a seat, Chuck encountered a reflection of himself and he shuddered.

For a critical mass of the U.S. population, it was literally impossible to go through a day without encountering the Bank of America. "It's hard to overestimate the profile of Bank of America for Californians of Chuck's generation," says Larry Stupski. "To a kid who grew up in California, Bank of America was a huge presence, a colossus that permeated every aspect of daily life. It was difficult to go through a day without having at least one interaction with the bank."

The bank was founded in 1904 by A. P. Giannini, the son of an Italian immigrant family that settled in San Jose, California. After a successful start as a produce wholesaler, Giannini started a bank to help other Italian immigrants, many of whom found that mainstream commercial banks refused to deal with them. He called his institution the Bank of Italy and focused on serving the immigrant farmers and working-class people of the area. In many ways Giannini, like Chuck many years later, had a sense of stewardship for "the little fellow." By 1918, the Bank of Italy was the fourth largest bank in California. By 1945, it had a new name—Bank of America—assets of $5 billion, and bragging rights to being the largest bank in the world.

Bank of America, like Charles Schwab & Co., was a beneficiary of its California roots. In no other state could the bank have been so successful. Not only was California the fastest-growing state with the most adventurous population—the very demographics that would feed Schwab's growth—but it was one of the few states in the country that allowed statewide branch banking. The branch strategy that so benefited Schwab also promoted Bank of America's success. By 1980, there were more than 1,000 branches and its Bank Americard (later VISA) credit cards were being issued all across the state. The bank had inserted itself into the very lifeblood of California. Thus when Bank of America expressed interest in buying Charles Schwab & Co., Chuck couldn't believe it.

To Chuck, Bank of America was the very embodiment of the financial establishment. It had unlimited wealth, its executives hobnobbed with the cream of California economic, social, and political might. It represented a world that Chuck wanted to have in his pocket. On a more pragmatic level, the bank had cash— lots of it—and if Chuck and the bank joined forces, Schwab could surely tap the funds, presumably without the embarrassment of filling out an application. Chuck was still smarting from being turned down for a bank loan by Bank of America, not just once, but twice. How ironic it would be to enjoy an unlimited line of credit from the same bank that had so recently deemed him uncreditworthy. Moreover, as long as we're in the realm of irony, an encounter from the murky past of Giannini and Chuck's grandfather was also said to inform Chuck's decision. Revenge is a dish best consumed cold, the proverb states, and many of Chuck's closest associates believe the Schwab–Bank of America deal happened because of a recipe that was supposedly first cooked up in the years before World War II.

What's in a name? Everything, Giannini understood. Bank of Italy was a fine name if you wanted to be a regional bank catering to working-stiffs of Italian descent, but if you had ambitions, as Giannini did, to own the largest bank in America . . . well, the name of your bank better have the word "America" in it. There was just one difficulty. The rights to the perfect name for Giannini's institution—"Bank of America"—were held by a bank in New York. To secure the rights to the name, Giannini dispatched a seasoned San Francisco lawyer, none other than Chuck's grandfather.

The elder Schwab was successful in his mission, the legend continues, and on his return to the Bay Area duly presented an invoice for his services. Giannini found the bill excessive and initially refused to pay it. After going back and forth, the bill was eventually paid, which is when a disgruntled Giannini is supposed to have made the angry pledge that "No Schwab will ever work for the Bank of America again!"

Was it worth it to Chuck to sacrifice his independence in order to avenge his grandfather's alleged humiliation and stick it to the long-departed Giannini? That's the speculation some of Chuck's executives indulged as they tried to figure out why he sold out. To be sure, it was the kind of sweet revenge that only a good legend can craft: *Up yours, Amadeo Peter Giannini. A Schwab not only works at Bank of America, but sits on the damned board of directors and, get this, is the bank's largest individual shareholder!* The legend requires Claire Hoffman, the founder's daughter, to declare upon Chuck's election to the board, "My poor father must be spinning in his grave." It also requires Chuck to be guilty of spite, a trait that among all his faults is the least observed.

In the end, practicality, not sentiment, ruled the day. Chuck sold his company because he had to. And he sold it to Bank of America because it offered the most upside. Two years after the failed IPO, true to the financial forecast Larry Stupski commissioned, Schwab's need for cash outstripped its ability to generate it. The constraint was the same as before—the minimum net capital rule—except that now Schwab's scale meant the company's capital needs ran to the tens of millions of dollars. According to some, this requirement proved to be a constant irritant, not only to Chuck in his capacity as chief executive, but in his relationship with his wife, Helen, who resented the occasional raiding of private funds to bail the company out. "There was nothing in Helen's privileged upbringing that prepared her for the kind of high-end scraping that Chuck was used to," a former executive close to Chuck says. "Helen pushed Chuck to take the Bank of America deal because she was never comfortable having more money than her husband."

The merger represented immediate relief for each one of those headaches. Chuck's biggest worries would be over. The money that he would put in his own pocket didn't hurt either, but that was not the main point. His wife would be happy for Chuck to finally be accepted by San Francisco society. Chuck also appreciated the credibility that would attach to the entire discount brokerage industry by the bank's action. Chuck was weary of running the largest company in an industry still considered somewhat sleazy. He never again wanted to hear the phrases "fly-by-night" or "bucket shop." He was tired of being turned down for credit because banks didn't understand his business. The bank that insiders called "MotherBank" must certainly understand, Chuck hoped, and if Bank of America approved, then his work would finally be validated. Chuck understood that the moment the news broke that Bank of America bought Schwab would be the moment the industry he helped create would, finally, be legitimate.

In a way, it was Stephen T. McLin's honeymoon that created the conditions for the Schwab–Bank of America deal. McLin, a rising star in the bank's strategic planning and corporate development department, had his eye out for profitable business opportunities the bank could enter. But in June 1981, the only strategic planning a newly married McLin had on his mind was how to pay for a Hawaii honeymoon. He decided to raise the funds by exercising 300 stock options for Bank of America stock. Merrill Lynch quoted a fee of $250 to sell the options, which seemed exorbitant to McLin. He had seen an advertisement for Schwab and was pleasantly pleased by the discounted $80 commission it quoted. But then he learned that Bank of America, like many organizations, provided a service that assisted employees in trading the company's own stock. "That's what I did, but it wasn't great execution," he recalls. "That started me thinking about the possibilities."

For some time, McLin had been analyzing the benefits of the bank buying a brokerage. Now he shifted his sights from Dean Witter & Co., one of the nation's biggest full-service stock brokerages, to Charles Schwab & Co. The advantages to the bank in acquiring Schwab were twofold. First, Sears, Roebuck & Co. also had its sights on Dean Witter (Sears would buy Dean Witter later that year) and McLin didn't want to get into a bidding war with the giant retailer. Second, and this was more critical, Bank of America had to deal with the restrictions of the Glass-Steagall Act, a law Congress passed after the 1929 stock market crash prohibiting commercial banks from owning a brokerage. McLin as well as Dean Witter officials (who thought it undignified to have "stocks and socks" under one roof and preferred to be acquired by Bank of America) struggled mightily to find a way around Glass-Steagall.

Then McLin flashed on a telephone call he had received from Peter Moss, his counterpart at Schwab. At thirty-three, just a year younger than McLin, Moss had quickly become Chuck's strategic planner. Years earlier, Moss was an options trader and Schwab customer who ingratiated himself with Chuck by jumping over the counter and reconciling his own account. By 1981 he had proved himself the most committed of Chuck's soldiers in the discounting crusade. Moss believed in the absolute righteousness of Schwab's mission and put his considerable intelligence and creativity in Chuck's service. He was brilliant at times, yes, but also reckless and impulsive, a deadly combination that would bitterly end his career at Schwab. But for now, he was tight with Chuck and more than anything wanted to solve his boss's capital requirement problems. A few weeks earlier, having heard rumors that Bank of America was looking for an entry into the brokerage business, Moss had picked up the phone and put two words in McLin's ear. The two words were "discount brokerage."

It's a fact that Glass-Steagall specifically enjoined banks from buying a brokerage. But about a bank buying a *discount* brokerage that didn't do securities underwriting, the act was silent. Of course, discounting did not exist when the restrictive Depression-era banking laws were written. If you had asked 10,000 East Coast lawyers, they would have said forget it; Glass-Steagall applies. But to a loophole artist like Moss, the assumption was that if the law did not explicitly prohibit an activity, then that activity was, by definition, kosher. Congress eventually closed this loophole, but not before grandfathering a number of banks that acted quickly to exploit the opening. Bank of America was among the first.

"A light bulb went off," McLin says. He called Leland Prussia, on Bank of America's board and the finest out-of-the-box thinker he knew. How far was the bank prepared to push the regulatory envelope? McLin made his case: "If a bank is permitted to buy and sell stock like I just did through the trading desk, and Schwab does not do underwriting, why shouldn't a bank be allowed to buy a discounter?" It seemed to Prussia that, indeed, the bank would be technically within the law in buying a *discount* brokerage. But Prussia warned it would not be a cakewalk. Even if the Federal Reserve approved, the bank would almost certainly be challenged in court, if not by the government than by one of the bank's competitors. Still, Prussia encouraged McLin to go forward.

Events half a world away have a habit of creating the conditions that, by making all things seem possible, make them in a sense inevitable. On January 20, 1981, a former movie actor and governor of California took the oath of office of the presidency of the United States. The sucking sound you heard was the number of fat-cat Californians gravitating to Washington, D.C. to become foot soldiers in the Reagan Revolution. At the head of the line, grabbing the plum prize of the presidency of the World Bank, was Tom Clausen, for 10 years chief executive of Bank of America.

Chuck's magic timing held. He couldn't have asked for a better replacement than Samuel H. Armacost, appointed chief executive by BankAmerica in its November 1981 board meeting. Only 42 years old, two years younger than Chuck, Armacost was predisposed by education and training to reclaim the bank's early reputation for risk taking, technological innovation, and leadership. Chuck and Armacost shared a number of similarities. They both were lackluster students in college before getting M.B.A.s from Stanford. Both were natural salesmen and passionate marketers. Golf for both men was more than just a hobby. Both came out of small-town middle-class families. Each one believed that computer technology was the key for success in financial services.

The new CEO's determination to focus the bank through bold new acquisitions and partnerships quickly brought Armacost into contact with McLin. The supremely confident Armacost saw in McLin a kindred spirit and he became Armacost's closest lieutenant. McLin's name regularly appeared in the newspapers, making him the unofficial spokesman for Armacost, earning him the envy and distrust of many in the bank. But backed by the CEO, McLin's star rose without opposition. As executive vice president of BankAmerica Corporation, McLin negotiated the bank's acquisitions of Schwab and more than twenty other companies. It is doubtful that the Schwab acquisition would have been successful without McLin's influence over Armacost. McLin left the bank in 1987 shortly after Armacost's departure. A native of St. Louis, McLin has an M.B.A. from Stanford University and is chairman of STM Holdings. He is currently a member of the board of directors of The Charles Schwab Corporation and chairman of its audit committee.

Jurors waiting for assignment have a lot of time on their hands. Called for jury duty in the U.S. courthouse in San Francisco in early August of 1981, McLin couldn't sit on his idea any longer. From a pay phone at the courthouse, he called his boss. "What do you think about exploring a discount brokerage?" he asked Armacost. The open circuit hummed as Armacost digested the idea. After a short pause, he told McLin to take the next step and set up a meeting. McLin had plenty of time to strategize about how to make the deal work. It had been years since Bank of America intentionally did anything risky, much less audacious. No other bank had ever bought a brokerage. To do so would unleash a major regulatory struggle. Were the bank's lobbyists up to the fury of a powerful securities industry determined to keep banks out of their territory? However, if the deal succeeded, Armacost's reputation for bold leadership would be assured. The deal seemed perfectly aligned with Armacost's strategy. Much depended on the chemistry at the table when Armacost and Chuck Schwab would first sit down.

It worked out pretty well . . . for McLin. For Bank of America and Charles Schwab & Co., the outcomes were mixed. McLin went on to become executive vice president, one of seven principal officers of BankAmerica Corporation. After McLin resigned from the bank in January, 1987, Chuck was quick to call and ask him to join the Schwab board. McLin has been on Schwab's board since 1988. Serving on the powerful audit and compensation committees, he has enjoyed a unique perspective of Schwab in all its glory and despair. On McLin's watch the company made the largest gains in Wall Street history, growing from $392 million in 1988 to $ 5.7 billion in 2000.

Although the Schwab–Bank of America marriage was fraught with difficulties (what marriage isn't?) and ultimately ended in divorce, McLin is convinced that the experience was critical for Schwab's eventual triumph. "The deal was momentous in pushing Schwab forward," he says. "The acquisition solved two problems that Schwab battled: lack of capital and credibility. But it also prepared the company to manage success." McLin argues that the bank imposed badly needed discipline on a company that was flying apart. Of course, the Schwab people resisted the bank's discipline. Cultural incompatibility is a fact of life when big bureaucratic companies buy small entrepreneurial companies. "But if the Schwab of today bought the Schwab of 20 years ago, it would insist on the same reforms the bank did," he adds.

McLin sat down with Peter Moss for the first time on September 11, 1981, at the Banker's Club on the fifty-second floor of the BankAmerica tower, an unlikely venue for private negotiations, but perhaps McLin wanted to give his counterpart a sense of Bank of America's perspective on every other enterprise. Moss was there on the pretense of talking about a $7.5 million subordinated line of credit for Schwab. McLin played along, asking about Schwab's balance sheet and performance. Moss was proud of Schwab's numbers. More than 370,000 customer accounts, revenues of $150 million, 800 employees in 50 branches. McLin was unimpressed. Schwab's revenues were not even a rounding error against Bank of America's $120 billion. And as for profits, the company's return on investment was, frankly, miserable.

But McLin saw that Schwab, with a little help, was ready to scale upward. The basic economics of discounting, McLin had learned, were a function of scale. The fixed costs of enabling securities trading are enormous, requiring huge investments in computers, telecommunications, and branches. The commissions earned on the first N trades of the day pays the overhead; the rest is profit. Plus economies of scale kick in when the brokerage gets larger; the costs per trade not only drop but drop right to the bottom line.

McLin was through fencing with Moss. He told Moss there wasn't going to be a line of credit but the bank might just be the source of the "ultimate capital infusion." Gary Hector recounts the ensuing conversation in his 1988 book, *Breaking the Bank: The Decline of Bank America.*

Moss: What are you really interested in here?

McLin: I think we can find a way to get together.

Moss: You mean some kind of joint venture, a minority interest?

McLin: We haven't been too happy with joint ventures. It's been especially difficult where we were a minority partner, but even when we hold a majority interest it has been difficult.

Moss: What would you like to do?

McLin: We'd like to own you.

Inwardly, Moss glowed with self-importance. He was spinning McLin! An equity offer and infusion of credibility from the world's most famous bank was exactly the outcome Moss was secretly hoping for. Of course, selling out completely was a different matter, so Moss allowed himself to express some reluctance. "Chuck wouldn't be interested," he told McLin. "He's independent-minded, aggressive. He's really so much of a maverick that it would be hard to see him in a large company." As it turned out, Moss called it right on the money, but, for now, he indulged in the fantasy that Chuck might see Moss as the savior of the company.

Not for an instant was McLin fooled by Moss's bravado. Far from Moss spinning McLin, the reverse was true. So their meetings would not be noticed, McLin proposed that the men continue their discussion as they commuted to work. He knew exactly what he was doing. The cloak and dagger secrecy would appeal to Moss's sense of bravado and narcissism. Moss lived in Lafayette, a close-in suburb across the bay from San Francisco, and rode the Bay Area Rapid Transit (BART). McLin's residence was in a town a few miles farther out. Over the next few weeks, McLin picked Moss up and as the men made their way downtown through San Francisco's rush hour traffic, they discussed the merits of the deal and how best to present it to Chuck. By September 21, 1981, McLin had convinced the Schwab strategic planner that the bank was serious, and Moss agreed to take the deal to Chuck.

"No and hell no." Those were Chuck's immediate sentiments on hearing of the Bank of America overture. "After all the struggling we've done," he said to Moss, "why should we sell our birthright now?" But the fact remained that he needed money. Confused about what to do, Chuck reached out to friends and colleagues. He received a variety of opinions. "I told him he'd be a fool to tie his destiny to an institution that would have huge problems in the next few years," said an associate with ties to Bank of America. However, Anthony Frank, who owned 20 percent of Schwab, was definitely interested in selling. "The company was not doing that sensationally then. I suppose my stupid feeling at the time was that if you could get an enormous windfall of capital, take it," he said. Eventually, Chuck decided to take a meeting with Armacost.

On September 25, 1981, in Armacost's private dining room twelve floors below where McLin and Moss first spoke, Chuck and Armacost broke bread and took each other's measure. Each liked what the other saw. Events moved quickly after that. McLin briefed BankAmerica's managing committee on the pending talks. With a green light from the bank's senior managers, Armacost and McLin sauntered over to tour Chuck's offices four blocks away. Armacost was impressed by the automation and paperless processes that he saw, absolutely transfixed by the sight of brokers entering trades on a computer terminal and then hitting "execute." "We're doing that 20,000 times per day," a proud Bill Pearson said. On the walk back, Armacost told McLin to buy Schwab.

Chuck's ambivalence became evident during the negotiations. BankAmerica offered $40 million; Chuck asked for $80 million—twice the company's annual revenues. Chuck sounded out other banks for a better offer. None came close to what BankAmerica was offering; one suggested $25 million might be a better number. Meanwhile, Schwab was out of money. A disastrous foray into insurance sales erased much of the company's profits in 1981. Chuck really had no choice. On November 22, 1981, Chuck shook Sam Armacost's hand. People at every level of BankAmerica cheered. "Everything stopped when we heard about it," one bank executive recalls. Armacost was hailed as a hero. After a decade of sluggish existence, BankAmerica finally had at its helm a Big Swinging Dick, the term Tom Wolfe coined in *Bonfire of the Vanities* to describe fearless creators of wealth.

For the first time, Chuck was rich. First-order rich. Not as rich as he would be, but rich enough to be able to look his father-in-law in the eye without blinking. And if things went his way, he could be even richer. At the end, Chuck had accepted $53 million for his company. Unfortunately, the $53 million was not in cash, but in BankAmerica stock: 2.2 million shares at the current price of about $26.00. Chuck would be the largest individual shareholder. Another sweetener: Armacost agreed to nominate Chuck for a position on BankAmerica's board. Now all they had to do was wait. Since the deal required approval by the Federal Reserve and would likely be challenged in court, McLin gave Chuck a choice. Behind door number one: $53 million. Chuck could fix the price and accept however many shares of stock that might be when the deal closed. Or he could take what was behind door number two: 2.2 million shares. Chuck could fix the number of shares—taking a risk that BankAmerica's stock would decrease in value or reaping a windfall if it should rise. Chuck, the eternal optimist, took the stock.

He should have taken the cash. As the approval process ground on, BankAmerica's internal contradictions started catching up with it. Chuck watched with horror as the stock which represented his entire fortune began to lose value. In the fall of 1982, BankAmerica's stock fell from $26.50 to $19.50. In other words, the value of the 2.2 million shares for Schwab shareholders dropped from $53 million to $43 million. Meanwhile, a bull market had *improved* his company's fortunes. In 1982, Schwab picked up more than 100,000 customers. Phones were melting down with the rush of trades. The branches had lines snaking out the door. A company that had never made as much as $20 million per year was suddenly clearing $30 million per *month.* In the last 5 months of 1982, Schwab earned more money than it made in its entire 7-year history. The deal that seemed so necessary the year before suddenly looked a lot less desirable.

Chuck is too much of a gentleman to back out of an agreement he has made in good faith. With the circumstances so profoundly different in 1982 than they were when the agreement was originally signed in 1981, he conceivably might have renegotiated more favorable terms. That is what Pete Moss urgently recommended. Moss, who initiated the deal, now undertook a one-man scorched earth campaign to derail the agreement. When Chuck rebuffed him, Moss went to Armacost to find a way out of the deal. Armacost would have none of it.

"What does Chuck think?" Armacost asked.

"Chuck has some discomfort with it," Moss recalls replying, "but he's a gentleman and he thinks a deal is a deal." Armacost just shrugged. Moss was starting to become a nuisance.

In January 1983, after 2 years and a ruling from both the Federal Reserve and the U.S. Supreme Court, BankAmerica got the green light to buy Schwab. But Moss kept up his relentless opposition to a deal he felt no longer represented the best interests of the company, in whose fortune he was vested to the tune of 1.5 percent. He had initiated the deal and now he wanted Chuck to put the kibosh on it. Now he claimed that the disclosure filings sent to the SEC were so incomplete that they may have bordered on fraud. Stupski listened to Moss's list of facts that should have been—but were not—in the disclosure documents. But even when Stupski issued a new set of SEC documents, embracing many of those points, Moss was not satisfied. "Larry told me to keep my nose out of it, but I had initiated the deal. I was one of five corporate officers. And I was pissed," Moss says.

That's when perhaps the most celebrated memo in Schwab lore was penned. "It is my personal and moral duty to inform you that I formally oppose the merger," began the memo to Chuck. Moss's increasingly shrill objections filled up two pages. Chuck could have lived with that. He still respected Moss and wanted to keep the relationship. But Moss went too far. This time, his strategic planner pushed a button on his computer and sent the memo to every officer in the company, all the way down to the branch managers. Chuck could not ignore such insubordination. As averse to conflict as he was, Chuck called Moss into his office and did the thing he hated most: He fired someone he considered a friend. Although it was too late for Moss, his criticisms of the agreement prompted BankAmerica to issue 2.6 million shares for Schwab instead of 2.2 million. Given the deflated value of the stock, the additional 400,000 shares brought the purchase price up to $52 million. For Moss, it was a bittersweet triumph. "No doubt about it. I hung myself out to dry," he says.

Life at Schwab after the merger went on pretty much as it did before. For the vast majority of Schwab employees, the only change was that they were offered free Bank of America checking accounts. "No myth at Schwab is stronger, or less true," says Larry Stupski, "than the myth that Bank of America imposed draconian changes on Schwab." The companies consolidated financials and identified 128 projects that would leverage the synergies. But the links between the companies were more opportunistic than strategic. For example, Schwab put some mini-branches in Bank of America lobbies in San Francisco, Modesto, Fresno, Bakersfield, Stockton, Beverly Hills, and Los Angeles. "When we bought the business back in 1987, it was easy to also back the company out of these projects, evidence that the links were peripheral," Stupski says.

The cultural mismatch was evident from the beginning. At one of the meetings at Bank of America, Stupski indicated that the mean tenure of all Schwab employees (then about 1,000 strong) was about 6 months. "The Bank of America managers' mouths hung open," Stupski recalls. "They couldn't imagine running a company under those conditions." Those conditions, of course, are what allowed Schwab to be so innovative. Stable? No. Predictable? No. But innovative? Out the wazoo.

Schwab's marketing and market research were also much stronger than the bank's. Dave Pottruck and Larry Stupski recall a bank off-site meeting where the keynote presentation seemed to demonstrate only that rich people have more money than poor people. Chuck was amazed at the lack of sophistication of the bank's executive information systems. Chuck would ask Armacost, "Sam, how much does it cost you to acquire a customer?" And Armacost would say, "Gee, Chuck, I don't know. We have so many businesses; I couldn't quote you a single number." That conversation was reconstructed by a former manager who overheard a conversation between Chuck and Armacost. Both men would come away from those encounters with a bit of a headache. For Armacost, Chuck's questions confirmed that he did not have the strategic vision to run an organization as intricate and multidimensional as Bank of America. Chuck would simply shake his head when he came back to his office and say, "How can you run a business if you don't know your customer acquisition costs?" The men who seemed to have so much in common were becoming estranged.

Earlene Perry is perhaps the most durable legacy of the Bank of America merger. She was an operations manager at the bank when her boss said, "We need a liaison officer to work with our Schwab acquisition. Do you want the job?" At Bank of America the only correct answer to such a question is yes. "My responsibility was to protect Schwab from being overwhelmed by the bank and to educate the bank on how it can leverage Schwab," she says. She fell in love with Schwab and stayed for almost 20 years. She helped create the BASH—Bank of America and Schwab—team to educate bankers on the brokerage industry. But her lasting contribution was as a customer service fanatic. To the extent that Schwab enjoys a reputation as a company that actually does walk the customer-truly-does-come-first walk, Perry has a lot to do with it. She worked on quality assurance, sending out customer satisfaction surveys with order confirmations. She dispatched secret shoppers to the branches to evaluate their performance. She created the service enhancement department to handle the complaints of last resort, the issues that customers could not get resolved at the branch level. "Chuck wanted to give customers a place to escalate issues so they could feel they received some personal attention," she says. But with millions of transactions, even a small fraction of complaints resulted in 2-week backlogs and huge costs as the staff investigated the issue, made a determination, and communicated the results.

Here is a good example of how Schwab's putting the customer first drives management decisions. As long as the company was invested in making incremental changes—how can we shorten the complaint resolution process from 2 weeks to, say, 1 week—little progress was possible. But what if the company reframed the question this way: "How could we respond to these complaints in 48 hours?" Now the company began to question all its assumptions. "In this case, we redefined the problem as 'customer retention' rather than 'complaint response,' " Pottruck says. "What did the customers want? They wanted to have the complaint resolved in their favor, as quickly as possible. This conclusion then goaded us to analyze the cost of our responses. We concluded that we could concede any dispute that we could resolve in the customer's favor for less than that cost and make our target. Eighty percent of the complaints could be handled in this way," he says.

Some problems even Perry's service enhancement department couldn't resolve. One customer had mentioned to a branch manager that if the option trade Schwab was about to execute didn't work out, he, the customer, would kill himself. The manager refused to take the option order. The customer appealed but the branch manager was adamant. No way would he accept the order. Then the customer demanded Schwab pay him the value of the trade he was denied. The branch manager said no. The customer's complaint eventually reached Earlene Perry, who confirmed that the branch manager's decision was final and there would be no payment. A little later, Perry was notified that the suicidal option trader was in the lobby and wanted to come up. The customer became a major pest. "But at least I was able to sleep at night. Taking that trade was not in the customer's best interest," Perry says.

Lending officers have a saying. If you owe the bank $100, it owns you; if you owe the bank $100 million, you own the bank. From his perch on the Bank of America board, Chuck got a disturbing view of how badly his biggest investment was mismanaged. It quickly became obvious to Chuck that the supposed synergies between the bank and the discounter were elusive. Either the synergies were straight-out fantasies or, for the handful that actually had some potential, the glacial pace of decision making at the bank made it impossible for them to get any traction. More sobering was his estimation of the board. The board he first regarded with a sense of awe, for it included the crown princes of American financial might, soon seemed to him to be dangerously passive and, with thirty members, cumbersome. Chuck's open unassuming manner soon collided with the board's glacial respectability. "There should have been a defibrillator in the boardroom," an executive close to the BankAmerica board laughs, recalling Chuck's attempts to rouse his fellow directors to action. "Poor bastard, he never realized the board was in a coma."

Chuck's break with Armacost was inevitable. By the second quarter of 1985, loan problems and mismanagement had created the real possibility that the bank would just break even or possibly lose money. Chuck's instincts were to say it like it is. Armacost's were to obfuscate. As it turned out, the results were far worse than anyone expected. The bank announced a second quarter loss of $448 million. It was not only the first quarterly loss in BankAmerica's history; it was the second largest quarterly loss in the history of U.S. banking. Chuck felt Armacost's "assurances" that the bank would break even represented an unforgivable breach of trust. The honeymoon was over.

It just exacerbated matters that the fortunes of the partners now dramatically reversed. Schwab was now on the upward trend. By the end of 1985, it had 1,500 employees, 90 branches, assets of almost $1 billion, and a profit of $11.3 million. Still peanuts by the bank's standards, but momentum was with Chuck and against Armacost. BankAmerica was, says Rich Arnold, "consuming itself." The bank was in the worst kind of trouble, insisted Schwab's former VP of finance: confronted by impossibly difficult loan and regulatory problems and headed by a CEO who was in denial. "Few people dared to tell Armacost that he had a disaster in the making, but when anyone did, he practically pressed his hands against his ears," Arnold says. Chuck says he couldn't get Armacost to acknowledge the bank had problems, much less to take action. According to Chuck, the board basically tuned him out. "What a naïve, dumb guy I was to think I could persuade an institution like that to do anything," Chuck said. He decided to get Armacost's attention and he knew just how to do it.

He began selling his BankAmerica stock. Between June 13 and June 26, Chuck and Helen sold 307,500 of the one million shares they controlled at an average price that was about $3 below what it was worth on the day of the merger. By law, whenever a director or officer of a publicly traded company sells stock in that company, it becomes public information. When investors learned that the bank's largest individual shareholder had, in effect, lost faith in the bank, the downward pressure on the bank's stock increased.

Chuck paid a high price for this act of rebellion. Whatever support he had on the board evaporated in a firestorm of recrimination and his relationship with Armacost was over. Ironically, Chuck was sued by investors alleging that in selling his shares, Chuck acted on insider information about mounting losses. In fact, the board was as surprised—and outraged—by the losses as anyone. Chuck's signal to Armacost to be more forthright with information was now used as evidence that Armacost's board possessed and acted on "material information not available to the public." It was over. In August 1986, after a board meeting in which the main order of business was installing golden parachutes for the board, Chuck resigned. "It was a great liberating thing to be free from the bank's problems," he said.

Now all that was left was to make the behemoth cough up Charles Schwab & Co. Fortunately, three realities converged to make the extrication possible. First, mounting losses created pressure on the bank to divest assets. Second, 2 months after Chuck resigned, Armacost resigned. A new president—Tom Clausen, back from the World Bank now that the Reagan gravy train was over—eliminated any personal resentments that might have thwarted the separation. Chuck's fabled timing was good as gold. Armacost's fabled "strategy" of which Schwab was such an integral part need no longer be defended. Schwab, it turned out, was not really a "core business" after all. Clausen would be pleased to divest the bank's discount brokerage operation.

Good news for Chuck? Not quite. Clausen didn't just plan to sell it; he intended to offer it to the highest bidder. Schwab was going to be auctioned off like a foreclosed warehouse.

This is where the third reality came in. No way was Chuck going to stand in line for a shot at his own company. Chuck told Clausen to take a close look at his contract with BankAmerica. The agreement gave the bank rights to Schwab's name, but *not* to Chuck's face and personality. Moreover, even the name "Charles Schwab & Co." would revert to Chuck after a mere 60 day non-compete term if he chose to leave the firm he founded. He would say later, "I could go across the street and, in two months, open up as 'The Charles Project.'" Given this reality, what did Clausen actually have to auction? Many years later, the company closed that unforgivable oversight. Today, an employment agreement between Chuck and the company explicitly prevents him from opening up a brokerage using his name should he and the firm part company. Appendix 2 gives the text of the controlling 1995 employment agreement between Charles R. Schwab and the company.

Clausen folded on the auction, but he rebelled at the $190 million Chuck offered for his old company. With profits of almost $60 million in 1986, Schwab was worth in the neighborhood of $300 million. The two parties launched an army of lawyers, negotiators, and analysts to value the company. But that was an infernally hard thing to do. What, exactly, are a discount brokerage's assets? Enter junk bond king Michael Milken, before he was convicted of criminal racketeering for securities fraud and insider trading. Milken was, Quackenbush says, "an absolute genius in understanding how to put value on *the customer* as asset. Our one million active customers were, in fact, our *only* asset." In the end, when the papers were signed on March 31, 1987, the bank was able to announce a sales price of $280 million—five times more than it paid for Schwab 6 years earlier. But Chuck knew that the true price was $190 million. The difference constituted accounting smoke and mirrors, the stuff of leveraged buyouts.

It was done. As everyone at Schwab celebrated and the champagne corks popped, Doug Farson in Schwab's purchasing department distributed buttons that he had made up for the occasion. "Schwab . . . Free at Last!" the buttons proclaimed. Herb Caen, the legendary columnist for the *San Francisco Chronicle* picked up the item. The effort to extricate the company exhausted everyone, which was a shame because the phones were always ringing. The problems didn't seem to go away; they just seemed to get bigger.

Once again, Chuck's timing was propitious. The sale couldn't have happened 6 months earlier, with Armacost still fighting for his failed "strategy" nor 6 months later, when market conditions would be toxic. And although it was delicious to be at the helm of his own company again, Chuck knew that he could rest but for a moment. Even as the champagne flowed, he called Rich Arnold into his office and said, "I want you to get started on a public offering." He didn't want to hear Arnold's objections that the company should get a few years of solid earnings under its belt and then go for the brass ring. "I know markets," a supremely confident Chuck Schwab said. "You never know when the top is coming." Chuck had put his finger to the wind and in the distance his instincts told him a storm was brewing.

9

Market Crash

October 19, 1987

Passionate highs to fearful lows. In less than a month, the men and women of Schwab saw the company they cherished go from the triumph of a successful initial public offering to the edge of despair as the Crash of 1987 threatened to sweep away everything they worked for.

Eight months after it won its independence from Bank of America in one of the first leveraged buyouts (LBOs) to become once again a private company, Schwab successfully became a public company. The company issued 8,050,000 shares on the New York Stock Exchange at a price of $16.50 per share. The company with the trading symbol SCH raised $132 million in capital. Within four weeks it would need every cent of it and more.

Was Chuck smart or just lucky to insist on taking the company public immediately after the LBO? There are those who believe that Chuck's instinct in reading the market is second to none. But no one, not even Chuck, can time the market—hence his

144

enthusiasm for index funds—so let's look at the market facts Chuck was working with. The country was clearly in a bull market. He saw the Dow Jones average rise from 776 points in August 1982 to a high of 2722 points in August 1987. Even though the day that Schwab went public the Dow Jones average was tending down (it opened at 2492), Schwab's entering the market may have helped the market leap an unbelievable 75 points. In fact, Chuck's timing was equivalent to a hole in one: He sold Schwab's shares into nothing less than the biggest one-day gain in the history of Dow Jones up to that point. Chuck surely wanted Schwab's IPO to ride that wave as far as it would take him. On a more pragmatic level, Chuck understood that much of the time-consuming and expensive legal and accounting work done for the LBO could be also used for the IPO. The company would save millions of dollars in fees by not having to duplicate much of this work.

However, Chuck would nod in agreement to the song in the musical *Pippin* that suggests "It's smarter to be lucky than lucky to be smart." It's an endearing trait of Schwab's leader that he resists claiming credit for the decisions that come out right while insisting on taking responsibility for the decisions that go south. Lucky or smart, Chuck would need them both, for while everyone in San Francisco was celebrating, half the world away a fuse was already burning. Oblivious to the signals that something was dreadfully wrong, Schwab and his teammates celebrated their good fortune. They had a scant 18 trading days to enjoy it.

"**I** thought that we should take the opportunity that the market presented," was all that Chuck had to say. Most observers at the time thought that Chuck pulled off a near miracle. For one thing, he neatly demonstrated what a move he pulled on Bank-America. By the market's incontrovertible estimation, the company that he had recently paid the bank $190 million for was really worth $400 million. Investors in early October 1987 demonstrated that the company was worth twice what its executives had paid the bank to buy it back the previous March.

All in all, it was a vote of confidence from the market that Schwab had finally arrived. Chuck liked to point out that the $16.50 price meant that SCH sold at a price/earnings ratio of 16, significantly higher than other brokerage stocks. Other executives were happy that much of the offering was gobbled up by Schwab's own customers. Even the investment banks who turned their noses up at Schwab in 1981 now lined up to underwrite the IPO. In the end, the underwriters were the most prestigious of the bunch: Morgan Stanley & Co. and The First Boston Corporation.

Chuck helped develop a new financial tool for taking a company public without risking significant assets beyond those represented by the target company. For the most part, Chuck took his company public using other people's money. The Schwab IPO represented a classic model of a process that Corporate America would repeat thousands of times in the following years: the LBO. In an LBO, the earnings and assets of the target corporation are used to pay off the money borrowed to finance the buyout. The executives then purchase stock in the new company with loans secured by the very shares they are buying. The assets of the target company not only serve as security for the loan, but the loan itself is repaid out of the cash flow of the acquired company.

The LBO represented another Schwab first: This was the first time that an issuer of stock was a distributor of its own offering without being part of the underwriting group. In other words, Schwab's customers could buy or sell Schwab stock using the services of the brokerage. It was a heady experience for Schwab employees to have a ringside seat the day the stock went on sale and see their customers trade in the future of their company. It felt good that, buy or sell, Schwab made a commission on each transaction.

"At the end of the day, I thought it was a good time to convert debt to equity," Chuck says. So let's take a look at the equity. The management team at the company became instant millionaires. Chuck, who had put up $9 million during the buyout for a little less than a third of the company, was now worth north of $100 million. The other executives fared pretty well, too. From the prospectus filed with the SEC, we learn that the principal stockholders and their percentage of ownership were:

| | Shares Beneficially Owned | | |
| | Prior to Offering | | After Offering |
Beneficial Owner	Number	Percent	Percent
Charles R. Schwab	7,215,000	41.5%	29.6%
Schwab Profit Sharing Plan	2,100,000	12.3%	8.6%
Lawrence J. Stupski	2,085,000	12.0%	8.5%
Joseph I. O'Neill	1,080,000	6.2%	4.4%
Anthony M. Frank	59,211	<1.0%	<1.0%
All other officers and directors	11,843,211	67.7.0%	48.4%

Chuck was extraordinarily generous in sharing the wealth. Although we don't know the number of shares received by individual officers and directors, it's fairly certain that no one felt cheated. "Chuck is one of the original non-zero-sum thinkers," Stupski says. "He knows that by treating people well, even if it dilutes his share, everyone comes out a winner." Nothing demonstrates Chuck's generosity and loyalty more than his performance when he took the company private from BankAmerica.

One thing had gnawed at Chuck in buying the company back. Between the time BankAmerica agreed to buy the bank and the time the merger closed, as described in Chapter 8, the value of BankAmerica stock had dropped by 25 percent. "Better [Chuck and his executives] had taken cash instead of shares in BankAmerica," wrote *San Francisco Chronicle* columnist Donald K. White. "Soon after the big transaction, the company's big subsidiary, Bank of America, ran into serious trouble and the value of the shares acquired by the Schwab high-ranker gang went down the tubes."

Chuck had made the decision to accept the risk of letting the stock float. He was okay with that decision as to his own fortune. But he was not comfortable knowing that his decision penalized the management team whose profits were also pegged to the decreased value of the BankAmerica shares. So Chuck decided to make the "high-ranker gang" whole. He calculated the losses that each member of his team incurred by holding their falling BankAmerica stock. Chuck then transferred that value to warrants or contingent rights for new Schwab stock. He made sure everyone was whole, even, remarkably, Peter Moss, whom he had fired for opposing the deal.

Chuck assembled a strong management team to take the company public. Many of the executives grew up with the company and participated in its success. David Pottruck had joined the company from Shearson in 1984. They were a team dedicated to Chuck and his vision of financial services with integrity. The company's years as a subsidiary of a larger organization taught it a lot about governance issues. "Bank of America was a much more mature organization than we were," Richard Arnold says. "They had gone through designing complex budgeting systems, transfer of pricing systems, structuring of policy committees. Everything that we built was affected by what we saw working—or not working—there." The divisions of responsibility broke down as follows:

	Position
Charles R. Schwab	Chairman and chief executive officer
Lawrence J. Stupski	President, chief operating officer, chief financial officer
Barbara A. Wolfe	Executive vice president—administration, corporate secretary
Richard W. Arnold	Executive vice president—investment banking
Robert W. Fivis	Executive vice president—operations and finance
Woodson M. Hobbs	Executive vice president—information systems
David S. Pottruck	Executive vice president—marketing and branch management

Position

Phyllis Kay Dryden — Senior vice president and general counsel

Hugo W. Quackenbush — Senior vice president—communications

Robert H. Rosseau — Senior vice president—retail service delivery

Elizabeth Gibson Sawi — Senior vice president—marketing and advertising

Barry G. Snowbarger — Senior vice president—trading administration and operations

James F. Wiggett — Senior vice president—human resources

For its first board of directors as a public company, Chuck recruited Donald G. Fisher, chairman of The Gap, Inc., and M. Kenneth Oshman, former CEO of Rolm Corporation. Fisher, who continues on Schwab's board, brought a retailer's experience to the company, underscoring Chuck's vision of his firm as essentially a consumer services company. In the following years, the board would be filled out with executives such as James R. Harvey, CEO of Transamerica Corporation; Stephen T. McLin, late of Bank of America; and Roger O. Walther, President and CEO, AIFS, Inc.

If one ever doubted the wisdom of Chuck in moving quickly to take the company public, one had to wait not even 4 weeks to be convinced of his golden touch. Had he waited even a month, Charles Schwab & Company would not have survived "Black Monday"—October 19, 1987—when the Dow Jones Industrial Average plunged 508.32 points, losing 22.6 percent of its total value. That fall far surpassed the one-day loss of 12.9 percent that began the great stock market crash of 1929 and foreshadowed the Great Depression. And if that weren't bad enough, the Dow's October 19th dive triggered events half a world away that would bring Schwab to the brink of catastrophe. Those events are described in Chapter 10.

It was going to be a long weekend. The market had been jumpy all week and on Friday, October 16, the center finally gave out. It was the first day in which the Dow Jones Industrial Average ever fell by more than 100 points in a single trading session. The 108.35 point drop brought the Dow Jones to 2247, a 4.6 percent loss for the day. More than 600 million shares changed hands that day, a volume record that would not be equaled for 10 years. The loss wiped out $145 billion in stock value, according to the Wilshire Associates index—a figure equal to almost 15 percent of the entire federal budget for the year. Friday was also the first day that investment professionals began to be really afraid that the hedges they developed—program trading, index arbitrage, portfolio insurance—would come back and bite them.

John Gambs, deputy treasurer at Merrill Lynch, spent that weekend at the American Bankers Association in Dallas. The bankers were already jittery that what happened on Friday was just the tip and the whole iceberg would be revealed when the markets opened on Monday. They didn't need government bureaucrats blowing hot air. When the you-know-what is hitting the fan, the last thing you want is more of a breeze. So they gathered with trepidation to watch CNN's *Newsmakers Saturday*. The guest that October 17th: Treasury Secretary James Baker, the senior voice for the United States on economic issues. To the uninitiated, Baker said all the right things. He defended the American economy. He told Americans that Wall Street losses appeared to be reactions to several forces, including possible tax increases, proposed legislation to limit foreign imports, and fears of inflation and rising interest rates. To the bankers, however, Baker's comments signaled that Washington would permit the value of the U.S. dollar to fall. In fact, investors in Germany, England, and Japan began to worry that a falling dollar would lower the income that foreign investors could expect to earn from American securities. Foreign investors prepared to bail out of stocks underpinned by the dollar. By coincidence, Margaret

Thatcher, the prime minister of England, was visiting Dallas that Sunday. During dinner one of her guests called Asia, where it was already Monday morning, to see how the markets were doing. Like stars going out one by one, they were collapsing.

Gambs left the convention early to fly back to Merrill Lynch. Within a year, he would be the CFO at Schwab. Gambs would be one of the few beneficiaries of the very dark days that Schwab was to face. Chuck would be so shaken up by what was to land on his desk that he admitted the company needed better financial management controls and risk management disciplines. Gambs took Chuck's desires to heart. On his first day at Schwab, Gambs ordered a three-sided sign made out of wood. It was to be on his desk for visitors to see. "No Surprises" was the message on the first side of the sign, "Keep it Simple" was on the second, and "Find the Right Way" was the third. Of these management sentiments, the most important is the first. " 'No Surprises' doesn't mean no bad news," Gambs notes. "It means that if we are on top of our responsibilities we need not be taken aback by developments. We are paid to lead and manage, not to be spectators."

For the financial services industry, the weekend offered a taste of what they would see on Monday. At the branches and call centers, the phone lines were jammed all weekend. And not just at Schwab. It was the same at Merrill Lynch, Fidelity, Dreyfus, and Vanguard. Fidelity alone received 80,000 calls from customers that weekend. Schwab's phones were melting down, but 99 percent of the calls that did go through were orders to sell stock and redeem funds. Chuck quickly understood what Monday would bring. The company, along with Merrill, Fidelity, Dreyfus, and everyone else would be dumping hundreds of millions of dollars worth of sell orders into an already fragile market. With everyone selling and very few people buying, it doesn't take a market genius to determine with absolute certainty the direction the market will take.

Monday itself . . . well, books have been written about Monday, October 19th, so we won't dwell on the carnage. Suffice it to say it was worse than anyone imagined. It was like a roadside accident from which you want to but somehow can't avert your eyes. John Gambs quit smoking that day and hasn't picked up a cigarette since. "There were times that day when stock traders felt as though they were standing outside their own bodies, watching themselves with a bizarre detachment as they frantically attempted to unload stocks," observes Nocera. The small investor was completely locked out. At Schwab, the computers were overwhelmed by 8:00 a.m. The Schwab toll-free phone system also fell victim to the incessant calls. For several days, all customers got when they called were busy signals. The best Chuck could do in the aftermath was to run advertisements apologizing for his company's performance. They were masterpieces of understatement: "If you tried to call Schwab in the past two weeks to place an order or get information, you may have had difficulty getting through immediately." By the time the bell mercifully ended the carnage, the Dow Jones average fell 508 points, a staggering 22 percent loss.

Business, like life itself, is not for the faint of heart. Just as the market began to regain equilibrium and the computers and phones at Schwab fluttered back to life and Chuck calculated the commissions on the 300 percent increase in trading volumes, he received word from BankAmerica that it needed $14.45 million from Schwab. BankAmerica had suffered badly in the crash and now, 2 days after the market's plunge, exercised one-third of the rights it had under the buyout to liquidate some of the Schwab stock it received to supplement the cash. To add insult to injury, the amount of the payment was a function of the average closing price of the stock in the 20 days before the rights are surrendered. With the stock market's plunge, Schwab stock dove to around $8 per share. Nevertheless, it would have to redeem the BankAmerica shares at the higher prices that prevailed before the crash. The company managed to come up with the money, but was forced to obtain a waiver of a provision of its bank loan agreement because the stock market downturn had put it in violation of its loan covenants.

It was the telephone calls to the wives that broke Kathy Levinson's heart. Every branch manager had the unpleasant duty of phoning customers whose accounts were not only wiped out by the market downturn, but owed Schwab money. Branch managers like Levinson, in charge of the Midwest branches, now had to contact these customers and make arrangements for collecting the debts. It was always the men who lost the money and Levinson was the last person they wanted to talk to. "The hardest part was calling and talking to the spouses," she says. She couldn't believe that the investors mortgaged everything—their homes, the college funds for their children, retirement savings—in pursuing the euphoria of the markets. "I really felt for the spouses as they began to comprehend the reckless decisions their husbands took with the family finances." Many of those families were wiped out. After each phone call, Levinson would sit in her office and let the tears come. Then she arranged for the customers to sign multiyear promissory notes.

But it's to the credit of Schwab values that even when the company was at the abyss, compassion for customers did not disappear. Every department had a story about Schwab employees going out of their way to protect customers. Mark King, a manager for Schwab 500 accounts, had a customer who was on a cruise when the market crashed. The customer had left strict instructions for King not to disturb him. That was an unnecessary request, for Schwab brokers weren't supposed to call customers; customers were supposed to call Schwab. Nevertheless, given the exceptional circumstances, King disregarded the customer's instructions as well as Schwab's norm and phoned the cruise line to reach him, faxing the customer details about the positions that needed to be adjusted. At every port, the customer found overnighted materials from King waiting for him. "He was my customer for life," King says.

The grandest story of Schwab's values in action involved a customer in the Newport Beach branch. "He was a retiree in his late eighties and couldn't be nicer," recalls former branch manager Rhet Andrews. "He was the ideal Schwab customer. He invested wisely, built a financially secure nest egg for his golden years, and was now comfortably retired. It made our day when he and his wife walked in. Everyone in the branch loved them." Andrews would never reveal a customers' identity, so let's call him Mr. Roberts, which happens to be his real name. A very conservative investor, Mr. Roberts had an account worth over $7 million in treasury bills, the safest investment an investor can have. But at some point he allowed himself to be persuaded to sell naked index puts. The advice certainly didn't come from Schwab. In 1987, Schwab wasn't in the advice business, nor did it question the decisions, however questionable, its customers made. And selling naked index puts was a risky, even reckless form of stock speculation. So when the market crashed and Schwab had to sell the T-bills to cover the loss, Mr. Roberts's $7.5 million dollar account was not only wiped out, but he was in the hole to Schwab for an additional $1.5 million. Andrews made the unpleasant call. Beside himself with worry and humiliation, Mr. Roberts told Andrews that he didn't have the money to pay the debt. All that was left was an IRA account and his Malibu home overlooking the Pacific Ocean.

With other brokerage firms, standard operating procedure in cases such as this would be to seize the IRA and if that didn't settle the debt, to attach a lien on the home, and, if necessary, foreclose. If it meant an elderly couple would be thrown out, well, that was too bad, but the shareholders had to be protected. Andrews knew that Schwab values would preclude such a course. He consulted with James Losi, the senior vice president responsible for collecting large balances after the market crash. What happened next tested the character of both Losi and the company he represented.

Losi was unhappy at Citibank when he took a $25,000 pay cut to join Schwab as employee number 777. "For the first time in my life I felt I was part of something grand," he recalled. "I was excited to work for a company that actually put the best interests of customers before profits." Now he would get an opportunity to test the limits of Schwab's commitment to that proposition.

In an effort to work out a payment plan, Losi and a Schwab attorney met with Mr. Roberts and his attorney. To make the situation even sadder, Mr. Roberts had terminal throat cancer and with his vocal chords surgically removed, he talked with difficulty through a hole in his windpipe. Mr. Roberts came right to the point. "I acknowledge the debt," he growled through the wound in his throat. "I will make it right, I don't know how, but

I'll make it right." To Losi, it was a heartbreaking sight. "He knew he was dying. All he wanted to do was protect his wife."

"What assets do you have?" The Schwab lawyer's question was predictable.

"Just my IRA and the house. I lost everything else."

"Well, I'm sorry, I don't see any other way," the Schwab attorney said. "We're going to have to take the house."

"But that house is all we have left. My wife and I have lived there for 47 years. What's going to happen to her?"

It was too much for Losi. Chuck had appointed him to head Schwab's recovery efforts because of his banking experience. Pottruck expected him to come back with cash for the ailing company, not real estate. But this felt all wrong. There was no way he would repossess this man's house. Pottruck would have to fire him first. "You can live in the house for the rest of your life," Losi heard himself say. "If your wife is still alive, she can live there for the rest of her life."

The Schwab lawyer was beside himself, desperately kicking Losi under the table in an attempt to shut him up. The lawyer for Mr. Roberts just sat there in stunned silence.

Pottruck insisted that Losi call as soon as a deal was hammered out. This was one of the largest collection efforts the company was pursuing. Losi called Pottruck from a phone booth near the famous statue of John Wayne at the Orange County airport. He took strength from The Duke's determination in countless films to stand up for the right thing, no matter the odds.

"We had successful conclusion to the Roberts matter, I think," Losi began. "I did what I think is the right thing. It's the way I'd want to be treated." And then he told Pottruck the discount brokerage was now in the real estate business, as well, and it would have to wait for its $1.5 million. The customer needed the house more than Schwab needed the money. As he waited for Pottruck's response, Losi honestly couldn't be sure if he'd be second-guessed or even fired for his judgment.

Losi could feel his heart racing as he waited for Pottruck's response. "Jim, you did the right thing," his boss said.

The parties came to the following agreement: Schwab would not touch the Roberts's IRA account. As far as the house was concerned, Mr. and Mrs. Roberts would have a life estate. They could continue to live in their home until they no longer needed it. When they died or moved, the house would be sold and Schwab would use the equity in the house to recover the outstanding balance it was owed.

If this story were turned into a Disney movie, the customer and his wife would live out the balance of their lives in security and die in dignity. The executor of the estate would use the proceeds of the sale of the house to settle the debt. Family members would praise Schwab's generosity to the heavens and a number of grandchildren would be named "Chuck."

It turned out to be more like a soap opera. A couple of years after the agreement was hammered out, Mr. Roberts passed away. Mrs. Roberts continued to live in the house. Six years after the original debt, there was a fire in the Malibu hills that burned the former customer's house to the ground. Schwab could have insisted that its debt be paid from the insurance proceeds. But she wanted to rebuild and live out her life where she was comfortable. Schwab worked with her family to negotiate a settlement with the insurance company, rebuilt the house, and she moved back in. Mrs. Roberts lived in the house until she died in 1998, and then the debt, 11 years later, was finally repaid.

By then the story, retold by one generation of Schwab employees to the next, had assumed the trappings of a genuine legend, which Schwab enshrined in a 1998 corporate video. The company got permission to tape the video in the rebuilt Malibu home, as the son of the couple emotionally narrated the story. At the end of the video, with a photo of his parents in the background, the son concluded, "There is a lot more to life than the bottom line. There are other things that are important, like faith, forgiveness, love, and family . . . and I think that is part of the way Schwab dealt with our family."

Such stories cemented the self-image of the company as a caring organization. But it made good business sense, too. Schwab was much more successful in its record of collecting unsecured margin debts, eventually recovering 77 cents on the dollar. By contrast, the securities industry as a whole recovered 23 cents on the dollar. Schwab's compassion and flexibility went straight to the bottom line. But it's as an example of Schwab compassion in action that the anecdote is trotted out at every opportunity. "We could talk for a long time about the abstraction of fairness and empathy, but we could not possibly have the impact that this story has," Pottruck says. "We use the story now to recruit and to illustrate to new employees just how far we will go to live our values, to sustain our culture."

Schwab emerged from the market crash of 1987, bruised but shaken. As always, Schwab people performed spectacularly and the crisis drew them even closer together. The company did make some needed structural changes. Risk management became central. John Gambs, the company's first CFO, came on board with a mandate to prevent similar excesses. The company beefed up the credit and margin department and backed off from a compensation system that rewarded reckless behaviors. The company moved to a more profit-centered approach in which the power of the branches, responsible for the top line, was balanced by the power of the credit and margin department, which was responsible for the bottom line. The branches also learned to be much more skeptical of the exceptional deals that customers occasionally presented. "These 'one-off' situations usually involved vast sums of gold and customers who just had to have numbered accounts," Levinson says. "Of the six such offers I subsequently considered, only one turned out to be real; the rest were phony." She credits the 1987 crisis for Schwab's increased scrutiny.

What's amazing is that Schwab kept itself together through such haphazard living and emerged the stronger for it. It was brutal, the hits to the company's confidence. The crash, the computer and phone systems failing, the telephone calls—when they got through—from devastated and angry customers and the stock now down 60 percent at $6.50 a share. Everyone's options were underwater. At other firms, executives would have been jumping ship. Yet with a couple of exceptions everyone kept the faith. Those who took the long view, like the investors who sat on their portfolios, came out looking good. Within 6 months, the market recovered from the devastating loss. Through such crises, the Schwab spirit took shape. Chuck apologized and asked for forgiveness. He received it. There were tough times ahead and everyone did what they could. Executives took pay cuts. Others agreed to work 4 days a week. They stayed and worked harder than they had ever worked before.

The drop in the value of Schwab stock definitely hurt. There were lots of pissed off customers. The company ate a few million dollars of errors and took a large hit to its reputation. Chuck would have to do some fence mending. In the Newport Beach, California branch, all the employees gathered around as branch manager Rhet Andrews opened the *Wall Street Journal* for October 28, 1987. There were two full-page ads, one thanking customers for their patience, the other appreciating employees for their dedication and service. "We were all blown away. We had never seen a Schwab ad bigger than a quarter-page, so this made us proud. The ads told us that the family was still together and we would move forward," Andrews recalls. "To all customers of Charles Schwab, we thank you for your patience and understanding," read the headline of the first ad. Chuck's bespectacled face sporting a wide glass-is-half-full smile, offered contrition.

On the next page: "A heartfelt 'thank you' to all the employees of Charles Schwab." The photo was exactly the same, but now Chuck's smile said he felt your pain. The ad listed the events beyond anyone's control: the 300 percent increase in trading, the inability of the market makers and exchanges to keep up. Chuck underscored the dedication and sacrifice of employees. "I know that many of you labored around the clock—not even taking a break to return home, but instead working through the nights. A special thanks must also go to Schwab employees who set aside their regular jobs and joined our traders and branch employees in processing orders, updating account records, and making thousands of additional calls to customers across the country, confirming their transactions." Not one to pass up an opportunity to plug customer service, the ad included a P.S.: "Let's not forget to answer phone calls with a 'thank you' to every Schwab customer for his or her patience, support, and understanding."

But if that was the worst punishment the market crash offered, Schwab would get over it. Investors, after all, have short memories. But it was far from the worst of it. Now Chuck received word that one of his customers had margin calls totaling . . . well, it couldn't be possible. A single customer couldn't possibly accumulate an unsecured margin call liability totaling $124 million!

Margin Call

October 19–29, 1987

Only 10 days after Black Monday, Schwab announced that it had lost $22 million in the crash. What really stung is that just one customer in Hong Kong was responsible for $13 million of the damage. And it was almost a lot, lot worse.

Not only was it possible, it was the reality. One Hong Kong investor had, unbeknownst to anyone at Schwab, accumulated liabilities representing more than a third of the company's total revenues for the year. Unforgivably, the situation had slipped past Schwab's admittedly primitive risk management alerts, allowing a single customer in Hong Kong to generate option trades that now exposed Schwab to calamity. Just one customer had borrowed money to trade options, lots of options, and because of the market crash, owed Schwab $124 million. When a customer owes money on a trade, the brokerage "calls" for the investor to fund his or her account to cover the liability.

If the Hong Kong customer wouldn't or couldn't pay the margin calls, Schwab would have to cover the $124 million itself.

Even today, Schwab has never acknowledged the name of the investor. By Chuck's lights even a customer that ripped him off deserves to have his confidentiality protected. The *New York Times* had no such reticence. There was nothing exceptional about the investor, Teh-huei "Teddy" Wang, except for the scale of his trading. With his wife Nina, Teddy operated a network of businesses controlled by a mysterious property and construction company called the ChinaChem Group. Trading and speculating in options and arcane financial instruments were popular activities among Hong Kong investors. Schwab had opened its first international branch in Hong Kong in 1981 precisely to exploit the island population's predilection for such trading. Of course, even by Hong Kong standards, Teddy Wang was off the chart. A serious options trader can juggle hundreds of contracts at a time. When the crash came and Schwab started counting—it took five accountants several days just to unravel his positions—Teddy had upwards of 42,000 contracts outstanding. Chuck's jaw dropped when he heard that number. "No one knew he was going around holding that kind of atom bomb in his hand," he said. Schwab's computer system couldn't even generate an integrated account statement for Teddy because the system was not programmed to display account values over $99,999,999.

Chuck had to—and did—accept responsibility. No way should Teddy have been allowed to expose the company to so much liability. In retrospect, it was easy to see how the situation developed. For much of his 3-year relationship with Schwab, Teddy spread his biggest trades among three brokers, with the bulk going to Drexel Burnham Lambert. But in the months before the crash, Teddy moved all his business to Schwab, spreading it out across hundreds of separate accounts. How did Schwab get to be so lucky? Some believe Teddy had a falling out with his Drexel broker, which, given the millions of dollars in commissions a trader like Teddy generates, must have temporarily created one very pained stockbroker. Perhaps Teddy responded to

Schwab's constant advertising about lower commissions. What is clear is that the Hong Kong branch manager had lost control of its biggest account. The risk management process at Schwab had utterly failed.

And the risks Teddy took! He didn't just buy options contracts outright—a significant risk by itself—no, his preferred strategy was to leverage his bets as much as possible by shorting put options. Since a put option is a bet that the market is going down, Teddy's trades would pay off big only if the market went up, which it had obediently been doing for 5 years. If the market went down, his losses would be just as big. By short-selling options contracts, Teddy was making bets on bets—betting against the speculators who were betting against the market. The market, of course, not only went down, it crashed. It would be one thing if he were betting with his own money, but he had borrowed the cash from Schwab.

Yes, Chuck admitted, the company should have had controls to flag and rein in mavericks like Teddy. At an early morning news conference on October 29th, just 10 days after Black Monday, a very glum Chuck took to the podium to disclose that his firm had lost $22 million in the crash. "I am profoundly unhappy," Chuck announced to the reporters. The harsh broadcast lights on Chuck's normally tanned and youthful face now revealed a weary fifty-year-old executive at the limits of his resources, both personal and financial. For the past 10 days, the firm had waged a frantic full-court press with Teddy in an attempt to recover as much of the money as possible.

Now the full import of Chuck's decision to take the company public was obvious. The financial cushion provided by the IPO allowed Chuck to go before the cameras and insist with more or less total sincerity that the firm would weather the storm. As a public company, Schwab was for the first time obliged to disclose bad news promptly. By law, he had 10 days to do so. And despite Chuck's reassurances, this was as bad as news gets without involving a body count. In the best case, Schwab would eat a loss equivalent to most of its 1987 profits. In the worst case, the firm would have to announce a loss of $100 million or more, an outcome from which the firm would not be able to survive. It was reminiscent of a graduation speech Woody Allen once gave, which begins: "Today we are at a crossroads. One road leads to hopelessness and despair; the other, to total extinction. Let us pray we choose wisely."

In its defense, Schwab had little reason to be suspicious of Teddy. He had always been a dream customer. Whenever there had been a margin call in the past, Teddy had promptly honored it. In fact, as a result of the Friday drop, Teddy had a $27 million margin call due Monday morning and well before the market opened, he had wired the funds to Schwab. As Monday opened and the market further eroded Teddy's positions, Schwab requested and Teddy provided another $13 million, on top of the $27 million he had paid earlier. But by the end of that wrenching day, Teddy owed Schwab much, much more. And now he promptly and perhaps understandably disappeared, leaving Schwab holding the bag for $84 million.

By the eve of the news conference, the outcome was still unresolved. Schwab's team in Hong Kong was close to getting an agreement, but it was not yet in hand. The Schwab communications staff had to prepare scripts for two developments. Plan A called for a loss of $22 million, after tax, a loss that the company could swallow with minor indigestion. Under Plan B, the loss was $100 million, pretax. Chuck would rather gargle with rusted razor blades than swallow such a loss, for he knew the company would probably not survive. Taking such a loss, the company would be in immediate violation of its loan covenants and minimum capital rules. Even if it survived those, the weakened company with its depressed share price would be like shark chum for acquisition-minded predators.

Mavericks flock to Schwab. That's one of the company's strengths, as well as the source of its limitations. The history of Schwab is replete with stories of individual employees, some known by name, some anonymous, who literally saved the company. So it is with Robert Rosseau who is assigned by Schwab lore to the role of the hero of Hong Kong. By all accounts, he earned the tribute. But while Schwab is good at recognizing extraordinary performance, it has failed to evolve a protocol for rewarding it. Less than 8 months after Rosseau saved the company, he was gone.

Rosseau did not come up through the ranks of Schwab. His hiring as vice president of retail service delivery was a result of Chuck's desire to beef up operations with experienced managers from the outside. Predictably, Rosseau was treated as the outsider he was. "Rosseau was never totally accepted by the insiders," says a Schwab confidant. Rosseau is a plain-spoken, compact man who radiates a vibe of the street fighter. Of his service in Viet Nam during the hottest days of the U.S. incursion, Rosseau avoids all questions. He gives off the aura of a former intelligence operative or perhaps military Special Forces. He speaks fluent Italian and seems to be at home in every corner of the world.

In describing Rosseau, two former colleagues both use kindergarten metaphors. "He wouldn't color inside the lines," says one; "he doesn't play well with others," says another. Both comments say more about the maturity of the Schwab organization than it does about Rosseau. "Rosseau could be confrontational and antagonistic, and in Schwab culture that's a big no-no," says another Schwab executive, acknowledging that it's just those characteristics that made Rosseau so effective in Hong Kong.

Schwab culture is provincial. It rebelled at Rosseau's New York mannerisms, military lead-or-get-out-of-the-way bearing, and refusal to accept Schwab dogma as the final word. The first two traits people could live with, but Rosseau was rejected as one of the team because he asked questions that challenged accepted wisdom at Schwab. At Schwab, anyone challenging the dogma stands out like a Picasso figure in a Rembrandt painting. Insiders considered him insufficiently indoctrinated in the Schwab way of doing things. "When the emperor has no clothes, Rosseau will say it," says Tom Seip, another former executive who was himself no stranger to holding Schwab dogma up to the light.

When the news came out that Schwab was in deep financial trouble in Hong Kong, Rosseau did what his training in Viet Nam prepared him for: He went into combat. Even before the markets closed on Black Monday, Rosseau was on a jet to Hong Kong. As soon as he heard the news, Rosseau understood that if Schwab wanted the money, someone would have to go to Hong Kong and make Teddy cough it up. Sending Rosseau to go mano a mano with Teddy Wang was one of Stupski's smartest decisions. "Okay, Larry," Rosseau told his boss. "But if I go, we'll do it my way. Can you live with that?" All Stupski could do was swallow hard and feel a moment of pity for Teddy. An unsupervisable force was being unleashed on the unsuspecting Hong Kong trader.

As he jetted to Hong Kong, Rosseau considered his strategy. With an M.B.A. in finance from the Wharton Graduate School and a postgraduate program courtesy of the U.S. Army, Rosseau understood that the only way to succeed was to get leverage. And the only legal way to get leverage was to seize Teddy's assets or tie them up so tight that Teddy would have to negotiate. On such matters, Rosseau agreed with his former commander-in-chief, President Lyndon B. Johnson, who said, "Never trust a man unless you have his pecker in your pocket." Rosseau landed in Hong Kong late Tuesday, October 20, 1987.

First came the courtesy call, choreographed by the precise demands of Asian formality, to ensure that all parties saved face. Rosseau was well acquainted with the rituals of Asian culture. It was in that spirit that Teddy sat down with Rosseau Wednesday morning. Teddy had lost the most face and it was critical that Rosseau show complete respect. "I bring you greetings from Chuck Schwab," Rosseau began, acting as the undemanding ambassador of the company's chairman and CEO. After exchanging small gifts, Teddy demonstrated his understanding of the situation: "Well, Mr. Rosseau, it appears that Schwab is worth $72 million and I owe the company $84 million." So the battle was set. With that thrust, Teddy retired from the negotiations, leaving his wife Nina to do the heavy lifting.

Rosseau's second action was to fire Schwab's Hong Kong law firm. They were the classiest legal outfit in Hong Kong and perfectly useless for what Rosseau had in mind. Rosseau enlisted a team of hungry lawyers to work the daylight hours and private detectives to work the nights. He systematically put the best law firms in Hong Kong on retainer, denying their services to Teddy. At night, a Chinese lawyer reviewed the work the American and British lawyers did during the day. If anyone didn't perform exactly right, he summarily fired them. He went to the mattresses. For the first week Rosseau rarely left a temporary office with paper taped over the windows. He periodically swept the telephones for signs of bugging. He recorded his phone conversations with lawyers, police, detectives, and informants. He spread a lot of Schwab's money around in an effort to get some dirt on Teddy. It was a covert operation and he relished the adventure. "It was by far the most interesting thing I've ever done in my life," Rosseau says. "The work required all of my skills and demanded the most from me professionally."

"Nobody beats Teddy," Nina Wang had warned Rosseau. In fact, Teddy's assets were as slippery as its owner. Teddy's company, ChinaChem, was akin to Enron, with assets hidden in hundreds of off-the-book partnerships and shell corporations. But Rosseau was just as slick in pinning down his adversary's assets. A major challenge was ascertaining Teddy's secret bank account numbers—no easy task in Hong Kong's supersecret banking industry. Rosseau still won't reveal some of the methods he used, but apparently one piece of social engineering involved going to a bank where Teddy had an account and telling the manager he was there to deposit money—and not just a trivial sum—into Teddy's account. In that way he got the unwitting bank manager to divulge account numbers. It's ironic that Schwab ended up seeding Teddy's account with even more of the brokerage's money before Rosseau eventually reclaimed it, or most of it anyway. But with account numbers, Rosseau could unlock the secrets of Teddy's suddenly not-so-secret financial empire.

Quickly, Rosseau's unconventional efforts and full-court press found traction in the Hong Kong courts. As soon as he determined where Teddy had accounts, he got court orders tying up his assets. By that weekend, Rosseau had locked up Teddy's assets so tight, Nina had to ask Rosseau for spending money. To spook his adversaries even more, Rosseau seeded the courtroom gallery with characters who also had claims against the Wangs.

Now Rosseau knew the Wangs would have to negotiate. But Teddy was a jumpy kind of guy—and for good reason as it turns out. Six years earlier, he had been abducted by Hong Kong kidnappers and held for 8 days until his wife negotiated the ransom down to $17 million. Teddy was nervous. He owed a lot of money to a lot of people and some of them would apply collection methods that even Rosseau rejected. Teddy sent Nina to meet with Rosseau.

After a few days of round-the-clock negotiating with Nina, Rosseau felt sorry for the kidnappers. Prior to joining Schwab, Rosseau had organized Interlink Network, the first multi-bank-sponsored debit card business in California, an effort akin to herding cats. At American Express, he managed the decentralization of the credit card, travelers checks, and travel business units to form the highly profitable Travel Related Services Company. He was used to dealing with tough cookies, but nothing had prepared him for Nina Wang. As a negotiator, Nina was in turn intimidating and seductive. She understood that she held some powerful cards. Her ace of spades was time. The brokerage, she knew, was under time pressure to settle because, back in San Francisco, Chuck had just 10 days to disclose the extent of the damage.

In fact, Chuck was under desperate time pressure. But Rosseau's strategy had to appear to be relaxed and willing to wait it out. One of the rules of negotiating is that he who cares least, wins. Rosseau understood that Teddy and Nina Wang had time pressures of their own. Teddy could not take the risk that his assets of over $500 million, now tied up by Schwab's demand for $84 million, would be plucked by other creditors. And there was Rosseau dangling the key to unlock Teddy's assets. Of course, the key would cost Teddy $84 million, or, because this was the real word, a bit less.

Meanwhile, Rosseau also had to deal with his colleagues back in San Francisco who were hounding him with questions and trying to micromanage events in Hong Kong. Rosseau quickly put a stop to that. "Look, guys, I don't have time to *entertain* you people," he recalls telling them, further cementing his reputation as "someone who doesn't play well with others." "You get

fifteen minutes for a conference call. This is a *war* over here
. . . ." The Schwab executives backed off, but they never forgave
Rosseau for his autonomy.

"Robert Rosseau pulled a classic Schwab hustle," is how
John Gambs describes what Rosseau accomplished. Over the
next 5 days, Rosseau and Nina Wang met every day. They both
knew that a settlement would happen, just as they knew that the
Wangs would not have to pay the full amount of the margin
call. They both knew they were better off resolving the matter
privately, instead of dragging their business through the
courts, an outcome that terrified the Wangs more than it did
Rosseau. After hours of negotiations, Rosseau called Chuck
with the best settlement he could get: 80 cents on the dollar, or
$67 million. Chuck thought about it for a minute and then
said "take it." Perhaps Chuck flashed on an anecdote making
the rounds about that time. The story was how Thomas J. Watson, chairman of IBM, confronted an executive who had made
a mistake that cost Big Blue $5 million. "Are you going to fire
me?" asked the petrified executive. Watson is said to have responded, "Fire you? Why would I fire you? I just paid $5 million
for your education."

As the ultimate validation of what a tough negotiator Rosseau
turned out to be, Nina Wang offered him a job with her organization. In quiet moments, Rosseau speculates on how his life
would have changed had he accepted her offer. *Forbes* magazine
ranks the sixty-four-year-old Nina, who is also known in Can-
tonese by the nickname "Little Sweetie" as the richest woman in
Asia (estimated wealth: $3.7 billion). The pigtailed tycoon has
a weakness for red vinyl miniskirts and other outlandish outfits
intended to put her adversaries off guard.

Nina Wang catapulted into the ranks of the world's super-
rich on April 10, 1990, when Teddy, then the thirteenth-richest
man in Hong Kong, was kidnapped yet again from his Mercedes
outside the elite Hong Kong Jockey Club. Despite the payment
of a $37 million installment on a $66 million ransom, he has not
been seen since. A year later, a member of the Sun Yee On triad
pleaded guilty to participating in the kidnapping and testified

that Teddy had died during a sea chase with a police motorboat. Teddy was finally declared legally dead in 1999, although many people still believe he is alive and in hiding.

As for Rosseau, he stayed in Hong Kong until February of the following year. The deal he struck with Teddy called for the debt to be paid out over a period of time. But Schwab couldn't wait for the money, so Rosseau took a few months to securitize the debt and structure a deal that would give Schwab an immediate cash infusion. Because Rosseau's exploits in Hong Kong were such a carefully guarded secret, there were no ceremonies on his return. Even the senior executives were muted in their congratulations. Chuck presented Rosseau with a ceremonial watch. As for stock options, which Chuck generously awarded to his favored executives, those were not forthcoming. While the executives were awestruck by what Rosseau achieved, they didn't open the inner circle to him. There was simply no future at Schwab for a cowboy like Rosseau. Chuck never again wanted the kind of crisis for which Rosseau's experience would be most pertinent. Within 6 months, he was allowed to quietly slip away. Over the years, as the veil of secrecy over the Hong Kong adventure lifted, the Schwab myth machine created some entertaining legends around Rosseau's accomplishments and with time the drama of Hong Kong took on mythic overtones.

In 2000, Schwab again tested Rosseau's reputation as a miracle worker. Pottruck had decided that Schwab's problems in its international operations were incapable of internal solution. But bringing on a new executive at a vice-chairman or senior-vice-president level was not something Schwab politics could tolerate. Pottruck's solution was to invite Rosseau back. From 2000–2001, as senior vice president of Schwab International, Rosseau tried to clean up the messes he found in England, Australia, Japan, and elsewhere. His conclusion: The Schwab business model could not be profitably exported outside the United States. It was a conclusion that bucked Schwab dogma, so once again, Rosseau was out.

The $22 million write-off was the cost of Schwab's continuing education. Everyone at the company chipped in for the tuition. Chuck was gratified, as he faced the reporters on October 29th, that Plan A succeeded. "We don't like it," he read from the script, "it will never happen again, but that's the way it is." Forthright as always. The facts are friendly. They may not always be attractive or convenient. But you deal with them.

11

Earthquake

October 17, 1989

California has infused Schwab with a sense of friskiness, an in-your-face, us-versus-them 'tude, a tilt toward innovation and risk taking, a culture that is inclusive even as it tolerates chaos. But the cost California imposes on its residents is also ample. Californians must pursue their lives knowing that the "Big One," the inevitable upshot of building their fortunes on one of the world's most active seismic fault lines, will render everything they do futile. It is a testament to Californians that they can ignore the most powerful natural agent on Earth while simultaneously being shaped by it. An earthquake, the company discovered, can be a constructive force as well as a catalyst for destruction.

Tuesday, October 17, 1989, was not a normal workday. If it had been, the earthquake that hit at 5:04 P.M. would have resulted in far more loss of life. By 5 P.M. on a normal workday in San Francisco, the afternoon rush would have seen commuters scurrying to trolleys, ferries, and Bay Area Rapid Transit

(BART) trains. Glass, brick, and marble from tired old buildings would have rained down on the crowds in the streets. Motorists would be bumper-to-bumper on the overpasses, double-decked freeways, and bridges. The collapse of even one section of freeway would have doomed hundreds of commuters.

But as everyone who was in town that Tuesday remembers, October 17 was far from a normal workday. All of San Francisco was in the grip of World Series Fever. It was an unprecedented event: a contest pitting the Oakland Athletics and the San Francisco Giants—the two local major league teams. The excitement of the event claimed everyone's free attention. That day, many workers had left work early, either to be at the game or at home where they could watch it on television. The afternoon commute was visibly less busy. Thus, when the city lost its footing, most residents were no longer in the most vulnerable, congested areas.

Charles Schwab & Company, 2 years into its run as a public company, was now clocking revenues of $553 million. It was by far the largest brokerage in the West. But its reputation for stability was far from established. Chuck knew that any disruption to its operations would cause many investors to lose faith in the company. The company was gradually working to decentralize its computer operations, spreading the risk around, but for now all its eggs were still in one basket.

A millisecond after the earthquake shook the financial district, the disk drives that served Schwab's IBM mainframe computer crashed. There are hard crashes and soft crashes. This was a hard crash, the worst kind. Disk drives house rapidly spinning magnetic disks. A millimeter above and below the disks float mechanical pickups that dart back and forth to read the data. When the building shook, the pickups came into contact with the disks. What happened inside the disk drives is not pleasant to imagine; it can best be described by imaging bits and bytes encountering a food processor set on grind. With the computers down for the count, Schwab was effectively out of business. The markets would open in 13 hours and 26 minutes.

Neither Schwab nor the city of San Francisco was prepared for the earthquake. Both Schwab and the city had plans in place; in both cases, the plans proved inadequate. Contingency plans necessarily focus on unknowable acts that are nevertheless anticipated. The random nature of what nature threw at Schwab and the city rendered the best-laid plans virtually useless. Electric power went out, stopping elevators and locking electronically secured doors. Telephone switchboards were inoperable. Passwords didn't work. The smell of natural gas filled the air. Firefighters could hook their hoses to hydrants but water pressure was not there. It was low tide, so the city's lone fireboat ran aground. Improvisation became the order of the day.

It was harrowing, Barbara Heinrich remembers, the 2 worst days of her career at Schwab. And the earthquake was still a few hours in the future. The 2 days before October 17 were a nightmare for the stock market in general and Schwab in particular. The Friday before the earthquake, there had been a 300-point market correction. That Monday, there was a fourfold surge in trading—45,000 trades in one session, a record for Schwab. By the time Heinrich knocked off on Tuesday to take a few Schwab customers to the World Series, she was exhausted.

"I was most surprised by how loud it was," she recalls. Everything seemed surreal. "The players were running out to the field and they couldn't seem to run in a straight line. The very concrete in the stadium seemed to turn liquid. Then the stadium lights went dark." A momentary silence filled the stadium. And then, typical of San Francisco crowds, people started stomping their feet and singing the Queen anthem, "We Will Rock You."

Heinrich was glad there was still an hour of daylight left. "If the stadium had to be evacuated in the dark, a lot of us wouldn't have made it," she says, offering another appreciation for the timing of the earthquake. She knew she had to get home for a few hours of sleep; everyone at Schwab had an emergency earthquake assignment. Hers was to report for work at 4:00 A.M.

Earlene Perry was on a BART platform when the ground started shaking. As people scurried up the stairs to the ground level, Perry assisted a visibly pregnant woman. Most people were desperate to make their way home. But Perry was determined to return to the office at 101 Montgomery. The downtown streets were orderly but filled with rumors about bridges collapsing, looting, and mayhem just around the corner. She wondered what she would find back at headquarters.

"I thought I was going to die," says Tom Taggart, who was on the twenty-fourth floor of the twenty-eight floor building. "When it hit, the movement was so violent it stunned me. The building must have moved 5 or 6 feet off the vertical." Screams from the employees around Taggart filled the air as shelves spilled their contents to the floor. Taggart was in an interior cubicle and he held onto the partition for dear life, grateful that it was bolted to the floor.

Tom Seip got out of his car and looked around. His was among thousands of cars stuck dead in traffic on the Bay Bridge. Nothing was moving. As far as Seip could see, it was gridlock. Without a second thought, he locked the car and started walking back toward the financial district. He could see the smoke from buildings burning in the Marina District in the distance. The streets were filled with the bricks, glass, and marble cornices that had been shaken off buildings. Seip looked at his watch. The markets would be open in less than 13 hours and he knew that if Schwab wasn't ready to do business, investors would get spooked and start dumping Schwab stock. Seip figured the mainframe computer had crashed and crashed hard. It was going to be a long night.

Kathy Levinson must have spaced out. That's the only way she can explain why she didn't realize it was an earthquake. "I thought it was a blackout," she says. "I mean, it just didn't register that I could look out the window and suddenly see buildings that normally were out of view." Levinson raced down the stairs and went into crisis mode. Her responsibility was to ensure that as many of the Bay Area branches as possible be open for business the next day. Most investors, she knew, really didn't believe that their money was kept at the branches, but nonetheless they wanted the assurance of business as usual. She didn't leave the building for 3 days.

John Gambs, the recently hired CFO, was on the twenty-eighth floor. What filled him with dread was the noise he didn't hear. "As soon as the building stopped rocking, the lights went out and the diesel generator on the roof kicked in nosily," he recalls. "It was comforting to hear the generator growl." But the moment was short because soon there was silence again. The generator had failed. It was unseasonably hot that October afternoon, causing the generator on the roof of the Schwab building to overheat. Technicians reduced the load on the generator and once again the purring on the roof continued. As the sun set, the Schwab building alone among the buildings in downtown was lit up. For 3 nights, the balance of downtown San Francisco was awash in darkness.

As Perry walked up and Taggart walked down the stairs, a command center was already being established on the fourth floor. The switchboard was out so most phones were dead. Someone found one working telephone, and a Schwab employee was deputized to commandeer the line and keep it open. In a world before ubiquitous cell phones it's difficult to remember how dependent people were on land lines. The first order of business was to locate the decision makers. Chuck was in Pebble Beach at the Transamerica Seniors golf tournament with, as fate would have it, the senior executive of Pacific Bell, a good person to have at your side during an emergency. Stupski, Mark Barmann, Jim Wiggett, and dozens of other Schwab executives were at Candlestick Park. Tom Seip was still stuck in traffic on the Oakland Bay Bridge. Fortunately, a full complement of senior executives was in the building at the time and immediately swung into action. The senior executive, David Pottruck, president of the brokerage subsidiary and executive vice president of the company, coordinated the recovery efforts.

The World Series games themselves were lackluster. There wasn't a pitching performance to stir memories of Sandy Koufax (1963). There wasn't a spectacular catch along the lines of the one made by Willie Mays in 1954. No crucial fielding blunder to remind fans of Mickey Owen (1941). There wasn't an edge-of-your-seat moment on which the Series outcome was hanging. And yet the 1989 World Series ranks as the most ground-shaking Series ever. While the action on the field was, in fact, mostly devoid of excitement, the activity under the field was another matter. Mother Nature hit a grand slam that day.

By 5:04 P.M. many of the 60,000 fans on hand that day were in their seats or entering Candlestick Park. As the throng awaited introduction of the lineups, an earthquake measuring 7.2 on the Richter scale rocked the Bay Area. The Candlestick press box swayed, the ballpark shook, and the lights went out. At first, fans, players, and the media remained generally calm and exhibited West Coast lightheartedness. People gathered around the many battery-powered portable radios and television sets to get the news. The news reports of death and destruction around the area turned the mood of the crowd somber. Baseball Commissioner Fay Vincent made an immediate decision to postpone game three. His decision ensured that everyone could vacate Candlestick before darkness set in.

The Loma Prieta earthquake took its name from a mountain that was not the epicenter but was the most prominent landmark in the immediate area. Less than 24 hours after the earthquake, Vincent announced that major league baseball's "modest little sporting event" would be postponed for at least a week. Later, after finally meeting with San Francisco Mayor Art Agnos and being apprised of continuing logistics problems, the commissioner disclosed that the resumption of the Series would be delayed for another 3 days, to October 27. The 10-day postponement and 12-day gap in games were the longest in World Series history. While some observers called for cancellation of the remainder of the Series in deference to the earthquake victims, most favored its continuation and even viewed the competition and resumption of all other normal events (sports and otherwise) as crucial to the area's healing process.

As the spectators, scared and edgy, filed out of Candlestick Park, they looked back toward the city and saw the first plumes of smoke rising over the Marina District.

As bad as it was, the Loma Prieta earthquake could have been much, much worse, and it was—on television. For a variety of reasons the 1989 earthquake was electronically magnified past the point of all reason, further raising the stakes for Schwab. Eyes around the nation were now on San Francisco. In retrospect it's not hard to see why TV reports blew reality out of proportion. This was the first earthquake to be covered on live TV. The World Series had congregated a critical mass of journalists and their cameras ready to jump on the story. The Goodyear Blimp itself provided live coverage of the calamity. Because the event was broadcast live, it magnified the event even to the people who were in the middle of it. A worldwide audience of more than 100 million people was cued in; the networks were ready to provide the melodrama. It's what the media wait for— a fire on steroids.

An earthquake is more than just a seismic event. It undermines the most cherished assumptions about our world and thereby becomes a screen onto which everyone projects their fears and anxieties. Around the country, Schwab shareholders must have been wondering about their investment. Gazing at the TV, they could be forgiven for thinking that their investment was slowly sinking into the sea. Many of them were likely to have made the decision that if Schwab wasn't ready to do business when the market opened, the company was toast. Schwab stock would be unloaded faster than Enron junk bonds.

Darkness was setting when an anonymous Schwab employee had the keen judgment to grab a man and ask for a piece of paper. That unknown employee probably did more than anyone to save the company. When people all around were wondering if they were going to die, this employee remembered that a San Francisco city building inspector was in the building on other business. The Schwab employee grabbed the inspector before he could leave and insisted that the inspector issue a provisional certificate of safety for 101 Montgomery Street. The inspector could see that the building was structurally sound. He had just one problem: the power was off and without power, there were no water pumps. Without water pumps, there was no water above the fourth floor. And without running water, for sanitary reasons, a building may not be occupied.

The employee invited the inspector into an upper floor washroom. Voila! A flush. And another! Fortunately, in this regard, Schwab had thought ahead. The generator on the roof powered the water pumps as well as one elevator. Satisfied, the building inspector allowed the Schwab building to remain occupied. Without that certificate of occupation, the building would have been evacuated and no one would have been allowed to return. As it was, employees began arriving after midnight to try to get Schwab ready for business by the time the markets opened. Schwab was the only brokerage in the downtown area that opened Wednesday morning.

Tom Seip started working the computer recovery issue. He declared an emergency and activated the backup computer disaster recovery site in New Jersey. As part of its routine business continuity practice, Schwab made a daily backup tape of its database and customer information records. Those tapes were shipped each night for safekeeping to a secure location in Colorado. Recovering that tape would allow the company to restore its operations as they were on the close of the previous business day. Someone was dispatched to charter a plane to Colorado, make a copy of the backup tape, and personally escort it to the backup facility in New Jersey.

In the seventh floor data center, teams of computer technicians worked through the night to breathe life into the computer. Sheri Anderson, senior vice president of information systems, was gratified that the quarterly disaster recovery drill paid off. But it wasn't just seeing Schwab people handle their assignments that impressed Anderson. It was the initiative that Schwab people showed. Using a garden hose, an unsung Schwab employee spent the first night on the roof, spraying water to cool down the struggling generator. An employee named Awk Umbay took it upon himself to drive to a grocery store and come back with three grocery carts full of food and beverages for the team. A disaster is made up of exceptions and unanticipated contingencies. Anderson watched with pride as employees solved problem after problem to initialize the mainframe. Only when the disk drives were once again spinning could the recovered data be loaded back into memory and the network brought back up. One by one, like stars in the night sky emerging from the clouds, Schwab branches around the country flickered to life.

In Branchland, uncertainty filled the silence. Branch managers fielded phone calls from concerned account holders but had very little news to report. Everyone knew that if Schwab wasn't ready for business when the market opened, then Schwab would be universally regarded as not ready for prime time.

In New York City, it was 8:04 P.M. Alan Diener, regional branch manager for the East Coast, was at home watching the World Series. "The cameras shook and then the view cut to shots of the Bay Bridge. It didn't seem like a big deal until the news started to run with the story," he recalls. After trying and failing to get directions from San Francisco, Diener made his way to the Schwab regional branch, arriving at 3 A.M. to establish communications. His heart sank to discover the computer system was down and there were no estimates of its recovery. One encouraging development: Schwab executives had established voice communications, initiating conference calls on the hour to provide updates. "There were tears in everyone's eyes to learn that everyone was okay," he says. Meanwhile, there was little to do but pray. Diener knew there'd be concerned customers waiting when the doors at the three New York City Schwab branches opened in less than 4 hours.

Without the computer system, the company would take a huge blow to its credibility, but Diener was determined that business would continue. The investment reps would take orders manually and then reconcile the orders based on bid and ask time. Customer trades would be "locked in" and customers would be protected from price swings. In other words, if a customer placed an order for IBM at 10 A.M. at a price of $60 and then IBM rose to $65 by the time Schwab got around to actually executing the order, the company would eat the difference. If the price went down, the customer would get the lower price. "We knew that if the market went against us, we'd have huge risk exposure," Diener says, but that's the way the company played it when the system went down. When the screens of the computer system finally flickered to life a few minutes before the doors opened, everyone gave out a collective sigh and got ready for another busy day.

Fort Lauderdale branch manager Jim Skinner was also watching the World Series. Within an hour, the regional branch manager in Tennessee had called with contingency plans. The Miami branch would be the fallback center for all Florida operations. In case the computer did not come up, every branch would phone orders into Miami for consolidations and reconciliation. Skinner reported to the branch and waited. He was touched that most of the customers called with concerns about the Schwab people in San Francisco.

Mark Thompson, manager of investor relations, was confident that the team working feverishly on the computer system would prevail. But investor relations is about managing perceptions. Thompson understood that investors couldn't wait until the market opened to test Schwab's survival. They needed reassurance now. Something had to go out on the wire immediately. Thompson dialed the Dow Jones News Service in New York. It was a difficult conversation. The editor on night duty didn't know Thompson and was reluctant to put something out on the wire without checking it out in the morning. But it will be too late by then, Thompson pleaded. Dow Jones relented. A report that Schwab was alive and well went out over the business wire. On Wednesday, investors awoke to a friendly story in the *Wall Street Journal.* The stock kept its value.

CFO John Gambs was doing everything he could to ensure that from a financial perspective, Schwab not only had sufficient liquidity and access to funds but that as many people as possible knew about it. As soon as phone service was restored, Gambs was on the horn with its banks, regulators, and Wall Street analysts to reassure them that Schwab was fine and ready for business. "Then I held my breath for the systems people to do their magic," he says. "Coming so soon after our difficulties in 1987, people might not have been so forgiving of us if our problems had been so conspicuous again."

Kathy Marshall, a manager at Schwab, lived in one of the Marina District apartments that were destroyed. She lost everything. Sometimes it's nice to work in an organization with deep paternalistic traditions. When Chuck and Pottruck heard about her plight, they immediately issued a five-figure check and instructed her to check into a hotel, buy whatever she needed, and return to work only when she was ready.

Schwab sought to use the experience to make itself stronger and smarter. In the aftermath of the earthquake, Schwab immediately began investing in backup systems and distributing a substantial part of operations outside the fault line. They would never again be caught with all their IT eggs in one basket. "We always wanted to and hoped to distribute our information processing infrastructure," Stupski says. "The earthquake accelerated all that." Within months, Schwab put a backup data center in Phoenix and then made it the company's primary data center. Over the next few years, additional data centers in Indianapolis and Denver sprang up, each capable of mirroring the others. With the flip of a switch, the entire company could be run from any one of these data centers.

Over the next 5 years, Schwab spent unprecedented sums to beef up its IT infrastructure, improve reliability of computer operations, and implement contingency plans for various scenarios. "The 1989 earthquake tested Schwab in every way and taught us to have a great sense of urgency about disaster recovery," Levinson says. "As a result, it gave us a blueprint for how to do crisis management." These investments would prove invaluable as the company scaled up to grow with the longest bull market in the history of the country.

OneSource

1992

*Only subversive questions create new wealth. Schwab has always had
the culture to entertain subversive questions and the guts to act on them.
Aside from the introduction of discount brokerage, the innovation that
Chuck holds closest to his heart is the development of the Mutual Fund
OneSource program.*

The crash of 1987 was the best thing that ever happened to
Charles Schwab & Co. If Nietzsche's dictum that "What
doesn't kill you, makes you stronger" holds, then Schwab
in 1988 was a very strong company, indeed. For a while, Chuck
was certain that everything he worked for was falling apart. In
the days after the crash, after it was clear that financially, at
least, the firm would survive, Chuck feared the loss of something perhaps just as vital: his bond with his customers. It was
his name on the door; Chuck was their broker; the customers
were his. It was mortifying to Chuck to review just how miser-

ably his firm had served the customers for whom Chuck had an almost magical affiliation. On almost every level, the firm had missed the mark.

The company came out of the crisis shaken to its very core but, as Chuck and his executives discovered, that core was sturdy enough. The employees, dispirited as they were, in personal gestures large and small, renewed their commitment to Chuck and the business. By pulling together and doing whatever it took, the people of Schwab determined to enter the new decade a more focused and humble company. Schwab had always been a company that was well led but badly managed. With its core values intact, the company made difficult management changes that would, for good and bad, reverberate to the present day.

The trickiest change was for Chuck to finally acknowledge to himself, his associates, and the world that his limitations as an executive had brought Schwab to its difficulties. As hard as it was, Chuck agreed that it was time for him to relinquish day-to-day control of the company. It would have been better for Chuck at this point to take the next step: to accept that the best way he could serve the company was as a hands-on chairman, visionary guru to the staff, and plenipotentiary to the customer. Instead, while retaining the title "chairman and chief executive officer," he finally surrendered most real day-to-day control of the company to Larry Stupski, who in turn, promoted David Pottruck, executive vice president of marketing and branch administration, to head the core discount brokerage business.

The decision was long overdue, it tore Chuck apart, and in the end it wasn't enough. "I saw him agonize about the decision whether or not to hand Stupski the CEO title that we all knew Larry would in every practical sense of the term occupy," a former vice president says. But in the end, Chuck could not let go of the title. The same issue, with essentially the same outcome but with much higher stakes, confronted Chuck 10 years later. "Chuck's need to serve as a CEO must have a religious basis because it cannot be defended as rational," says a former member of the Schwab board.

Liberated from the demands of managing the business, Chuck's vision now soared. The company's celebrated innovations—like Telebroker, the Mutual Fund Marketplace, and the no-fee IRA—were now as much as 8 years in the past. With Chuck distracted as he was by the rigors of financing the business, there had been of late precious little innovation from the company. To associates, Chuck expressed frustration that the company had lost its edge as a powerhouse of innovation. To his friends, he sometimes shared a sense of gloomy unrest. But contact with customers visibly improved Chuck's disposition. Now he started spending more time away from headquarters, visiting branches and meeting with customers. Perhaps it was out of recognition that good things would happen if Chuck went on extended road trips to visit customers that Chuck received such encouragement from Stupski and the other executives. Or perhaps they just wanted him out of the way.

Unfettered, Chuck's vision now realized a concept so revolutionary that it stands on par with the development of the discount brokerage itself. When the final history of Wall Street is written, Schwab's Mutual Fund OneSource program will go down as the innovation that most liberates do-it-yourself investors from the constraints imposed on them by an industry less interested in service than exploitation. It may be Chuck's most durable legacy: OneSource changed the way people around the world bought and sold mutual funds.

Chuck had been watching the amazing success of mutual funds since the beginning. Of course, he had always been a champion of no-load funds. He had even started a family of mutual funds (no load, of course) called SchwabFunds. By 1981, he had the concept for a centralized market for mutual funds. But at that time, Schwab wasn't big enough to implement a concept as radical as OneSource. Schwab's Mutual Fund Marketplace, introduced in 1984, was a very limited Version 1.0 of OneSource. But by 1992, even Chuck was in awe of the public's insatiable demand for mutual funds of every variety and description. There were more funds now than equities. There were days when Fidelity, the largest mutual fund company, accounted for up to 10 percent of the volume on the New York

Stock Exchange. Alone, Merrill Lynch's mutual division held about $125 billion.

Even so, from a customer's point of view (the only perspective comfortable to Chuck), getting into mutual funds was anything but convenient. Now Schwab had enough clout to release Mutual Fund OneSource, the first no-load, no-transaction-fee mutual fund supermarket. Fund supermarkets allow investors to pick and choose among no-load funds from competing families and gather them all in a single account. It was the first financial supermarket where investors could buy funds as easily as they pluck items off the shelf at Wal-Mart.

"In the days before supermarkets, to buy a mutual fund," Chuck explained in a 1996 *Forbes* article, "you had to write or call the fund distributor. On Day Six, you'd get a prospectus. On Day Seven or Eight you call up and they say you've got to put in your money. If you're lucky, by Day Ten you've bought it. Multiply that by the four or five other funds you saw in *Forbes* that month and were going to buy. It was even more cumbersome when you redeemed. You had to send a notarized redemption form. We brought all this into modern times."

Mutual Fund OneSource took the hassle out of owning funds. With one phone call, visit to a branch office, or, for the computer literate, with Schwab's brand new StreetSmart software for the PC, a customer could buy more than 200 different funds from 25 fund families, compare their performance, sell the funds, and switch between funds. Investors who diversified and bought funds from several different fund families no longer had the frustration of dealing with a confusing variety of statements, rules, and sales representatives. Investors in the OneSource program received one statement that consolidated the performance of each fund, individually and by family. An analysis in *Fortune* put the choice this way: "In the past, anyone who wanted a diversified portfolio of no-load mutual funds had two options: Either commit to a single fund family, which meant sacrificing choice for convenience; or else set up multiple accounts, which brought a monthly paper avalanche, delays in switching, and bewilderment at tax time. Now that same investor can consolidate holdings in one account. Life is simpler."

A tremendous advance in customer convenience, to be sure, but revolutionary? To appreciate how truly subversive One-Source is to the balance of power between the investor and the fund management industry, one needs to go under the covers a little. Remember that it was in the interests of fund managers to make it difficult for investors to get out of funds. In traditional marketing terms, they wanted high switching barriers. In dot-com terms, they wanted the money invested in their funds to be "sticky." By eliminating switching barriers, OneSource gave investors more control, more opportunity, and more real power than they ever had before.

And it really was free. Not "free" in the Wall Street tradition of hiding the costs, but literally without cost to the customer: Schwab imposed no fee at all on the investors for the One-Source service. Chuck's brilliance was leveraging the increasing value of Schwab's distribution clout. The fund companies would *pay* Schwab for the privilege of participating in OneSource. The company would charge the fund families the 25–35 basis points (25–35 cents per $100 invested) fee formerly borne by customers. In return, Schwab provided value almost impossible to resist: "shelf space" in Schwab's supermarket of funds, lower marketing costs, cooperative advertising, and exposure to the independent financial advisors increasingly using Schwab as a platform to serve their own clients. Fund managers could also outsource onto OneSource the headaches that come with record keeping and account servicing.

But there was a risk to Schwab. Before OneSource, the company charged its customers a fee for the convenience of buying funds. And now the decision before the company was whether to undermine yet another tidy revenue stream. The analysis showed that adopting OneSource would cut the profitability of the company's mutual fund business in half. The analysis on the upside was ambiguous. Could Schwab attract the incremental assets it would need to compensate for the loss in fees? The showdown came in a meeting in Schwab's twenty-eighth-floor boardroom. There were heated words on either side of the issue as the executives tried to paint OneSource as a blessing or a curse. Then the low-key Chuck spoke up. "Damn the marketing research, we need to do this," he said. "People will bang down our doors to use this product."

Some fund managers immediately got it. Tom Seip, the Schwab executive who brilliantly implemented Chuck's vision, recalls being summoned to an October 1993 meeting by Barton Biggs, the celebrated chief of asset management at Morgan Stanley. Biggs listened carefully while Seip and John Coghlan, now a Schwab vice chairman, laid out the details. "Gentlemen," Biggs said, "it's time for me to retire because this program will change the world of mutual funds as I know it." Seip didn't tell him that until Chuck made his decision it was touch and go for One-Source. "Sometimes it took Chuck to cut through the indecision," Seip says. "Someone with less courage and vision wouldn't have done it."

Seip assembled a sales team to hit the road and start evangelizing. "We knew we had to get at least seven solid fund families on board to launch OneSource," he says. Most fund managers resisted at first, but ultimately succumbed to the plan's win-win fundamentals. "I did a lot of begging with Tom Baily at Janus Funds. I wore out the knees on at least two or three suits" says David Pottruck. Over the space of a few months, Seip collared names like Dreyfus, Federated, Denver Funds, Founders, and Neuberger Berman. The bended-knee routine eventually won over hundreds of fund companies, including Janus.

It was like pouring gasoline on a fire. "No one, not even Chuck, anticipated the success of OneSource," Seip says. It's not surprising. Schwab's approach to product development is untraditional. Where most companies develop a product and try to find a market for it, Schwab identifies a customer need and then attempts to meet it. Considerations of profit come later. For market research, the Schwab product developers tapped their own experience as investors. "We invented OneSource for ourselves," Seip says. "We knew that this was how we wanted to buy mutual funds, and we figured there were millions of other people who did too."

Schwab's integrity, as always, was tested as it tried to get One-Source off the ground. David Pottruck recalls a conversation with an executive from the "hide-the-cost" school of fund management: "Oh, this will be easy. We'll just give Schwab a different class of shares with higher expenses for customers. They'll barely notice and we'll pass it on to you," the fund manager suggested. Pottruck turned him down cold. "Our intention was that our customers were getting exactly the same product they would get from the funds directly without any transaction fees. Selling them a different class of shares would have made our offer of 'no transaction fee' a lie, and inconsistent with our values."

Other fund managers would participate, but only if Schwab restricted access to financial advisors. Chuck insisted that One-Source be available to all customers, retail as well as institutional. He was sensitive to the fund managers' desire to avoid conflict in their channels, but not at the expense of imposing it on Schwab's.

What had shifted for Schwab between 1981, when the Mutual Fund Marketplace was introduced, and its eventual success as Mutual Fund OneSource 11 years later? One difference: Schwab had grown more than 500 percent, from 300,000 accounts in 1981 to 2 million accounts in 1992. But the biggest difference was the critical mass of independent financial advisors who came to use Schwab's platform to serve their own clients. These financial advisors tended to use mutual funds as the investment vehicles of first choice.

The fund managers really had little alternative. Intense competition had ended the clubby fraternity of fund managers. Many understood that, going forward, the balance of power in the mutual fund industry would now tilt away from manufacturers (the fund families) and would now favor distributors (like Schwab). Greed would ensure it. Fund managers were desperate for fast, efficient asset growth. They needed access to shelf space in Schwab's national marketplace so bad they were even willing to risk being disintermediated by an account aggregator. Of course, it was 1992, and those terms wouldn't come into common usage for 5 more years, but make no mistake, that's what Schwab was doing.

OneSource surgically removes the control the fund managers had over their customers and transplants it into Schwab. "To take advantage of Schwab's marketing and distribution prowess, fund managers must forfeit control of the customer relationship," says Adrian Slywotzky in *Value Migration.* "When Schwab sells a fund for a money manager, it passes along the assets, but not the customer's name. This destroys the ability of a fund family to cross-sell and establish a deeper relationship with the investor." Schwab now neatly inserted itself between the fund manager and its customers. OneSource maintains a single omnibus account with each of its fund families, behind which may lie thousands of individual shareholders. Fund managers don't even know how many shareholders they have—much less what their names are. But Schwab does.

In the trenches, OneSource not only dismembers the ability of fund families to cross-sell shareholders with direct mail and phone calls, but actually encourages shareholders to defect by making it so easy to switch among OneSource funds. And a convenient destination for many of those panicky investors in market downturns? None other than a family of Schwab-branded funds. It's a bitter pill for some fund managers. "To gain access to Schwab's distribution network, fund families must accept all its conditions, which makes some fund operators extremely nervous. As one noted, going through Schwab is like 'dancing with the devil'."

Different is not always better, but better is always different. Chuck is the master of the win-win product. OneSource benefits investors, it benefits Schwab, and it even helped drag the fund industry into the modern age. OneSource opens the gates to innovative fund companies by eliminating switching costs and collapsing the time required to make decisions. "Chuck's genius is in shaking up the industry that not only serves the best long-term interests of investors but extracts value for Schwab in the process," says Guy Moszkowski, managing director of the

Salomon Smith Barney unit of Citigroup, Inc. "Chuck saw how investment management in mutual funds was becoming a commodity and distribution the new proprietary asset." OneSource, Moszkowski explains, exploits a characteristic of buyer behavior. "Customers are fixated on commissions or loads but much less sensitive to ongoing fees or interest on margin borrowing," he says. No wonder Chuck is smiling all the time.

13

Heart Attack

January 10, 1992

September 11, 2001. November 23, 1963. December 7, 1942. The events of certain dates enshrine themselves in our memories, establishing forever a sense of where we were and what we were doing and how afterward nothing could ever be the same. For the men and women of Schwab, one of those keynote dates is January 10, 1992, the day on which the universally admired and seemingly indestructible heart of Larry Stupski gave out, altering forever the company's center of gravity.

Even before Larry Stupski was out of intensive care, the legends had begun. This part everyone got right: He was playing basketball at the San Francisco Bay Club, the fitness center of choice for the city's most driven executives, a population for which Stupski served as poster boy. It was late on a Friday afternoon, January 10, 1992. That part they got right, too. But, of course, Chuck had sent out a company-wide E-mail announcing the news. Over the next few weeks, as Stupski's condition went from shaky to stable and then shaky again, the myths making the rounds all reflected the aspects of Larry Stupski individuals most wanted to preserve.

Let's start with Stupski's learning style. Only one word described it. Analytical. "Stupski is always ready to take a marker to a whiteboard to show you the steps in a decision," Jim Wiggett recalls. "Larry wants to go through the steps one by one." Often his desire to connect the dots slowed down the process, as one could tell by the line of people waiting outside his office. But no one could take this away from him: If a piece was missing from your presentation—an untested assumption, a slapdash guesstimate—Stupski was sure to zero in on it. No matter what was hitting the fan, Stupski was a rock. If anyone could keep thinking during a heart attack, he could.

So when Stupski felt chest pains, he told the front desk at the Bay Club that he was having chest pains and needed a taxicab. That's right, a taxicab. Stupski was so smart he knew that an ambulance is the last thing a fitness center wants pulling up to the front door. The drones at the front desk would probably waste precious minutes covering their well sculpted butts so as not to perturb the other heart attack candidates working out. Because he knew he needed to get to the hospital pronto, Stupski asked for a taxi. Pretty smart, huh? Okay, it doesn't make much sense and in fact the taxi story is utter baloney. In fact, he requested an ambulance and it was in an ambulance that Stupski's heart stopped.

From the day he arrived at Schwab in February 1980, Larry Stupski represented hope. To Stupski, Chuck attached his longing to let go of the day-to-day operations of the company that were driving him to distraction. In Stupski, he saw a world-class analytical mind, generosity of spirit, and scrupulous integrity. In Stupski, the executives saw a coach and mentor that Chuck for all his gifts did not provide. Even those he demoted or replaced found they could not dislike him. With Stupski providing a counterweight to the mercurial Chuck, the investment analysts covering the company found additional confidence to recommend the company and its stock. For the first time, Schwab watchers saw in Stupski the possibility of a Charles Schwab & Co. without Chuck Schwab.

Born in Houston, Texas, the eldest of five sons of a father in the Army Air Force, Stupski in early life developed the drive to outthink, outwork, and outhustle everyone around him. When he was 13, the family moved to blue collar Jacksonville, Florida where his father took a job as an electrotyper and he played high school football. A scholarship took him to Princeton and then Yale Law School. When law school seemed irrelevant, as it did much of the time, he could be found on the Yale athletic fields. He worked out with the Yale rugby club and later became its captain. "We did not bother with exams in my second year because of the tear gas," he says. "There were lots of issues on people's minds: Cambodia, Kent State, Viet Nam, civil rights. The place was very, very yeasty." The war in Viet Nam was winding down but not fast enough. Rather than risk being drafted, in 1968 he enlisted in the navy and entered Officer Candidate School in Newport, Rhode Island. Commissioned as an ensign, he served a year on active duty and when the war finally did wind down, the Navy excused 2½ years of his 3½ year obligation. Stupski reenrolled at Yale, graduating in 1971. By then he was married and had a child.

At the age of twenty-six, he took a job in New York City with Bradford National Corp., a kick-ass entrepreneurial company in the emerging field of computer services. His job: analyzing deals and negotiating agreements. Bradford National was the quintessential "Type A" company staffed by Type A managers and Stupski felt he was among kindred spirits. "Larry always seemed to be in a chronic state of hurry," a Bradford coworker recalls. "He needed to be an expert on every subject. He was determined to win every game, even when playing with people who were less skilled or experienced." Bradford had a raw, in-your-face culture that thrived on conflict. Stupski never relished the clashes for their own sake, but always saw them as a battle of ideas. He was usually oblivious to the hard feelings that resulted. "I liked figuring out how I could make things work faster, more cheaply, more accurately, and take the white space out," he says. As for the people who occupied the white space in Stupski's crosshairs, many came away with a grudging respect for him but nevertheless could breath easier when he resigned.

Today, Stupski ruefully concedes that many of his work attitudes were unhealthy and counterproductive. "My law school training heightened an already unhealthy sense of perfectionism," he says. "It encouraged me to expect that things could be made perfect and that I had the right to criticize the work of my colleagues. After all, I had had this wonderful education, and I could figure out how to poke holes in everything. It took a few years and a number of confrontations for that really to be brought home," he says.

After leaving Yale, none of Stupski's jobs required a law degree. But that doesn't mean that he left his legal training in New Haven. For better and for worse, the disciplines he learned in law school informed his management style. As a student he hated the case method of training lawyers, in which the essence of a problem was extracted from precedents. Two decades later he realized how the case method mirrored business. "The heart of the problem is the concealment of the real issue," he says. "In business, things always come to you with a spin, with a view, with a partial set of facts. I came to believe that the relentless, questioning effort of the case method, a kind of pounding for 3 years, really helped me better understand issues and problems in the business world."

Another attribute of Type A personalities—a personal commitment to having, rather than being—made Stupski restless after 5 years with Bradford National. He had learned a lot and now wanted to make a lot of money. It was the 1970s, a tough time for the economy in New York. "I was in the business for 10 years before I had any idea what the words 'bull market' meant," he says. It wasn't greed. Stupski has never been one to covet material possessions. It's just that men saddled with a certain set of assumptions need to validate themselves by jumping socially sanctioned hoops. In this culture, those expectations involve accumulating wealth, power, and privilege. Such opportunities seemed limited in New York. So like many other restless men before him, Stupski turned his sights westward to California, where at least the white space was tanned. He arranged for Bradford to transfer him to the Bay Area. In 1979, he sent out resumes to 200 companies. Charles Schwab & Co. was not one of them. As it was, only one of the recipients, a headhunter, responded, and after six months with no callback, he forgot about that one, too.

It was Chuck's notorious inattention to detail that sparked Stupski's introduction to Schwab. Serendipitous is a word that's often overused, but in this case it fits. Let Tom Seip, a critical figure at Schwab, tell it:

> I was the junior partner in the San Francisco office of Korn/Ferry International, an executive recruiting firm, when I received a call from Chuck's secretary. They needed to recruit an executive to head the company's growing branch network. I went to meet Chuck at his first building, a location that's now occupied by the Citicorp building. Only later did I learn the true story. Chuck had been at a Young Presidents Organization cocktail party when he said he needed a recommendation for a recruitment firm. The recommendation he got was for Heidrich & Shendrich, our biggest competitor. But by the time Chuck got back to the office, all he remembered was that the search firm sported a pair of funny names separated by an ampersand. He asked his secretary to search the yellow pages. Well, Korn/Ferry had a slash, not an ampersand, but Chuck said call them anyway. That's why she picked up the phone and since I was the junior guy, I was the one who answered it.
>
> As the search went on, the job description morphed from branch office manager to chief operating officer. None of the people I could find fit the requirements or wanted to join something as untested as discount brokerage. And then I literally woke up in the middle of the night. I knew we had the right guy. But where? Was he a walk-in? I remembered a conversation but little else. For the life of me, I couldn't retrieve a name. By 5 A.M. I was at the office pulling out resumes one by one. When I saw it,

I knew we had our candidate. The name on the resume: Lawrence J. Stupski.

"**C**huck, I have just three questions for you," Stupski said during their initial meeting. Chuck just nodded his head shyly and smiled, waiting.

"Do you have any plans for an IPO?"

"Does Schwab have any financial difficulties?"

"Is the company facing any regulatory difficulties?"

The answers came in quick succession, "No, no, and no."

Alas, Chuck's determination to reel Stupski in may have inspired a level of veracity appropriate to fishing stories. But then Chuck was only telling Stupski what Stupski was hoping to hear. Where was the cross-examination? In any case, it would have taken Stupski only two phone calls to determine the truth of the matter. And the truth of the matter was that the situation was, in one of his more descriptive terms, "yeasty."

As he started work, the first thing he noticed was the investment bankers, the guys with the suspenders working on the S-1 registration statement required for an IPO. The second thing he noticed were the regulators from the Philadelphia Stock Exchange who were inserting themselves so deep into the bowels of the company that executives had to turn their heads and cough. The third thing he noticed was Rich Arnold warning that in 6 months, the company would be out of cash. And that was all in the first 60 days. "It was my first introduction to how quickly things change at Schwab," Stupski says generously.

In the beginning, he spent the mornings running the San Francisco branch and attending to the needs of the eighteen or so other branches in the region. When the markets closed, he went upstairs and handled duties in a cross section of areas. One of his first tasks was to persuade all the branches, some of which were still relying on incompatible computer systems, to move to a common computer platform. He quickly earned Chuck's confidence and helped him think through some of the toughest decisions facing the company.

To franchise or not to franchise, that was the question. Franchising was the sexiest business topic of 1980. For a company running out of money, franchising Schwab branches offered a number of benefits. Franchising, as operationalized by McDonalds, Household Finance, Midas, Culligan, Century 21, and others provided another source of capital. Expansion of any business is risky and requires significant investments of capital and human resources. Franchising the branches would inject the company with much-needed capital from the franchisees and allow the company to penetrate markets much more quickly than it could by organic expansion alone.

Ultimately, Chuck decided that if his name was going to be on the door, only company-owned branches could guarantee customers the quality and integrity that he demanded. In addition, no brokerage ever tried the franchising route before. Normally, this alone would not have stopped Schwab, but it is also true that capital markets fund only activities they understand. When you have a brand-new concept, it can be an impediment to raising money. This decision would prove consequential 2 years later when the company sold itself to Bank of America. Had Schwab taken the franchising route, there would have been much less to sell.

In 1982, when Stupski was promoted out of the branch management job, Tom Seip asked him for a shot at the open position. Stupski turned him down in favor of Bernell V. Flath, an inspired manager who led the most intense period of branch expansion in the company's history and helped transform the branches into a well-oiled machine for generating wealth.

A year later, with Schwab now a part of Bank of America, the company needed someone to bring its human resources department up to the bank's standards. Stupski called Seip, who said, "No, thank you. Been there, done that." Stupski looked pained. "He read me the riot act," Seip recalls. "'Look, dummy, you're thirty-two years old,'" he told me. "'You have no business degree. You haven't managed anything but HR. Come and do a decent job and I'll give you a shot on the revenue side.'" Seip proved to be one of Stupski's best hires. In his 15-year career at Schwab,

Seip held several key management positions, including CEO of Charles Schwab Investment Management, Inc. He is proudest of pioneering Schwab's revolutionary OneSource Mutual Fund Service and Schwab's highly successful Services to Investment Managers business. Seip very nearly succeeded Stupski as president of the company until Pottruck derailed his career, a conflict described in Chapter 15.

Over the next 10 years, Stupski's main role was to translate Chuck to the company and, in turn, translate the company to Chuck. For example, Chuck might look at a layout of a prospective ad and grunt something undecipherable. It was left for Stupski to explain to the bewildered art director and copywriter what Chuck objected to. Where's the offer? Where's the bid for action? Stupski would ask, putting words around Chuck's visceral noises. When Chuck said in a meeting, "Don't you understand what it means to be a growth company?" it was Stupski who unpacked that statement into concrete steps and measurable objectives that people could take on. "No one worked harder, was smarter, understood with more clarity, played more competitively, had more heart than Larry," Kathy Levinson says. "He was the glue that held the company together." Stupski became nothing less than a pillar of the organization, indispensable in ways people preferred not to think about.

Under Stupski's stewardship, the company prospered, transforming from a scrappy discount brokerage that succeeded in spite of itself, to an increasingly well-disciplined machine for growth. He helped the company take its present form, its organizational structure, presentation to the outside world, and its remarkable record of commitment to its employees. He spent 18 years at Schwab, 13 as chief operating officer (COO). When he joined Schwab, the company had 18 branches, 400 employees, and $30 million in revenues. On the day of his heart attack, the company had 175 branches, 4,000 employees, and revenues of more than $750 million. When Stupski's heart stopped, everyone said a prayer for his recovery. After that, everyone turned their thoughts to the same thorny meditation: What becomes of us if Chuck gets sick or dies?

No one dared talk to Chuck about succession plans. It was just assumed that Stupski would take over. Stupski out of commission was a concept quite unthinkable because everyone knew that the company had grown so large and complex that there was little possibility Chuck could manage it anymore. "When Larry got sick, the burden of sustainability fell squarely on Chuck's shoulders and it scared the derivatives out of him," a former board member recalls. Chuck was fifty-five years old; he hadn't operated as COO for over 10 years. "The scale of the company in 1991 put it quite considerably past Chuck's abilities to administer," is the way one Schwab executive put the situation. Chuck would prove the naysayers wrong.

After the break from Bank of America, the newly independent company confronted a fiercely contentious management team. As long as the company was a serf in the bank's feudal empire, the executives toed the line in an uneasy "us against them" consciousness. Now out of captivity, the ambitions, egos, and management styles of Chuck, Stupski, Pottruck, and the other members of the senior management team threatened to tear the company apart. Jim Wiggett understood that unless the executives could refocus their energies and find common ground, the company would never have the cohesion to achieve real success. A struggle was inevitable and struggle, if properly managed, could serve a constructive purpose. It seemed to Wiggett a perfect opportunity to be intentional about shaping the management team for the next period. He asked Joe Cutcliffe, an organizational psychologist and executive coach based in Los Angeles, to see what he could do. It was another way Wiggett quietly shaped the company for greatness.

Cutcliffe met with Chuck and, one by one, with each of the occupants of the executive offices on the twenty-eighth floor. In their first meeting, Stupski asked Cutcliffe to look at the company from top to bottom, find out what's wrong, and to make some recommendations. Everyone, including Stupski, welcomed Cutcliffe to the extent they assumed he was there to coach the other guy. Cutcliffe started slow, laying out some organizational theory, playing learning games. One exercise required everyone to imagine Schwab as a baseball team. Now, which position would each executive play? People started to awake to the reality that a team of nine pitchers is not much of a team. Gradually, Cutcliffe helped them grow into the reality that no executive could meet his or her objectives unless everyone met theirs, as well.

A skilled interviewer and sensitive listener, Cutcliffe won the confidence of the executives. Over a period of months, he developed a picture of the organizational dynamics at Schwab. He helped the Schwab team, now operating as an effective team for the first time, see that all organizations go through four phases—Form, Storm, Norm, and Perform—which are repeated in cycles as the organization evolves. "It didn't take much convincing for them to see that Schwab was in the Storm phase. There was a clash of Titans going on," Cutcliffe says. The central lesson he wanted the Schwab executives to learn: The problems they were experiencing were not the fault of any individual. The friction was not personal, but rather a symptom of the inevitable struggle over power that all teams must resolve if they are to move on to success. Schwab culture practically begged for this type of conflict because it was a founder company. It was headed by a genuinely beloved leader who had his name on the door. He was on a first name basis with everyone in the company, and everyone felt that they had a claim on what he stood for. Chuck inspired a sense that the business was about more than trading stocks. They loved the sense of mission. *Schwab is the guardian of the customers' financial dreams. Around here we're curing cancer.* That raised the ante for disagreements. Unless checked, the temptation was to regard people who didn't agree with you as not just incorrect or misinformed, but bad, almost evil. But although he was perceived as capable of doing no wrong, as a steward of the business Chuck was aloof and disengaged. He maintained a subtle control over his executives on the strength of his whispers.

So it's a paradox that although Chuck rarely raises his voice and absolutely abhors conflict of any kind, the managers he surrounded himself with were often contentious, boisterous, impassioned, and rarely hushed about it. Chuck's original management team—Peter Moss, Rich Arnold, Hugo Quackenbush, Barbara Wolfe—were types not averse to confrontation. As Chuck replaced that first wave of managers, the confrontation quotient generally went down. Stupski could be stormy, but he generally preferred to handle things in the low-key manner Chuck found most agreeable. But Chuck also saw the benefit of bringing on board executives with giant chips on their shoulders. Of no one was this truer than Pottruck, who was the most cantankerous, the most argumentative of all. With one exception, everyone on Chuck's management team tilted toward leadership and learning styles that were characterized by terms such as intuitive, impulsive, spontaneous, and discerning. Heading the list in these attributes were Pottruck and Wolfe. Taking up the rear on the intuitive scale: Larry Stupski.

This was the Schwab executive management team in 1990. Besides Chuck, who took the title of Chairman and CEO, the executives were:

	Title	*Tenure*
Larry Stupski	President and COO	1980–1992
David Pottruck	President of the brokerage and Executive Vice President (EVP)	1984–present
Mark Barmann	EVP and Chief Information Officer	1988–1994
Mark Brandin	EVP, Marketing and Advertising	1990–1991
A. John Gambs	EVP and Chief Financial Officer	1988–1996
Ronald Readmond	EVP, Operations, Trading and Credit	1989–1996
Barbara Wolfe	EVP, Chief Administrative Officer and Corporate Secretary	1974–1992

Making a cohesive team out of this crew would not be easy. In terms of ego strength and self-confidence, each one of these executives was off the chart. Some were obsessed with detail; others gravitated to the big picture; all were workaholics intolerant of anything less than total commitment. To their credit, they never expected more from anyone else than they expected of themselves. They could have convened a perfectionist's support group on the twenty-eighth floor. It would have been a thirteen-step program.

Two principal challenges for the Schwab team now took shape. First, to get some basic agreements about the goals everyone was struggling for. "The central challenge was for the executives to identify and agree on a transcendent set of goals to which individual egos would be subordinated," Cutcliffe says. Chuck's moral standing and the deep respect everyone had for the founder made that task go relatively quickly. Everyone signed on to the value of serving the average, individual investor by conformity to a few nonnegotiable principles:

- *Absolute integrity* in serving the best interests of customers to be worthy of their trust
- *World-class customer service* and consistent high-tech, high-touch convenience across all Schwab channels
- *Working from the customer in*, rather than from self-interest out
- *An innovation meritocracy* where excellent ideas win out no matter where they come from
- *Outrageously ambitious growth* objectives that are manifestly unattainable without everyone pulling together.
- *Relentless commitment* to improve processes and services

Second, Cutcliffe understood that Stupski would need to receive coaching if he were to be successful in directing such a muscular executive team. Everyone knew there was considerable friction around Stupski's relationship with the other managers. People were desperate for Cutcliffe to find a solution because the result was often management gridlock and bad feelings all around. Cutcliffe invited everyone to consider the following perspective. Stupski saw his colleagues as impulsive and lazy because they were not always willing to do the analysis he deemed critical. They perceived the Schwab president as an obstacle and resented being made to connect the dots for activities they saw as trivial and self-evident. He resented the others doing end runs around him. The others resented having to wait. No wonder it was getting personal.

Cutcliffe helped everyone understand that there was no right or wrong here. In engineering terms, it was an impedance mismatch, a clash of learning preferences and management styles. He helped people understand that analytical types, introverts, or perfectionists can't be pressured. The system is organic and feeds back on itself. When they feel rushed, analytical managers tend to slow down even more, and that slows down the organization. In response, the organization figures out mechanisms to go around the constraint. People felt relieved to hear Cutcliffe describe in terms of organizational development theory what they experienced. His coaching helped Stupski see that the organization's behavior was not personal and to help him find the balance between his needs for analysis and the legitimate needs of the organization to grow and act.

Four months later, Stupski was about to get the answer to his question. "Joe, do you now know what the problem is?" Stupski asked.

"I think so," Cutcliffe told the president of Schwab. "The problem is you." He was confident that Stupski would get it.

He got it. True leaders are so committed to the success of the team that they will face the possibility that their limitations are at least one source of the difficulty. "I was in a lot of pain," Stupski says. He had been trying desperately to get the management team to gel and it wasn't working. "I felt the whole weight of the company was on my shoulders. If the pain is bad enough, you can look at anything. I had been focusing on intent. I assumed that the people around me would notice how well-intentioned I was. The problem, of course, is that the world comes at us based on our behavior and the outcomes of that behavior. Failing to understand that distinction gets a lot of executives into trouble. It got me into trouble." With this logjam broken, the Schwab team made real progress. Stupski learned to delegate more and let go of some of the perfectionism. His colleagues learned how to talk to him so that he heard them. By the time Stupski's heart attack threw the company into chaos and another cycle of Form-Storm-Norm-Perform, Schwab was squarely in the Perform phase. The company was clicking on all cylinders and things were working better than anyone had dared hope. "Schwab had the most well-functioning executive team I ever saw," Cutcliffe says.

There are trigger events to heart attacks even as the reasons for those triggers remain a mystery. The most dangerous times in the lives of working men are 9 o'clock on Monday morning and the first few months following retirement. "One death is caused by the strain of carrying the burden, the other by the inability to live without the burden," says the poet David Whyte. Physical exertion, diet, heredity, and stress all contribute to the ache in uncertain measures. But research also shows that timing of heart attacks is often associated with painful emotion. Stupski's heart was heavy that Friday afternoon as he left Schwab for the Bay Club. Jim Wiggett, a beloved figure throughout Schwab for the depth of his caring, and someone he regarded as a friend, was being pressured out of the company, and Stupski decided not to interfere.

The company's HR policies mirror Chuck's aversion to conflict and his optimistic humanism that most situations can be made right. In HR circles, Schwab is renowned for the effort it puts into coaching, training, and mediating in an effort to correct a situation. Most of Schwab's enviable reputation in this area can be directly traced to Wiggett's own moral authority. However, all the coaching Stupski was receiving—don't micromanage, avoid being a bottleneck, back up your executives in their decisions—now seemed at odds with his instincts to mediate the dispute. He acquiesced and felt lousy about it. A workout was just the thing.

The Wiggett matter was just one of dozens of Schwab matters that weighed on Stupski as he went with heavy heart to the Bay Club that Friday afternoon. Although he thought the world of

Wiggett, Stupski decided not to interfere in a matter between Wiggett and his supervisor. Wiggett left the company shortly thereafter. Today Stupski dismisses the possibility that this one decision as opposed to any other was a trigger event for his heart attack, but our own hearts are often poor judges of what incites us most.

The Bay Club is crowded on an early Friday evening. Stupski is playing full-court basketball with men half his age. That's his way. He wants to run one more mile, do one more sit-up, give no quarter. Many Schwab managers who played basketball with Stupski in those days recall how intense and physical his game was. Every game counts, but this time someone is keeping score. A league tournament game raises the ante even further. After the game, which his team loses, Stupski is feeling uncharacteristically tired. Very strange after just one game. He limps off the court, exhausted. He has to wait for another game to finish before his team plays again. Despite his fatigue, he shoots hoops, trying to cool down, find his center. It's not working. The pain in his chest—like someone sitting on it—can't be ignored. He recognizes the warning signs of a heart attack. He asks the desk to call 911.

The firefighters arrive first. Before loading him into the ambulance, the firefighters stand around ogling the Spandex-clad hard bodies doing their aerobics. "Great," he recalls thinking, "I'm going to die because the firefighters can't tear themselves away from the show." Maybe he should have called for a taxi after all. The ambulance takes off but is soon stopped in traffic. In the back, the paramedics struggle to stabilize the patient. He's not going to make it if they don't get Stupski to the emergency room. Midcourse correction to another hospital. They are unloading him just as his wife, Joyce, arrives. The next few days are touch and go. It's a massive coronary. Immediate bypass surgery saves his life, but the prognosis is by no means assured.

Chuck, hearing the news, turned white, all the color drained from his face. This was not in the plan. After the earthquake, the company had made contingency planning a priority. The company moved the data center and other divisions of the company to cities with less seismic risk. Disaster recovery was built into every process. Computer systems were made redundant. Earthquake, fire, flood, power outage, computer attacks, sabotage. All contingencies accounted for. But this? This was out of left field. No one anticipated anything like it.

And that's what made Stupski's heart attack so shocking. Schwab was a vital young company in rapid growth mode. Chuck, fifty-five at the time, was seen as the oldest person on the team. If a few individuals were chronologically older, it was not by much. On the management team, most, like Stupski, forty-six at the time, or Dave, forty-four in 1992, were a decade or so younger. Elsewhere in the organization, the youth of employees was even more conspicuous. Engagements, weddings, births, yes. Funerals, except for those taken by AIDS, were rarities. The company, after all, had a truncated experience of the life cycle of executives. Recruitment and hiring preoccupied the company. Retirement? That was something intangible, for the future, something people provided for in their 401(k) plans and then gave no further thought. What came after retirement was literally unthinkable.

Stupski's heart attack inspired profound soul-searching within the company about the issue of work–life balance. In some cases, it forced individuals to confront their own workaholism. "It stunned me because I thought he was invulnerable," says Tom Seip. "I thought he had an endless appetite for work. For me, it started an examination about what was important." In others, it was a more spiritual inquiry into the fragility of life and the meaning of being alive. Beth Sawi was executive vice president and chief administrative officer when she took a year off so she and her family could live her dream of taking a sabbatical in Italy. She used the experience to write a book, *Coming Up for Air: How to Build a Balanced Life in a Workaholic World*. A self-confessed workaholic until her children were born, Sawi's dream might very well have remained just that had Stupski's heart attack not demonstrated the folly of putting off for a later date what we cherish today. Sawi retired in 2002 after 20 years at Schwab.

Almost everyone who counted Stupski as a mentor used his heart attack as an opportunity to take a good look at their own lives. Many of them didn't like what they saw. The heart attack caught everyone off balance. For Chuck, his absence created real terror. For those he mentored, he wasn't available. For everyone else, it challenged the terms of their relationship with the company. Some used it as an opportunity to slow down in an attempt to achieve balance. Others used the opportunity to take stock of their lives and perhaps calculate the value of their stock options. A number of long-time managers retired.

"Schwab was a workaholic's paradise," says Tom Taggart, whose own health suffered from the intensity of working for Schwab. "In the months after his heart attack, Stupski campaigned for more work life balance in the company," Taggart notes. Both Chuck and Stupski recognized that the company was out of whack and attempted to restore some proportion. "Chuck added his voice to Larry's call for balance, and I think he was sincere, but there were lots of mixed messages," Taggart says, adding that it's not easy to change the pace of an organization, especially when people keep being rewarded for producing. Taggart, director of corporate communications and long-time spokesperson for the company, took an extended leave from Schwab in 1996 after his own health failed. When he came back with a commitment to lead a more balanced work life, he found that he was out of step with the company's furious velocity. He left the company shortly thereafter.

Workaholism is a difficult addiction to interrupt. In *Clicks and Mortar*, Pottruck recounts a 1996 exchange that he offers as a gloss on change management and how critical it is for change agents to ask the right question. But the incident also provides an insight into Schwab attitudes toward overwork. In the story, an innovation consultant is attempting to persuade a group of 150 Schwab employees that it's a myth that people are resistant to change. "How many of you went to the same place on vacation more than once," the consultant asked. Only a few hands went up. He went on: "And how many of you went on vacation to the same place four times or more?" This time the hands remained down.

"You see," said the consultant, "it's not true that people don't like change. When we are left to do the choosing, we all like a certain amount of variety and change in our lives."

Then, from the back of the room came a raspy woman's voice: "You misunderstand, sir. We do not take vacations."

"Hopefully, she was kidding . . ." Pottruck comments. She probably wasn't. Not in 1996 when the market was white hot.

In the months following Stupski's heart attack, many executives concluded they were better off by not working for Schwab any longer. Appropriately, the wealth they generated by being workaholics at Schwab made such decisions possible. "My relationship with Larry was the best working relationship of my 30-year career," says Mark Barmann. "It's difficult to overstate the tumult his heart attack inspired in me. It was one of the reasons I chose to retire."

Kathy Levinson felt bonded to Larry Stupski from the same day they both joined Schwab. Twelve years later, she reflected on what it all meant. "Larry's heart attack made me conscious on a number of levels about my relationship with the company. In the year after his heart attack, I noticed I wasn't enjoying waking up and coming to work," she says. She wasn't leaving for another job. "It just wasn't the same without Larry," she says.

As for David Pottruck, while he was in some ways a beneficiary of the leadership vacuum created by Stupski's heart attack, he was also its most profound victim. Simply put, it arrested the development of Pottruck's learning. Chuck and Stupski were grooming Pottruck for higher office, but Pottruck gave them plenty of evidence that before he would be ready he needed more experience in other parts of the company. They had a plan to provide the experience and coaching that Pottruck needed. Then Stupski's heart attack short-circuited that process. It's true that Pottruck replaced Stupski as president of the Charles Schwab Corp. and, as co-chief executive officer, is heir apparent to Chuck. But Stupski's heart attack ensured that he wasn't fully ready for the former responsibility and still isn't fully ready for the latter.

14

eSchwab

1995–1998

The emergence of the Internet sparked an intense internal debate at Schwab. Should the firm go online—and, if so, what would happen to the existing channels? The full-commission brokers went through exactly the same debate when discount brokers like Schwab first emerged. The only difference is that now Schwab represented incumbency as it regarded competition for a new, lower-cost distribution channel.

I t is said that the truest mark of bravery is to challenge the practices that made you rich. For Schwab employees, executives to workers alike, the years leading up to 1995 were fat years in which people literally watched themselves getting rich. There was very little incentive to upset the apple cart. Nevertheless, people in various parts of the organization agitated to make the case for taking the Internet more seriously. Many individuals in Schwab's IT division saw the writing on the wall, but the bureaucratic walls the company by then imposed made it difficult for radical ideas to survive official channels.

So the story of a young software specialist in the bowels of Schwab's retail marketing department is instructive. His name is William Pearson and that he is still with Schwab says something about the organization's tolerance for mavericks. Note that this William Pearson is not the same person as the Bill Pearson (1975–1985, 1987–1989) who made an appearance earlier in the book. This Pearson, no relation, worked on the StreetSmart software package. He quickly saw the transformational power of the Internet and realized it would obsolete Schwab's packaged software business. As hard as he tried, Pearson couldn't get his supervisor interested. Here he ran into an aspect of Schwab culture that distorted one of its core values, that of innovation meritocracy where great ideas win out, no matter where they come from. Unfortunately, the company's culture penalized anyone who appeared to grandstand or call attention to himself or herself. Schwab's quarterly 360-degree evaluation process put a premium on being a team player; negative feedback from people who were upset at you could reduce your bonus for many quarters. Going outside of channels, bypassing your boss, was definitely a career-limiting move.

Nevertheless, Pearson took a chance and approached Anne Hennegar, a former Schwab manager and, after 1987, a consultant to the company. He rattled off the names of current executives he had approached without success and asked if she knew anyone else. Hennegar immediately thought of Executive Vice President Tom Seip, a manager known to reject the most rigid aspects of Schwab bureaucracy. Seip was immediately interested. "Set it up," Seip said. Hennegar assumed the meeting would include just Seip, Pearson, and her, so she was surprised when Seip popped his head in and said he was recruiting a couple of friends to join the meeting. The "friends" were Chuck, David Pottruck, Art Shaw, and Ed Rodden. Shaw and Rodden were in charge of strategic planning in the electronic brokerage arena.

The big news in brokerage circles in 1992 was the launch of Schwab's phenomenally successful OneSource program. But not far away, a small company named E*Trade began offering stock trading through such Internet services as America Online and Compuserve. Bill Porter, who had approached Schwab's Bill Gillis more than 15 years earlier with his Trade Plus proposal, now had a service company. The early E*Trade Securities provided online quote and trading services to other firms. This experience led Porter, a physicist and inventor with more than a dozen patents to his credit, to wonder why, as an individual investor, he had to pay a broker hundreds of dollars for stock transactions. He saw the solution at hand: Someday, everyone would own computers and invest through them with unprecedented efficiency and control.

Two years later, E*Trade launched the first dedicated Web site for online trading. For the few investors who were comfortable with the Internet, E*Trade was a godsend. E*Trade announced a flat $14.95 commission on stock trades. Schwab's average commission was $65.00. E*Trade and its brethren such as Ameritrade represented a direct challenge to discount brokers in terms of both convenience and price. The cost savings were considerable, yes, but what made E*Trade such a threat was the ease, speed, and flexibility of investing that digital investing made possible. Schwab was about to be Schwabbed.

Schwab was not overly concerned about losing first mover advantage to E*Trade, although the loss of bragging rights stung. The company has usually been averse to occupying the bleeding edge of technology. Its early implementation of BETA was pioneering work that paid off. However, efforts such as Equalizer and SchwabLine persuaded the company to let others do the difficult work of developing standards and protocols. Since 1990, Schwab has usually been a company that is first to be second, and its entry into Web trading was no exception. But two things were of concern.

First, top quality talent started to leave Schwab for E*Trade. Nor should this have been surprising. For information technology people, E*Trade was infinitely more sexy. It was a creation company while the more mature and much larger Schwab was operating as a compliance company. So many people, including Kathy Levinson who became its president, left to work at the E*Trade facilities in Silicon Valley south of the San Francisco financial district that it became known as "Schwab South."

Second, Schwab had a problem deciding how to answer E*Trade's challenge. The good news was that initial evidence indicated that online trading was not completely price sensitive. Schwab knew this because after two years of head-to-head competition, eSchwab serviced twice as many accounts as E*Trade despite the fact that eSchwab's standard commission of $29.95 was more than double that of E*Trade's $14.95. "Schwab's instincts, honed through years of competition in the off-line investment services marketplace, was never to compete solely on the basis of price," say the authors of *How Digital Is Your Business?* "Schwab had invented the new category of value-added discount brokerage to differentiate itself from discounters whose only selling point was low cost. Applying the same mind-set to the new online universe, Schwab became a value-added online broker. Rather than run the endless treadmill race of price competition, Schwab would (1) add value to its online offerings, thereby justifying a price premium, and (2) build a recognized brand name associated with customer service, integrity and quality."

The executives gathered around William Pearson's demo encountered something that shifted the way they thought about the future. Pearson demonstrated the experience of navigating through a logically organized Web site that integrated information and services from many sources. Although the demonstration used static instead of dynamic pages, the impact couldn't have been more powerful. What they saw harmonized with Schwab's core values. It was about empowerment. Schwab wanted to give customers control over the information, the processes, and the services needed to implement intelligent investment decisions. Moreover, the Internet offered unprecedented opportunities for Schwab to reduce the costs of delivering its services. Questions flowed furiously as the executives tried to get their minds around how well the Schwab experience aligned with the attributes of the Web: real-time information, personalization, customization, and interactivity. All advanced Schwab's commitment to the customer. As the group debated, Seip recalls, the executives got more and more excited. Eventually Chuck and Pottruck looked at each other and nodded.

Pottruck felt like a swimmer about to enter a pool that was uncomfortably cold. Was he the kind of manager who would wade in or would he jump? By nature, Pottruck is a jumper. After this demonstration, Pottruck knew it was time for the company to make the plunge to the Web.

As for Pearson, well, he had his moment of glory and he got the green light for his project. But he also paid a small price for his defiance of channels. The opportunity to present to Chuck and Dave was the highlight of his career. So what if the phrase "doesn't play well with others," appeared on his evaluation that quarter? His supervisors, upset as they were, really couldn't do much to punish him; Tom Seip saw to that. Suddenly, developers throughout Schwab announced their unofficial experiments and forays into the world of the Net. Deep in the bowels of Schwab's IT organization, various R&D efforts had been silently underway. The first initiatives focused on using the Internet as a common platform to get Schwab's systems to talk to each other. Interoperability of incompatible information systems was a huge issue at Schwab.

As chief information officer Dawn Lepore became aware of these skunk works, she brought them together. She asked for a prototype that would demonstrate some practical applications of the Internet for Schwab. The prototype that Lepore's department built leveraged the work Schwab had accumulated developing the Equalizer, StreetSmart, and SchwabLink. The developers wisely selected the application they knew would knock the ball out of the park. The application they built allowed a Schwab server to take an order from a Web browser on a PC, route it through all of Schwab's sophisticated back end systems and mainframes, execute it, and send a confirmation back to the PC. While other firms had Web trading systems, they were not integrated end to end, requiring that PC orders be printed out and entered by hand into the mainframe trading system. This was new. When Pottruck saw it, all remaining doubts evaporated. As for Chuck, "I fell off my chair" is the sentiment attributed to him when he completed a trade using the prototype. The race to the Net was now job number one.

Chuck's appetite for size and scale was finally within reach. By 1995, Charles Schwab & Co. registered assets of $181 billion with revenues of $1.4 billion and net income of $173 million. More than 9,200 men and women considered it a badge of honor to be Schwabbies. As it celebrated its twentieth anniversary, Chuck's company was universally admired as an engine of innovation, a model of the modern technologically driven, customer-focused financial services organization. Chuck himself had attained the highest honor that the establishment can bestow: He was an icon, an author, and an honored sage. Schwab's triple-channel strategy of telephone services, branches—a Schwab branch office was now less than an hour from 70 percent of the U.S. population— and most recently access to its mainframe computer network through the personal computer—seemed irresistible to cus- tomers as well as investors. Under the leadership of Chuck and Co-CEO David Pottruck, Schwab's stock soared, creating a com- pany whose stock price soared 74 percent that year. Clearly, the market approved of the direction they were taking the company.

And yet, Pottruck sensed a speed bump in the relentless race toward greater and greater success. In 1995 he realized that the number of personal computers sold in the United States for the first time eclipsed the number of televisions sold. He sensed the presence of a force, a discontinuity that could con- ceivably do to Schwab what Schwab did to Wall Street 20 years earlier. Computer-based trading was about to go mainstream. By buying laptops for all of Schwab's vice presidents and teach- ing himself how to type, Pottruck modeled the sense of urgency he wanted everyone to take. E-mail became a powerful commu- nications device at Schwab, and Pottruck proved himself a master of this new form of asynchronous communications. His middle-of-the-night E-mails on matters large and small became cele-brated throughout the company. Schwab employees looked for-ward to inspirational E-mails from Electric.Dave, the username he gave himself.

Ah, the paradox of incumbency. The ability for an organization to react nimbly to emerging opportunities rarely falls to market leaders. Why should it be otherwise? Any truly transformative vi-sion is a leap into the unknown. Why is it that most revolutionary companies are typically recruited from the also-rans of the in-dustry from which they emerged? Because industry leaders generally have too much invested in the status quo to ask the questions necessary to make radical changes. These organiza-tions suffer from a kind of institutional insanity brought on by their success. They want to change and grow, but their very suc-cess locks them in. These organizations hope for a different out-come by continuing to do what they have always done. The challenge for Schwab, if it was to emerge as a leader on the Web, was to surmount its success.

In the long run, things worked out pretty well for Schwab, but that doesn't mean it avoided mistakes. "Back in 1994, when the Net first gave inconspicuous signals that it might someday amount to something, Schwab managers settled into an intuitive view of the Net that was much like that of other companies," says David Stauffer in *Dinosaur to Dynamo: How 20 Established Com-panies Are Winning in the New Economy*. "This was a strange and different thinking that would be used, quite logically, by strange and different people. That meant the online customer would do business online, and the offline customer would do business offline, and never the twain shall meet."

The race for the Net was on, but luckily Schwab did not have to start from scratch. It could not have beaten Merrill Lynch to the Web without a succession of mini-innovations under its belt. The company launched its first foray into the online world in

1985 with a dial-up service called "The Equalizer." It was radical for its time, but with only 5 percent of the population using computers and a DOS interface, it stayed a marginal product. "But if we hadn't stumbled around with it for 10 years, we wouldn't have been in a position to see it take off with the Internet," Pottruck says. Later, as a Windows-based system now dubbed "StreetSmart," the product gained favor with a less skeptical audience.

Everyone understood that the race was crowded and the stakes were high. Most of the deep-discount brokerages, such as E*Trade and Ameritrade were pushing hard to nail Web trading. Pottruck realized that Schwab's competitors were start-ups: leaner, younger, more Net-ready. Start-ups always have two big advantages. First, they don't have legacy systems to which new systems must be integrated. Second, they are not constrained by channel conflicts representing the interests of their established businesses. They would almost certainly get to the finish line before Schwab. If Schwab lost first mover advantage with Web traders, Pottruck believed, it would be impossible to win them back. On the first point Pottruck was correct. On the latter he was wrong. Pottruck, like almost every other executive enraptured by the Internet, underestimated the value of physical infrastructure and mature customer service disciplines.

From his Citicorp days, Pottruck knew that established businesses can be inhospitable for new ideas. All the best companies struggle with the problem of developing good judgment without bad judgment swamping the effort. Pottruck was determined to do everything he could to avoid letting Schwab fall into that trap. Most organizations—and Schwab is no exception—are averse to failure. They all give lip service to welcoming or at least not punishing failure and Schwab is better at this than most companies. Schwab people speak of "Noble Failures," a category of experimentation that includes doing the analysis, playing to learn, starting small, and skewing the test toward success. And in the early days of Schwab, failures that resulted in real learning were actually welcome. But as the company grew in complexity, Schwab's arteries hardened. Schwab's culture of avoiding conflict combined with inevitable bureaucratic rigidity, making it difficult for radical ideas to find a receptive ear. By 1994, when the company really needed them, actionable radical ideas found it almost impossible to be heard above the roar of the company's success.

Schwab's best chance to rapidly develop the necessary Internet competencies would require a skunk works physically removed from the day-to-day constraints of managing Schwab. Organizations go crazy when engineers, managers, and sales people have to make decisions about serving new projects that threaten the established order or compete for limited resources. What are we going to take on first and what will we do second? These questions paralyze the organization until both the established and the new initiatives suffer.

When push comes to shove, a manager assigned to two development projects at once will always put priority on the one that's paying the bills. "The new enterprise was going to use a different model for making money than our traditional business, and we didn't want the comparisons to form the basis for measurement of success or failure," Pottruck says. "For example, eSchwab's per-trade revenue would be less than half that of the mainstream of the company, and that could be seen as a drain on resources rather than a response to what customers would be using in the future." Without a separate entity that has its own cost structure and own set of customers, Pottruck understood, the new initiative didn't stand a chance. Strategy determines structure and two strategies call for two structures.

There was another reason Pottruck demanded a separate structure, and it made him shiver to think about it. He was beginning to face the prospect of the new entity competing with Schwab. In Internet terms, Schwab was setting up a separate company to cannibalize the parent. It was a pattern to be repeated many times as the Net took off: Established company creates Web channel to compete with itself. It was called "eating your young" and Pottruck knew that if Schwab didn't do it to itself, someone else would be happy to oblige. "Breakneck change and a raft of Internet upstarts are threatening to overturn long-successful technologies and business models. There are two choices: Yield to your instincts and protect those still-profitable technologies and models. Or preemptively overturn them yourself, even if it means eroding the very revenue streams upon which your company is founded."

Thus a separate electronic-brokerage unit dubbed eSchwab was born. Pottruck staffed it with new talent, including Gideon Sasson, an Israeli engineer Lepore had lured away from IBM to be the team's head of technological development. The group bypassed Schwab's normal hierarchy and reported directly to Pottruck. "We had to figure out how to compete with these small brokerages," says Pottruck. "So we needed a group unshackled from the larger bureaucracy. All eyes, ears, and brains must be focused on the newborns."

A critical decision was the selection of the executive to lead the eSchwab project. Recruiting from outside Schwab was out of the question as a newcomer would never be trusted. Senior Schwab IT executives were also off-limits. They would carry too much incumbent baggage to do the outside-the-box thinking the job required. Moreover, few of the executives would resist seeing the assignment as a demotion. No, the job would have to go to someone with the following attributes: a Schwab veteran, well-liked, extremely credible, non-IT, and a rock-solid performer. When you put those attributes together, they led Pottruck straight to Beth Sawi, a trusted marketing manager who enjoyed a good relationship with apparently everyone at Schwab. Pottruck knew that such trust would be indispensable down the road. He was right. Well into the project, Sawi came to a Schwab executive management meeting and said the Schwab.com project needed a lot more money than had been budgeted. Because they trusted Sawi, the other Schwab executives each accepted small cuts in their own budgets to fund Sawi's. They all understood that getting to the Web was the priority.

Sawi set up shop in a development center physically separate from any other Schwab facilities. Her project had its own mission and a unique set of measurement criteria. The team, which grew to about 30 people, was encouraged to work in secrecy. They thought of themselves as elite and a notch sharper than the regular Schwab developers. Perhaps they were, and the sense of privilege probably helped spur their efforts, but it complicated the eventual integration of the effort.

eSchwab launched in 1996 without the customary hullabaloo Schwab attached to new product announcements. The only publicity for the launch was an announcement at the annual shareholders' meeting. The reality was that the company was ambivalent about this new channel. There was an element of caution in eSchwab's quarantine from the rest of the company. "We created eSchwab because we wanted to learn. But we did not want to risk the whole company," concedes Dan Leemon, chief strategy officer. Given the lack of fanfare, people were amazed at how quickly the new service attracted customers. In 2 weeks, people had opened 25,000 eSchwab accounts—"our goal for the entire year," says Sasson. Even though E*Trade had beaten it by over a year, Schwab quickly surpassed the upstart. By the end of 1997, the number of online accounts had grown to 1.2 million, bringing in assets of $81 billion, about ten times the assets at E*Trade. Schwab executives declared victory.

The battle with E*Trade was certainly won, but Schwab had to face a bigger obstacle: itself. In practice, eSchwab was just not very, well, Schwab-like. The good news was that once customers established an eSchwab account, they could log on to eSchwab's Web site and then trade any security available through a regular Schwab account—stocks, mutual funds, even options—and get immediate confirmation of the order. Another innovation that foreshadowed a future development: Schwab abandoned its sliding scale commission for a flat commission of $39 (quickly dropped to $29.95) for any stock trade up to 1,000 shares.

The bad news? Managing two separate channels into Schwab—one Net-driven, the other traditional—created contradictions that threatened the company's finely tuned sense of fairness. Schwab limited the access eSchwab customers had to Schwab brokers to one toll-free call per month. Schwab's regular customers, those who relied on the branches and the phone, couldn't access eSchwab at all. The people in Branchland found themselves saying "No" and "Sorry, we can't do that" far more than they wanted to. Schwab people hate saying no and they started agitating for a change in policy. Then there was the issue of the two-tiered pricing system. Traditional customers paid an average of $65 per trade; eSchwab customers paid $29.95. The pricing disparity distorted customer behavior. Some customers began keeping small sums of money with a traditional Schwab account to maintain access to live brokers, then executing their trades through eSchwab. "It was untenable," says a member of the Schwab board. "We found that customers were gaming the Schwab policies. Turning the customers into outlaws is not satisfactory."

Starting a separate Net business unit was one thing, maintaining it in parallel with an existing business was another. eSchwab, Pottruck realized, would have to be set free. If it ended up eating Schwab, so be it.

No one said cannibalization would be painless. The cleanest, most customer-friendly, most Schwab-like scenario would be for the company to give every customer online access, adopt a flat $29.95 trading commission across all its channels, and maintain the levels of in-person and over-the-phone customer service. Again, the company faced a wrenching choice. The costs of such a move were certain; the benefits a matter of conjecture. Dan Leemon's analysis demonstrated that the price cut would shave an estimated $125 million off revenues. It didn't take a rocket scientist to know that the company's high-flying stock would plummet out of orbit. With everyone at Schwab so fixated on the daily, even hourly, value of Schwab stock, it is difficult to appreciate what an immediate and fearful prospect it was to contemplate such a drop-off. Employees owned more than 40 percent of the stock. The preoccupation with the value of the stock concerned Pottruck to such an extent that at one point he ordered that all Schwab pagers be prevented from displaying the price of the stock. The point he wanted to make was that you can't play the game if you keep your eyes on the scoreboard.

Schwab had been here before. The situation was similar to what it confronted with the No-Fee IRA and Mutual Fund MarketPlace decisions, both of which traded certain losses for uncertain gains. Now the stakes were immeasurably higher. Employees worried that Web trading would result in a drop-off of business to the branches and they would be out of jobs. "Unfounded fears of being replaced or laid off did circulate among the phone reps," recalls Sherm Yee, a registered representative who joined Schwab in 1982. "But those concerns quickly dissipated when the reps saw that they were continuing to get more customer phone calls than they could handle." The board worried about revenue erosion. Even Pottruck himself wasn't quite sure of what he was doing. "I can't tell you honestly that I didn't lose a lot of sleep about it. Maybe all we're going to do is give away revenue, profit, and share price."

The company wrestled with the decision through much of 1997, a glorious year for the company. Revenues grew 24 percent to $2.3 billion. Its online trading business grew by 90 percent, adding $81 billion in assets. Online trades accounted for 37 percent of total trades, and that ratio was trending upward. As the pace of online trading accelerated, the bifurcated policy confused and annoyed clients. Pottruck came to a radical decision: All trades would be priced the same. He didn't know what that price would be, but he knew it would be low enough to make Schwab bleed. "You can't steal second base," says Pottruck, "with one foot on first." In essence, all of Schwab would become eSchwab. The first step was to enlist Chuck's support. As the largest individual shareholder (52 million shares worth some $2 billion), he would bear the brunt of the drop-off in the stock's value. That fall, Chuck heard Pottruck argue for a one-price trading scheme. Based on a number of contemporaneous sources, the conversation went like this:

POTTRUCK: We don't know exactly what will happen. The budget is shaky. We'll be winging it.

CHUCK: Are our customers being forced to make compromises they're unhappy about?

POTTRUCK: Yes.

CHUCK: Do you believe that the Schwab/eSchwab structure is sustainable for even 5 years?

POTTRUCK: No.

CHUCK: Will it ever be easier or less painful financially to put these companies together than right now?

POTTRUCK: I don't see any benefit to waiting. It will only be harder later.

CHUCK (after a fleeting pause): This isn't that hard a decision, because we really have no choice. Let's bite the bullet now.

In July 1997, a ten-member task force assembled to dovetail the old and new. Fierce arguments filled the air as the group debated a plan everyone agreed—it was the one thing on which they all did agree—would collapse revenues and instigate a cultural crisis within the firm. Now the elitism of the eSchwab team created friction within the room. Meanwhile, representatives of Schwab's incumbency mounted objections in the best tradition of incumbents protecting the status quo. Nevertheless, with Chuck's mandate filling the conference room at the St. Francis Yacht Club, there was no doubt about the outcome. Only the details were in play. Finally, a plan emerged. All of the company's electronic services would be merged into Schwab.com. It would be a complete triumph of the Web. Schwab.com would coordinate both Schwab's online as well as offline businesses. Customers would be charged $29.95 per trade whether they used the Web, a branch, or the telephone to make the order. The bricks-and-mortar branches would take on more sophisticated customer support and advice giving. It was the first articulation of Schwab's celebrated "clicks and mortar" strategy.

The task force considered the three levels of resistance to any new project: content, trust, and emotion. The content level was the easiest to deal with. Yes, the pricing move would lose the company as much as $125 million, but at least that was a known quantity. Besides, it could be demonstrated that the lost revenues could be recouped via higher transaction volume. "We knew the losses would make the Wall Street analysts nervous," said Susanne Lyons, Schwab's former president for retail client services. In response, the company consulted with the stock analysts and tried to minimize the damage. On the trust level, the decision to have Beth Sawi lead eSchwab proved decisive. She now called on the many relationships she had cultivated with people throughout the organization to build consensus for integrating the company with Schwab.com.

Schwab immediately tackled an issue that dooms many good ideas to failure: If people believe a change will mean less money in their pockets, they will sabotage the idea. Why should people in the branches be supportive of the Web? The key to making the electronic brokerage great was not the Internet interface but Schwab's branch offices. Clearly, Branchland had to have a stake in Schwab.com's success. But how? Pottruck's answer came quickly. Branch people were paid on the basis of the assets that accrued to their branches. The compensation system was changed so that they would be rewarded for directing people to the Web. It was a win-win. They would still be compensated for new assets, even when they came in via the Internet. "An amazing thing happens once you align the incentive systems," he says.

Absent such alignments, initiatives crash and burn. The economist Jeremy Bentham immediately understood this truth when he was asked to consult on a management problem with literal life-and-death implications. For many decades in the nineteenth century, England sent its convicts to Australia. The problem was the low survival rate of transported prisoners; only half the prisoners who boarded in England made it to Australia alive. Bentham solved the problem by suggesting a minor change to the contract the government had with the privately owned ship owners. Instead of the ship owner receiving payment for every prisoner who boarded the ship in England, make the payment for every prisoner who disembarked in Australia. On the first voyage under the new terms, the survival rate increased to 98 percent.

Schwab took its first step into the future on January 15, 1998. No one at Schwab was surprised to see the stock take an immediate tumble. Revenues dropped 3 percent as the average commission in the first quarter dropped to $57 from $63 the quarter before. Earnings came in $6 million short of expectations. Schwab's stock price plummeted. By late summer of 1998, Schwab's market capitalization fell by more than $2 billion (from $11.1 billion to $8.7 billion). These were not insubstantial hits. The company had prepared its troops well, although no one predicted that it would lose nearly one-third of its value before recovering. Pottruck dismissed the bad news as an artifact of a myopic market. "Wall Street is paid to recognize predictability, not breakthrough change," he says.

Just as Pottruck promised, the short-term pain harvested long-term gain. While Web trading reduced Schwab's costs, the number of trades doubled. Total accounts climbed from 3 million to 6.2 million. New assets of $51 poured in during the first 6 months of 1998 alone. The stock price stabilized, then recovered, then found new highs. By year-end, Schwab's market value had rocketed to $23 billion—more than twice its late summer low.

Less easily calculated were the opportunities it gained and avoided. In the former category, Schwab.com grabbed 42 percent of a new market that would otherwise have gone to E*Trade. In the latter, the efficiencies of the Web allowed Schwab to increase its call volumes without building new infrastructure. Without the efficiencies of "the Web dividend," the company would have had to build four new call centers and hire 1,500 more people. By the end of the year, Schwab stock not only recovered, it did something unthinkable. In December, Schwab's market capitalization surpassed that of Merrill Lynch, its staunchest rival and the personification of the traditional brokerage against which Schwab was created. For Chuck, nothing could have been sweeter.

PART THREE

Custodian of Uneasy Dreams

Balance of Power

1992-1995

His career with Schwab transformed David Pottruck from an ineffective leader into an inspired one, and he returned the favor by transforming Schwab from a struggling discount brokerage into an Internet-driven, wealth-generating business success story without parallel. A number of Schwab directors believed that Pottruck earned the right to be the chief executive officer of the company. Chuck was not one of them. Chuck and Pottruck became co-CEOs.

David Pottruck arrived at Schwab with a lot of what Chuck diplomatically labeled "East Coast baggage." He was brilliant, of that there was no doubt, but Pottruck's hard-driving personality, molded by growing up as the eldest of three boys in New York, and a management style refined by gigs at Citibank and Shearson, irritated a lot of people at Schwab. The Schwab culture was no less intense or competitive than at Pottruck's previous employers, but it demanded that displays of testosterone be downplayed. At Schwab the aggressiveness, the ambition couldn't be announced. In acting terms, you could have it, but you couldn't show it. At Schwab, above all, you acted nice, collegial, avoiding any hint of grandstanding. Pottruck came to Schwab with a streak of impetuousness, an eagerness to call a spade a spade, and a strong fondness for making wise-cracks. All three traits violated Schwab norms.

Born in Brooklyn in 1948, Pottruck was the firstborn in a Jew-ish family of four boys, in a predominantly Catholic neighbor-hood. His father was a machinist and his mother a homemaker. After the children left home, she went to college and earned a degree in nursing, inspiring in her eldest son a commitment to social activism. The Pottrucks soon joined the migration of many Jewish families leaving the crowded city in the quest for upward mobility for their children. The family moved to Levittown, Long Island, a community planned to accommodate the chil-dren of the veterans returning from World War II. "By no stretch of the imagination do I consider myself disadvantaged. Nonethe-less, my cultural uniqueness included some habit-forming ex-periences, including intense athletic competition, and the daily physical competition of three brothers," Pottruck recalls. The three Pottruck brothers were the first generation of his family to go to college. He attended the University of Pennsylvania, graduating in 1970 with a B.A. in psychology, and then going on for an M.B.A. from the Wharton School of Management in 1972. His first job was in health administration with the Depart-ment of Health, Education, and Welfare. After a stint as a man-agement consultant with Arthur Young & Co, he joined Citibank in 1976 as a division controller. In 1981, he moved to Shearson/ American Express, where he was senior vice president of con-sumer marketing and advertising.

Pottruck's first assignment when he joined Citibank in 1976 was as Barry Young's chief of staff. "At Citibank, you were ap-preciated for being as tough as you could be, giving no quarter to people you worked with," says Young, senior vice president at Citicorp from 1975–1982 and currently vice president and CFO of DisplaySearch in Austin, Texas. "It was so aggressive that you were more competitive with your coworkers at Citibank than with your competitors from other banks." The work was services management, supporting the back-office information technology requirements for the bank's accounting and check-processing activities. Eventually, Pottruck inherited a business unit that tracked revenues and other data across the entire domestic bank network. As controller for the unit, Pottruck managed a small staff in the subbasement of the Citibank building, two levels below the streets of Manhattan. He had his sights higher up, but for now he foraged for resources, protected his staff, and tried to get noticed. He would be like Citibank chairmen Walter Wriston and John Reed: tough as nails, conflict-driven, and absolutely committed to victory. Victory, he would come to learn at Schwab, takes different forms.

Citibank couldn't have been more different than Schwab. In the 1970s, under a succession of red-meat-eating chairmen, Citibank grew into the most innovative and feared bank in the country. It recruited very forceful, determined, and hungry managers to realize its own ambitious growth objectives. Citibank was known throughout the financial services industry as a breeding factory for Type A executives. The hero in Citibank lore was not the team, but the individual champion who vanquished all challengers for the crown. Walter Wriston rejected the gentlemanly culture of the banking establishment and began marketing financial services like Proctor & Gamble moved detergent. John Reed was even more deliberate about dismantling the gentlemanly culture that had long existed in banking, replacing it with a fiercely Darwinian eat-or-be-eaten jungle.

The organizations Pottruck worked for were fiercely hierarchical and conflict-driven. Rewards were for individual performance. As for teamwork, fine, but you had better be the star quarterback or the winning pitcher. Interdependence was not a highly valued concept, much less a practice. It was a world of men and it was every man for himself; workplace diversity was low on the priorities of anyone with power. "Until I joined [Schwab] in 1984, my work experience was really focused on my own learning and my own career growth," Pottruck explains in *Clicks and Mortar.* "I had worked for some great companies where the internal rules clearly encouraged individual accomplishment and internal competition for the top jobs. The cultures of these companies were expressions of the more traditional rules of business: make money, pay homage to the hierarchy, and promote yourself with hard work and exposure so that you could race your peers up the corporate ladder."

Pottruck joined Schwab in 1984, while it was still a part of Bank of America. His first assignment was marketing and branch management. He performed brilliantly in the former; less satisfactorily in the latter. It's not hard to see why. Marketing is like wrestling. You face a challenge and wrestle with it until the Big Idea surrenders itself. And in subjugating the Big Idea in the service of Schwab's retail brokerage activities, Pottruck was undefeated.

The pace of his marketing ideas was so relentless that his staff begged Pottruck for mercy. Barbara Heinrich joined Schwab in 1983 as VP of marketing, reporting to Pottruck when the entire marketing department had a total of fourteen people. "His marketing imagination was so fertile that the marketing staff was overwhelmed," she says. In self-defense, they had to develop a system to help manage the endless flow of marketing ideas emanating from the boss. The solution was to give Pottruck a pair of paddles. On one paddle was a picture of an illuminated light bulb. The other had a picture of a gun. Every time Pottruck introduced an idea he was to hold up one of the signs. The light bulb would indicate an idea for further discussion. If it was an action item, Pottruck would hold up the gun. "He listens," Heinrich says. "We were telling him that he was making it difficult for us, and he wasn't offended as other executives might have been. He used the signs."

Branch management was another nut altogether. Here Pottruck was sometimes tone deaf to the nuances of building trust, modeling sensitivity, and constructing interdependence. He was a corporate infighter rather than a team player. He viewed internal debates as battles to be won rather than opportunities to hash out important issues. He was just too . . . persuasive.

"Too persuasive? What the heck does that mean: I'm too persuasive? Am I not supposed to be persuasive?" Larry Stupski's performance appraisal caught Pottruck short. It was 1988, four years after Pottruck joined the company. "This performance evaluation marked the inflection point in my career," he says. "Larry told me that my peers didn't trust me. This was really devastating for me. I didn't understand why they didn't trust me and Larry said, 'Well, you're too persuasive.'"

Pottruck was devastated. At first he was defensive and argued, "Larry, how can a leader be too persuasive?" Pottruck marshaled his arguments, making Stupski's point. "I'm head of marketing. We're growing at 25 percent a year. I like to think some of that success is because I lead. Isn't persuasion part and parcel of leadership?"

"Well, when you want something, when you want a decision to be made a certain way, you present all the arguments for why it should happen," Stupski replied. "You never present the other side of the argument. You don't really invite people to participate in the decision. You sell them on what your decision is."

Pottruck reeled from the evaluation. He had heard Stupski say that he was a divisive executive; that he was failing as a leader. Nor was it just from Stupski. He heard it straight from Chuck—which was not easy for Chuck, given his aversion to conflict—and then from every other senior vice president who had the courage to tell the truth. "I heard my colleagues say they didn't like working with me. They said, 'You run over people. You don't leave much room for teamwork.' They said they often didn't trust my motives, and they thought I had an agenda."

Pottruck's undisguised territoriality nearly derailed the recruitment of Mark Barmann, CEO of a wholly owned subsidiary of First Interstate Bank, whom Chuck wanted to hire as chief information officer. "Everything was going well until I met with Pottruck," Barmann says. "He leaned across the table with this Greco Roman posture and told me, 'Don't think you're going to be president here!' I came away wondering if I wanted to work with such a street fighter," he recalls. Later that evening, the phone rang. "It was Pottruck, but it was a side of him I never saw at the interview. He apologized and was conciliatory. 'If I gave you the idea that you weren't welcome at Schwab, I hope you can forgive me for that was not my intention,' he told me. Pottruck's attitude allowed me to take the job and set the groundwork for a productive relationship," Barmann says. In retrospect, it's clear what happened. The company was sufficiently concerned about Pottruck's impact on recruiting that someone—probably HR manager Jim Wiggett—debriefed him after the Barmann interview. Wiggett probably helped Pottruck realize how he was perceived, hence the follow-up phone call that saved the hire. Wiggett won't confirm this sequence of events. All he will say is, "Dave is eminently coachable." Barmann was hired as CIO in 1988.

Slowly, Stupski's message sank in. Supervisors and colleagues could be outargued or outwrestled, but the facts always pin you down. His colleagues didn't trust him. Pottruck's life at home was filled with turmoil. His second marriage broke up. Pottruck took a good look at himself and he didn't like what he saw. He began therapy, seeking to understand how a man who seemingly had it all together could feel so out of control. "I needed to examine the extent to which my ego was driving my behavior," Pottruck said. With the help of a number of therapists, coaches, and friends, Pottruck disassembled his life and started building constructs that served him more faithfully. Pottruck began to pay more attention to the language that he used, the risks he took, and the ways he conducted himself. Meanwhile, he struggled.

Pottruck decided he needed to rethink his assumptions about leadership—a management makeover, if you will. He hired Terry Pearce, a former IBM executive turned management coach and communications consultant to executives. Pearce offered to guide Pottruck through a complete reexamination of what Pottruck knew about leadership, competition, and every other aspect of dealing with people. Pearce started by asking Pottruck to write an autobiography. Pottruck delivered more than 300 pages. "Terry said he wanted to learn the 'defining moments' of my life, to help him discover my values," Pottruck recalls. What Pearce wanted, of course, were the stories that we all tell about ourselves and use as an excuse to limit our possibilities.

Pottruck threw himself into renegotiating his life with the same frenzy he did everything else. Nothing was out of bounds. It was easy to examine his heroes, such as Senator John McCain (R-Arizona), who was shot down over Vietnam and held as a prisoner-of-war in Hanoi for more than 5 years and overcame physical injuries to run for president. And Don Gable, the great University of Iowa wrestler, who lost only one wrestling match in his entire college career. "He out-trained and out-worked everybody he ever competed against," Pottruck said. As an executive, that's what Pottruck did too—and he didn't let up even after his style cost him two marriages. As for his staff, "I emitted a vibe of 'don't come to me with your problems.'"

He faced his struggles with Stupski and Chuck in the context of his battles with early authority figures. Pottruck began to accept that he was responsible for all the decisions he made in his past but he was not limited by them. "It was like being on the inside of a box when the instructions are on the outside of the box, and you can't do anything because you're stuck on the inside," Pottruck says, describing the learning process. "So I realized I had to change if I was going to be more effective; that was the first thing I had to do.

Pottruck became convinced that the old take-no-prisoners, domineering style of management wouldn't work in the new economy, where success, more than ever, depended on people. "I needed to change and recognize that it was no longer appropriate for me to behave in the way I did when I was younger." Painstakingly, he began to take baby steps in trying on behaviors that seemed so odd: that there are other ways to get what he wants than by pinning someone to the ground; that interdependence actually offers more security than doing it yourself; that team building works better than divide and conquer; that leaders who are willing to be led are more likely to build loyalty than those who issue fiats from above.

Pottruck's learning continued. He wanted to be an inspired leader like Chuck. He watched Chuck lead by having more questions than answers. Ordinary leaders have answers. Inspired leaders have questions and understand that letting subordinates figure out the answers is sometimes more important than the answers themselves. Ordinary leaders contract for employees' time and effort. Inspired leaders know that people will work for money, but they'll give you a piece of their lives for meaning. Ordinary leaders seek team players. Inspired leaders seek allies. Ordinary leaders allow employees to keep growing. Inspired leaders care by kicking employees up to the next rung in their personal ladder of evolution. Ordinary leaders challenge employees by always being better. And this was the hardest lesson of all: The most daring way inspired leaders challenge employees is by being wrong, by occasionally losing arguments, and by acknowledging when they are wrong.

Much of the work Pottruck did with Pearce is described in *Clicks and Mortar: Passion Driven Growth in an Internet Driven World,* a book they coauthored in 2001. For a business book, it is uncommonly self-disclosing. One of the episodes most revealing about Pottruck's state of mind, the difficulties he faced, and the learning he embraced, concerns his dating a Schwab employee. He had just divorced his second wife. "My presumption coming out of two failed marriages was that I had a 'wife selection' problem. Clearly, I should not get married again because I couldn't trust my selection skills," he says. But that thinking leads to a dead-end. Pottruck didn't want to stay single for the rest of his life, so part of his therapy was to sort through why he was having so much trouble picking a suitable partner. "What I came to learn was that I didn't have a wife selection problem. I had a husband behavior problem," he says.

After his divorce, Pottruck began dating Emily Scott, a Schwab employee four levels of management removed from his circle of management. Now he couldn't understand why Chuck was picking on him and telling him he couldn't date any Schwab employees. Pottruck's first temptation was to bristle at the unfairness and feel singled out. After all, other Schwab employees were involved with each other, and some had married. But something inside Pottruck had definitely shifted, for he stopped arguing and accepted that he was wrong and Chuck was right. Chuck had explained his reasoning to Pottruck like this: "I don't want people in the company spending their time speculating about your relationship with an employee when they should be doing their work. You're a visible guy and it's just not right." Pottruck nodded in agreement. "Later, when I thought over Chuck's message, I came to realize he was right. The rules for me as president of the company were different from the rules for other people. They were tougher. Even though the woman— Emily, my wife—was pretty far removed from my circle of daily contacts in the company, it was difficult for people who dealt with her daily not to think, in the back of their minds, about her pipeline to the boss. She and I have talked about it since, of course, and it was difficult for her as well. It created a real problem for her manager, trying not to treat her special, but knowing that she was dating a top executive. All these issues made the situation turn on more complex ideas than just being single and available," he says.

Pottruck's coworkers watched with amazement at his self-transformation. "He's flat out the best learner I ever met," says a Schwab colleague. "I didn't think it was possible for people to change that much. I give Dave a lot of credit for showing himself." Pottruck developed a new sense of authenticity. "I watched David transform himself into the heart and soul of the company," says Barbara Heinrich. "People who were personally touched by Chuck felt his warmth. But Chuck could never articulate the guiding principles of the company on the large scale that by 1990 the company demanded. It was left for Dave to do that. Dave's contribution is his ability to vocalize and embody the Schwab culture and scale it from 300 employees to 20,000 employees. That is his legacy."

Pottruck emerged as a brilliant and emotional speaker. Jim Losi was running advertising when it was time for the company to launch a network TV advertising campaign. "We were struggling to create a sense of the brand and what the company stands for. We had never done it before and we had only one opportunity to do it right," he says. "Despite the fact that Dave had very strong opinions about advertising, rather than being dictatorial, he encouraged a group of smart people to craft the advertising strategy." Out of those meetings, came Schwab's first network advertising campaign. Two brilliant conclusions came out of this work. First, the decision to feature actual Schwab employees, not actors, to communicate the company's key promise to customers. And what was that key promise? To help investors take control of their own lives and their own futures, to serve as a catalyst, and to help make a difference. With Pottruck's facilitation, the promise found perfect expression: helping investors help themselves.

He had to set aside much of his earlier training. Pottruck recalled the way he prepared for speeches: "My staff and I would rehearse the answers to questions that we thought were likely to come from an audience, and then during the 'performance,' our measure of success was whether we had correctly anticipated the questions. Of course, the intention of that drill was to look good and 'fend off,' not to really engage. Pretty dumb."

The old Pottruck, for example, would have pushed through a badly conceived program to open branches for extended hours on weekends despite the objections of the branch managers. He would have dismissed employee resistance to relocating to a recently opened call center in Denver. If he did talk to the branch managers, the old Pottruck would have laid out the reasons why the moves were good for the customers. If employees had objections, he would listen only to find the flaws in their arguments. In his 1995 book about effective leadership, *Leading Out Loud*, Terry Pearce describes what happened next. While he does not identify this episode with Pottruck by name, Pearce is clearly referring to the Schwab controversy. Pottruck was about to address 200 Schwab branch managers. The first draft of the speech Pottruck wanted to give went like this:

> I am excited about speaking with you tonight regarding the changes we have planned. Saturday hours and the new concentration in the mountain states will make us even more responsive to our customers. As we grow into the next decade, we will be seeing similar changes for the same reason—to serve our customers better while we provide more leverage for our own growth.

Nothing awful about this approach, but the enlightened Pot-truck considered what he really wanted. In marketing terms, what was the bid for action? After this speech, what he would get from branch managers would be compliance. Pottruck wanted much more. He wanted everyone to commit themselves to something bigger than extended branch hours, something bigger than themselves. He wanted the branch managers to commit themselves to each other. The only way to do that was to make himself vulnerable. Pottruck began his reworked remarks like this:

> When I decided to speak to all of you about these changes, I was quite excited. As you know, we have been considering both relocation to the mountain states and opening the branches for a few hours on Saturday for some time.
>
> But as I reflected on the impact of these changes, it occurred to me that the relocation did not require me to move from my home, and, in fact, I was not going to work any more hours on Saturday than I already do. My kids are used to my irregular hours, yet I still value my time with their sports teams and the other weekend time we have together. For many of you, an occasional Saturday away from the family will be something new, and certainly, these changes will cause some disruption.
>
> It also occurred to me that I wasn't going to be telling my staff about moving or working Saturdays. Rather, I get to address the big issues, while you will be conveying the news to individuals and dealing with their very specific questions.
>
> Given these thoughts, I quickly realized that you might not be as excited about these moves as I am, even though these changes are for the good of the company and ultimately will create more opportunity for all of us.

"These changes did nothing to alter the logical content of the talk of the eventual action of the managers," comments Pearce, yet the new version set an entirely different tone for the speech, and required something entirely new from the executive." As for Pottruck, he was delighted that the feedback he received was more appreciative about the caring part of his remarks than the content regarding the changes. He says, "People wanted to be heard and acknowledged."

By 1992, the year of Stupski's heart attack, the company was too big and complex for Chuck to manage, and Chuck was the first to acknowledge that reality. For almost 10 years, Chuck had delegated increasing responsibility for running the business to Stupski. Chuck was comfortable operating as a visionary and an evangelizer, dispensing Big Ideas for his team to implement. Pottruck's management makeover was working, and he was enjoying positive working relationships with his colleagues, including Stupski, for the first time in years. Stupski's heart attack set Pottruck up for an uneasy ride. On the one hand, the heart attack created a leadership vacuum into which Pottruck diligently stepped. On the other hand, it denied Pottruck critical years of Stupski's coaching, additional experience, and seasoning. It ensured that Chuck wouldn't think Pottruck ready when it was time for him to lead the company.

In the wake of Stupski's heart attack, Chuck stepped up to the plate and, with Pottruck's assistance, took over the day-to-day management of the company. Many observers didn't think that Chuck was up to it, but he did a great job until Stupski recovered and returned to his post as president and COO. Everyone at the company let out the breath that they had collectively held since the heart attack and waited to see what would happen next.

Crisis always recalibrates the norm. Remember Joe Cutcliffe's four stages of organizational growth—Form, Storm, Norm, and Perform—described in Chapter 13? Before the heart attack, the company had been operating in stage four. Now the company was back to stage one. It was impossible for everyone to take their old roles, so new roles would have to be negotiated. Stupski came back with doctor's orders to take it easier; clearly some of his responsibilities would have to be offloaded to others. Moreover, Stupski was now an apostle for fitness and balance, telling people to leave at 5 o'clock, reminding them to be with their families on weekends. Noble sentiments to be sure, but Schwab culture still rewarded performance and, truth be told, Chuck was concerned. Stupski was just not the same after the heart attack. Chuck was at once concerned that Stupski didn't have the fire in the belly anymore, and if he did, the fire would kill him.

Chuck took his concerns to Cutcliffe. The bottom line: He didn't want the new improved Stupski at the helm of his company. He wanted the old, hard-driving Stupski. And if he couldn't have that, he wanted another COO. Growth is what Chuck wanted. With $750 million in revenues in 1992, the company was on the very brink of the multi-billion-dollar greatness Chuck coveted. The last thing he wanted was a COO advocating moderation. But any attempt to replace Stupksi so soon after his heart attack would tear the company apart. Chuck asked Cutcliffe for help in preparing his company for new leadership and identifying a new role for Stupski.

Cutcliffe went to work. He set up breakfasts, and off-line dialogues, meeting one-on-one with every Schwab executive. The main challenge was helping everyone through the denial that some important decisions needed to be made, decisions that would be wrenching for the company. There were three main decisions: One, was it time for the company to have a new president? Two, who should that president be? Three, what role would there be for Stupski? A fourth question should have been asked, but was not: Could a change in Chuck's role make sense for the company? Specifically, was it time for Chuck to name himself chairman of the company, opening up the CEO role for the next leader to bring the company into the twenty-first century?

Over the next year, the company struggled with a set of decisions everyone knew would roil the company. Corporate America had evolved a formula for handling these issues, and with the Stupski issue, Schwab dutifully followed convention: The company created the role of vice chairman, a title which Stupski willingly accepted. His health scare had inspired in Stupski a renewed interest in philanthropy; his new role would afford him more time for community service. The decision about the number two role in the company was harder. Chuck considered three or four people within the company, and even toyed with the possibility of recruiting someone from outside the organization. Every sign pointed for Chuck to give the nod to Pottruck. Any other move would surely make Pottruck bolt. The trouble is, in Chuck's mind, Pottruck wasn't ready. Could he bring the steady hand to balance Chuck's disengaged visionary approach? Could Chuck trust him? As a leader, Pottruck was making steady progress, but his rough edges and bad boy behaviors continued to raise serious questions in Chuck's mind. Cutcliffe organized an off-site retreat so that, once and for all, the issues could be worked out, reporting structures aligned, and responsibilities distributed.

In 1994, the company announced the main changes. Larry Stupski stepped down as president and became vice chairman. David Pottruck assumed the responsibilities of president and chief operating officer. Chuck retained the title of chief executive officer in addition to chairman. As the company approached its twentieth anniversary in the spring of 1994, Schwab customers held over $100 billion of assets in 2.5 million customer accounts. Revenues had surpassed $1 billion for the first time. The company, this "safe haven," where investors could find only the kind of products that Chuck would buy for his family and friends, had a new leadership structure. It was, everyone understood, a temporary solution that ignored the ultimate question of Chuck's long-term relationship with the company. The CEO role was sitting there, like the elephant in the room that no one acknowledged.

And as for the inevitable conflicts, well, they were inevitable and worse than Chuck imagined. Barbara Wolfe, chief administrative officer, refused to work for Pottruck. She was with Chuck when he founded the company in 1974 and she felt that would protect her, but she was wrong. Chuck is, above all, a realist, and he was backing the best candidate he had. Wolfe was offered a position at the Schwab Foundation but chose to resign.

For 23 years, Chuck had been the sole and undisputed monarch at Charles Schwab Corp. Now 5 years had gone by, 5 years in which Pottruck had matured as a leader and under whose stewardship Schwab had tripled to revenues of $2.3 billion in 1997 from $75 million in 1992. Since Pottruck has become president, the company's stock price has rocketed more than tenfold.

Chuck had set a high bar for Pottruck, and he outperformed in every way. He helped navigate Schwab to a dominant position on the Internet, the most exciting development the retail brokerage business had seen since the company was founded. His fingerprints were on every part of the company, from the monumentally successful AdvisorSource program to Schwab's increasing presence in the retirement plan market. With Chuck increasingly preoccupied with visionary duties and activities such as writing his book, *Charles Schwab's Guide to Financial Independence: Simple Solutions for Busy People,* Pottruck had been operating in every respect like a chief executive officer. Now it was time for Pottruck to be rewarded with what he indisputably earned: a shot at the chief executive officer role. It was time, many board members believed, for Chuck to make himself chairman of the company he founded almost a quarter century earlier.

Except it didn't happen. When it came time for Chuck, now 60 years old, to step back and give a new generation of leadership a chance, he blinked. He couldn't let go of the CEO role. During these years, a confidant had brought up the possibility—just the possibility—of Chuck taking the role of chairman. "I got a swift reaction, a no and a hell no. It was clear to me that, for Chuck, "chairman" is a titular role. This was his legacy. He would retain the leverage of staying the CEO," he says. The company announced that Chuck's second in command, David Pottruck, president and chief operating officer of the San Francisco discount broker, would get the additional title of co-chief executive, effective January 1, 1998. It was the lousiest decision of Chuck's career.

Schwab Mythology

1974–present

In the quiet hours, Schwab people celebrate the origins of their company and the stories that guided their corporate destinies and filled their work lives with meaning. Now, as the company dismantles critical elements of those old stories to build a new culture, it is finding how resistant to change even myths that no longer serve can be.

Every company manufactures stories about itself along with the products and services it builds. These stories tell people inside and outside the organization what it believes to be true, what it accepts as right and wrong, where the company starts and where it ends. A company's culture is the sum of the stories, myths, and legends it has cultivated. Schwab puts enormous resources into identifying, focusing, and cultivating its once and future stories, legends, and rituals. By "once and future," I mean the stories that not only describe the events that happened but also inform the events yet to be.

Call it mythological property. Akin to the concept of intellectual property—any product of the human experience that is unique, novel, unobvious, and has some value in the marketplace—mythological property may be an organization's most valuable yet least understood asset. While an organization may own and control its creativity and innovation in the same way that it can own and control its physical assets, it is far from clear that an organization can own or control mythological property. More likely, its mythological property owns and controls the organization.

The word *myth* derives from the ancient Greek *muthos*, which means to "murmur with closed lips, to mutter, to moan." And what is to be muttered or moaned? Those are the stories, legends, and tales about the beginnings of things. From start to finish, the Schwab experience is filled with myths, legends, stories, and rituals that uplift it and weigh it down. For the most part, they are a blessing. Occasionally they are an obstacle. Like most companies, Schwab finds it hard to distinguish between the two.

Here's the tricky thing about a company putting myth to work: We all live inside a culture; we don't see it because it is given. It is the water fish swim in. We don't know who invented water, but we can be pretty sure it wasn't a fish. In the same way, it's risky for humans to manipulate myth. The myths that define Schwab's shared purpose, the "nonnegotiable tenets against which we measure the worthiness of our choices" are two-edged swords. If Schwab does not acknowledge that its "mythological property" is a resource that imposes costs as well as benefits, the company risks being overpowered by its own invented legend.

Mythology at Schwab runs deep, much deeper than at most other organizations not yet even 30 years old, much deeper than even the cultural anthropologists within Schwab can realize. Schwab myth has definitely sustained the company on more than one occasion. It was the sacred narrative and the joined destinies of the Schwab family that kept the company from spinning out of

244 of CUSTODIAN OF UNEASY DREAMS

control during the various crises described earlier in the book. Schwab's mythic vision has allowed employees to step back from their own personal fears to catch a glimpse of something bigger than themselves to which they could dedicate their energies. This is the abiding benefit of Schwab's mythological property.

The most powerful myths all revolve around a common center. In the case of Charles Schwab & Co, the center of the universe is Chuck Schwab. There is nothing remarkable about this development. It would be more noteworthy if it weren't so, given that Schwab is an example of a founder culture. As human beings, we have a strong need to create community, build norms, and evoke eternal truths about timeless opposites such as good and evil, birth and death, now and then, and most important, us and them. Our organizations are built to help us find our places along those continuums. We look to leaders who have fixed their own positions to better help us find our own.

Chuck Schwab happens to display the characteristics that absolutely require a community to construct prodigious quantities of myth and legend. The words people use to describe him are invariably the same: quiet, shy, small of stature, wise of heart, remote, aloof, introverted, disengaged, passionate, emotional, grown-up, good-hearted, paternal, generous. His name and face are bigger than life, on every advertisement and building. These conditions provide a nutritious foundation for the mythological representation of the Schwab culture.

Corporate culture of founder companies is always a function of the founder. Had Chuck been cocky and charismatic, like Steve Jobs, then Schwab culture might resemble that of Apple. Had be been more physically aggressive and authoritarian, the Schwab culture would be much different, perhaps akin to the ruthless environment that founder Charles Wang built at Computer Associates International. Had he been younger and more intellectual, perhaps we'd see a culture like the one that grew up around Bill Gates at Microsoft. Were he more extroverted and fantasy-oriented, perhaps Schwab's culture would come to look like Disney's. But Chuck was Chuck and that has made all the difference.

By serendipity, and later with more intention, Schwab began its journey as a constructor of myths and legends. It starts, as all things do, at the beginning. There is a belief among many cultures that unless the origin of something can first be enshrined, one should not even talk about it. Telling a story about how things began, from the origin of the universe to the starting point of individual human lives, is a way of paying respect to its importance. Schwab enjoys the lucky break of having an exceptional origin story. It breaks down into a number of dichotomies.

Good and bad. Chuck was the good guy, the guy with the white hat, battling the forces of darkness, standing up for the little guy against the elites. We see these themes played out in literature as well as popular culture: *High Noon, Star Wars, The Magnificent Seven.* Schwab was the company that would end persistent inequalities based on class, gender, race, and sexual orientation in the financial services industry.

Old and new. The distinction between the way it is and the way it was. There is that magic day to separate the sacred and the profane. Few companies have origins one can fix in time. Can Microsoft people tell you the date of its formation? Does anyone care? How about E*Trade? But every Schwabbie knows the date by heart. May 1, 1975, the day the universe started.

Big and small. Schwab was Samson to the Philistines of Wall Street. Chuck was David to Merrill Lynch's Goliath. Yes. Once Schwab was small. Now it is big. But the legend operates to make it hard for Schwab to view itself as the significant company it is. To the extent the company persists in seeing itself as the little guy, the legend becomes a roadblock to Schwab leveraging its scale.

Up and down. The ancient legends of Schwab were all cemented by the triumphant highs followed in quick succession by perilous lows. Myth is easy to nourish when a history of crisis exists, because all crises require heroes who brought the company back from the brink. Chuck frequently occupies the role of hero, but occasionally finds it useful to cede that role temporarily to people we have met in the course of this narrative.

Young and old. Chuck was thirty-eight years old in 1975. For the original Schwabbies, especially those not in daily contact with him, Chuck seemed impossibly old. Most of the people Chuck hired in the early days were young, little more than kids. Many came to Schwab as a substitute for a college education, and they saw in Chuck a very definite mentor, often the only adult they respected. He was ancient, powerful yet unknowable, like Zeus on Olympus. For them, Chuck could do no wrong. When the company was in trouble, Chuck would always know the right thing to do. From this the stuff of legend is made.

Here and there. The entrepreneurial and spiritual attributes of San Francisco are deeply enmeshed in the organization and are best expressed in Schwab's commitment to doing right, diversity, tolerance, philanthropy, and social activism. Deeply skeptical about authority, the Schwabbies loved Chuck for his absolute commitment to doing well by doing good without being authoritarian about it. These practices, in turn, kept customers coming back again and again to Schwab when the company failed to deliver.

Us and them. Us versus them is the critical way communities define themselves because it defines the all-important question of membership. The difficulties of navigating the who's in and who's out issue haunt us in every organization from kindergarten to the board of directors. We never outgrow it. Much of the company's us-against-them culture can be traced to the company's acquisition by the Bank of America in the early 1980s. The skirmishes that took place between the two mismatched cultures are the basis of countless stories about how Schwab succeeded in maintaining its purity. The "Free at Last" buttons that Schwabbies wore when the company was again independent underscored its commitment to realign around a core set of the old principles.

The us-against-them stories a firm tells itself are critical for another reason: recruitment. This worldview sets up a company's success or failure in its recruitment of outside talent. Every company must have a core group with enough institutional memory to protect the integrity of the company. But it must also be open enough to accommodate newcomers who share the vision and, occasionally, newcomers who don't. Every company struggles with this issue. It's not hard to see why Schwab's difficulties with this issue have probably been more intense than other companies. From the beginning, Schwab culture has internalized its us-against-them legend. In addition, Chuck limited the number of people who had access to him, further setting up a competition to be in the inner circle. Today, executives recruited from outside the company face formidable barriers being assimilated into the community. The short tenure of executives hired after 1995 is evidence that the company has a problem with fully embracing the people it invites to join the cause.

Unless organizations develop a process to become aware of the myths that are running it, they run the risk of being consumed. This is happening to Schwab. All myths were true at some point; all had survival value for the company. But it's important that they be reexamined every once in a while to see if they still fit. "We need to reinvent our stories from time to time," says the philosopher Sam Keen. "The stories we tell of ourselves determine who we become, who are we, what we believe."

Running the underdog story continues to be important at Schwab. Yes, in its early days, the company definitely took its lumps from a brutal establishment. It was hard to get office space, seats on the exchanges, or even a place at the table. It's true that the company's identification with the average investor, the little guy, fits hand in glove with its image of itself as the perennial runner-up. It's reinforced by San Francisco's up-yours nonconformity. The underdog story was useful for building the brand. It moved people to stick together and work incredibly hard. But it's time to face facts. By no yardstick can Schwab be considered an underdog. In 1999, its Schwab market capitalization surpassed that of Merrill Lynch.

The downside of Schwab's underdog story is that it maintains an us-against-them energy that imposes obstacles on the company's ability to recruit outside talent and to nurture and sustain partnerships. It contributes to the continuing turmoil at the top of the organization. It explains the difficulty of the company to recruit top talent and, once recruited, to integrate them into the company. Combined with the legend about Schwab being a San Francisco company, this attitude is particularly off-putting to executives from New York.

The costs to Schwab of maintaining the us-against-them story are huge. It distorts a number of the company's principles. For example, the us/them energy interferes with the company's commitment to an innovation meritocracy where great ideas win out no matter where they come from. In reality, the company's need for control means if the idea doesn't come from a place approved by legend, it has a hard time finding an ear. Another example of this legend in action is the "What would Chuck say?" argument that Schwab people trot out when they feel threatened by a proposal. The problem is, this shorthand has nothing to do with Chuck, but becomes an unimpeachable tactic for cutting off conversation or rejecting inconvenient ideas out of hand.

Of course, Schwab's legends have the benefit of defining the company's core values and grounding the company in unchanging principles. But what happens to unchanging principles when they no longer serve? We saw Schwab struggle with the consequences of its original principles against giving advice or selling. All organizations find it hard to reexamine let alone abandon cherished principles. But many have an easier time of it than Schwab precisely because the Schwab values are so enforced by unspoken myth. In this context, embracing change is doubly difficult because the unspoken myths raise the ante on the debate. On a subconscious level, one's challengers become not only shortsighted, misguided, or misinformed but may be perceived as bad or even evil. This formulation creates the condi-

tions for protracted conflict because it escalates simple disagreements into battles of morality.

Schwab is working diligently with ritual and metaphor to craft
new legends to replace the old. In 1999, Schwab staged an elaborate ritual called VisionQuest in which every Schwab employee
around the world crafted elaborate maps to depict the current
state of the industry and Schwab's role in it. Over the course of
a day, more than 20,000 Schwab people worked with these maps
and a group of facilitators to gain a personal experience of the
vision and values of the company and to rededicate themselves
to sharing and shaping the combined purpose of the company.

As we saw in Chapter 5, Schwab created MarketStorm as a
ritual for the frenetically busy weeks when the entire country
was trading like mad. Part of this ritual requires that each of the
Schwab executives be licensed to answer phones and take trades.
It is part of Schwab's legend that every person pitches in.
MarketStorm participation reinforces these values. It doesn't
matter that it can never be economically justified to have phones
answered by executives pulling down half a million dollars per
year. But legend requires it, and woe to those who do not understand the requirement.

Myths are living entities and that makes them notoriously
difficult to replace. Schwab is determined to create a new set of
myths to support its recognition that a new class of wealthy investors wants not only much more advice of all kinds but expects Schwab to actively sell all manner of new products and
services. The problem is that the mythic is everywhere, and most
often appears when and where it is least expected.

The company grew up with the myth of empowering the average investor, helping investors help themselves, leveling the
playing field between us and them. The company grew successful by doing just that and earned enormous moral capital from
both customers and employees in doing so. Shifts in demographics made it imperative for Schwab to cultivate wealthy investors even as it distances itself from average customers. This
shift would be traumatic for any organization, but it is more so

for Schwab due to the deep-seated commitment people have to preserve the perceived culture. In large measure, the only way the company moved forward on this agenda is by systematically replacing the people in the branches who lived and breathed the old values. That's a pretty costly fix.

We saw throughout the book how difficult it has been for Schwab to find its path along the no-conflict-of-interest principle. The company originally articulated that value in the formula, "Thou shalt not give advice." For many years, the company enforced the no-sales imperative in an effort to end the addiction to advice giving that many traders brought to the company. One reason Schwab hired so many people without securities industry experience is to avoid that trap. But dogma is hard to put aside; even when it no longer serves it resists realignment to fit new cultural needs. The company's position that it's possible to provide advice without conflict of interest is correct and logical. But logic finds little foothold against faith, and even less against market realities.

So, too, the admonition against selling. The rule against selling wasn't just another rule, it was taboo. It grew out of the legend that Schwab would corrupt itself, like all the other brokerages routinely did, because selling securities turned honest people into . . . well, securities salespeople. The structural policy that Schwab representatives would be compensated by salary, not commission, also helped align the interests of customers and the company. It set up very tight teamwork at the branches because everyone shared in the pot. That is the legend and Schwab people are sticking with it, no matter how much it makes sense for the company to embrace some limited forms of sales and compensate people by the volume of assets they individually bring into the company. Revolutions happen when people's dogmas are upset. Again, Schwab found it could advance its agenda in this area only by systematically replacing people.

It's a messy process, this myth business. A company manipulates its own identity when it tinkers with its myths, no matter how necessary that becomes. However, it is imperative that a company see the stories it actually lives by so it can determine if particular myths are working for it or against it.

Unfinished Business

2002–Forward

In the end, Chuck abdicated his responsibility. By insisting on sharing the CEO title, instead of accepting the chairman role reality has persistently tailored for him, Chuck has failed the main test of a leader. For all of Chuck's accomplishments—and his place at the table of business visionaries of the first order is secure—he has been unable to transcend the limitation that has snared almost every company led by its founder.

Succession is perhaps the most critical responsibility of a leader. The reality is that Chuck has repeatedly stepped away from this responsibility. In this area, the Schwab board of directors has failed, as well.

On the subject of succession, Chuck refuses to engage. "The whole issue of Schwab's transition away from Chuck has not been dealt with," a source close to the board says in that passive voice that passive boards favor. One has only to look at the makeup of the Schwab board to see that this is true. The board has an audit committee, a compensation committee, and a customer quality assurance committee. Significantly, the Schwab board does not have a nominating committee, the venue where strategic succession issues traditionally get discussed. When a board member periodically inquires about why the company does not have a nominating committee, Chuck simply says, "I don't want one" and then changes the subject, according to the source. "Look, Chuck is an icon. It's his name on the door. He has a hard time letting go and is clearly in denial about this. Chuck continues to feel an enormous responsibility for his legacy," he explains.

In their attempt to protect their legacy, founders invariably damage it. Of course, if it were only their legacy at risk, that would be one thing. But a leader's inability to deal with the succession issue has consequences for investors, employees, and the management team. "When all is said and done," says John C. Maxwell in *The 21 Irrefutable Laws of Leadership,* "a leader's legacy is judged not by what you achieved personally or even by what your team accomplished during your tenure. You will be judged by how well your people and your organization did after you were gone. Your lasting value will be measured by succession." Schwab has a number of pieces of unfinished business on its plate, but the succession issue dominates them all and makes their successful implementation more difficult.

Chuck's unwillingness to take himself out of operating responsibility has had painful consequences for the company throughout its history. In the early years, he delayed acknowledging that others were more suited to managing the company than he was. In those earlier episodes, the scale of the company and Chuck's personal charisma made the resulting consequences manageable. Today, the stakes are much higher and Chuck is at an age where many companies enforce retirement. The company is simply not prepared for a post-Chuck reality.

Chuck's inability to deal with the inevitability of a Charles Schwab & Co. without him has created an awkward situation for the board and a toxic environment for the executive management of the company. The dynamics at the executive committee level has become so distorted by Chuck's insistence on sharing the co-CEO title with Pottruck that recruitment is difficult, retention problematic, and healthy executive development unnecessarily challenging.

Pottruck continues to pay the burden of Chuck's determination to keep the CEO role. How long will Pottruck put up with the situation? "Pottruck will leave before Chuck does," a senior Schwab manager observes. "He wants a shot at running a company and he's not going to get it at Schwab." Moreover, the lack of confidence that Chuck's decision demonstrates, makes it difficult for Pottruck to show confidence in the people that report to him. Pottruck has a hard time trusting others, when it's so clear that Chuck does not trust him. Having hit a glass ceiling, Pottruck is hypersensitive to anyone approaching from below. The result has been a revolving door at the number three position, resulting in subpar bench strength on executive row.

In 1995, the company hired an outsider, Timothy F. McCarthy, to rescue Schwab's money funds business. Schwab had a huge exposure following the default of bonds issued by Orange County, California. SchwabFunds, the company's money fund product, was in jeopardy of "breaking the buck," falling below its $1 share price, an almost unheard of event in the money funds industry and one not acceptable to Chuck, whose name, after all, was on the funds. In the end, Chuck fronted a $100 million guarantee from the brokerage division to shore up Schwab-Funds. It was a gutsy move because if the guarantee had been called, the viability of the entire company would have been on the line. As it was, Schwab could make such a guarantee because Chuck was sufficiently politically connected to understand that, in the end, Sacramento would bail Orange County out. Chuck's political performance was excellent. But by any standards of risk management, Schwab's performance in the money funds arena in the mid-1990s was a fiasco. McCarthy, a veteran of the securities industry with a reputation for cleaning up messes, restored credibility to SchwabFunds. His reward: Pottruck named McCarthy president and CEO of Charles Schwab & Company.

In naming McCarthy president of the brokerage company, Pottruck passed over Tom Seip, the architect of OneSource, and a 15-year veteran of Schwab with experience in virtually every area of the company, including retail, operations, institutional, mutual funds, information technology, human resources, and international. Some members of the board favored Seip for the president of the brokerage division, but Pottruck argued that promoting McCarthy, an outsider, created possibilities for the infusion of new ideas. "It was a very tough decision because Tom expressed interest in being president of the brokerage and had prepared himself well for the challenge," a former member of the board muses. "Looking back on the matter, it is clear the better course would have been to promote Tom." The opportunity that Pottruck offered Seip—to go back to mutual funds—was in every respect a demotion.

When he heard the news that he lost the race to be president of the brokerage company, Tom Seip felt his world collapse. He felt the sting of failure and the shame of humiliation. His first impulse was blame others and then to blame himself. What else was there to do but quit? Nine out of ten executives in his shoes would have resigned on the spot. But then Seip changed his mind and accepted McCarthy as his boss. It was a remarkable demonstration of how Schwab culture can inspire long-time employees to subordinate their personal ambitions in the service of a higher goal. In this case, that goal was loyalty to Chuck, admiration for the Schwab cause, and an elitist's certainty that working anywhere else would be a step down.

On October 16, 1977, Tom Seip addressed the Charles Schwab Senior Management Team at an off-site retreat in Burlingame, California. Tim McCarthy had recently been named president and speculation about the futures of Seip and John Coghlan, another senior executive, was rampant. It was a remarkable speech for two reasons. First, in its level of personal detail and private anguish, the speech was uncharacteristically frank. Second, students of Schwab politics and culture can find in Seip's speech nuggets of detail that speak to broad cultural dynamics and specific personal relationships. Pottruck thought Seip's speech so remarkable that in *Clicks and Mortar* he devoted four pages to an edited version of it. Because the speech gives readers a rare glimpse into the inner circle of Schwab, I am reproducing Seip's speech in its entirety, with my annotations in brackets. Note that Seip uses ellipses for effect; they do not indicate that material has been omitted.

Two weeks ago, Dave asked me if I would speak to the group this morning, and frankly, I was surprised. It just had never occurred to me, but then we talked a bit about potential elephants in the room during this meeting. For those of you who are new [to Schwab] we refer to "the elephant in the room" as the unasked, unanswered question on everyone's mind. In this case, perhaps there are some elephants regarding me and perhaps about John Coghlan [enterprise president for institutional services]. So John and I had a conversation and agreed there were some things worth saying that could be instructive to this audience.

We've been talking about our challenges and opportunities for the last 2 days, and I think by now we all agree we needed this change [Tim McCarthy's appointment as president] in organization. That said, I would not for one moment want you to believe that I didn't want the job that Tim is now doing. I did. I thought about it a lot, and I was terribly disappointed when I did not get the job. I was at first angry, of course, and because I was raised like you were, to put tremendous value on where I was positioned in the hierarchy, it was a fairly significant blow to my self-esteem. And to the degree my identity is linked to my job, the answer to the question, "Who am I?" in this case comes back very quickly, "You are not the President." And so now what?

And I had to deal with that; not only for myself, but for my wife and family. As most of you know, my wife is a former employee who worked for both John Coghlan and Jim Hackley [executive vice president, retail branch network], and, of course, John's wife, Patte, is also a former employee. Many of our friends were introduced through Schwab. So the implications of being, quote, "passed over," seemed to be social and personal. [Here we see the blurring of work and personal lives at Schwab; they were very much intermixed.]

And, for me, there was the issue of how all of you would perceive me. That, by the way, was the biggest hurdle. In a sense, I felt I had somehow let you all down, and that this was one glaring sign of it that I could never recover from. That idea was nearly unbearable. There was a part of me that just wanted to disappear.

But I didn't. And I wanted you all to know why. Why I've made the decisions as I have.

When Dave [Pottruck] was made President, after Larry's health emergency [even 5 years later, Seip was reluctant to call it for what it was: a heart attack], there was one person in the company then who could not let that promotion be. She couldn't deal with a former peer as her boss. She was in such pain that she totally lost her perspective. I didn't understand it then, but, in retrospect, I can understand how it could happen. The situation would not allow her to look at the changes with any objectivity, and the result was that it hurt her, it hurt our team, and it hurt the company. She abandoned her job, made a new career out of highly personal attacks on Dave, wrote letters to the board vilifying him, and sued her company.

I vowed if that ever happened to me, I would not be hurtful to the company, even if I felt betrayed and set upon . . . both of which this woman clearly felt, and by the way . . . I felt neither.

So I have been and will continue to be totally supportive to Tim [McCarthy] and to the new organization in every way I know how.

A tougher decision than that one, though, was the decision to stay. After all, we are all at a very high level of achievement. There are few people in this room who could not land another job in the time-frame they wanted, in the place they wanted, at roughly the pay they wanted. I'm no exception. Also, given the success we all have enjoyed in the last 15 years I've been here, I suppose I could have simply retired.

So the decisions were to stay or go, retire or find another job.

Let's take retirement first. When I first learned of my proposed role in the reorganization, I called Buzz Schulte, a senior partner at the executive search firm of Korn/Ferry International where I was working when I recruited Larry Stupski to Schwab [see page 195]. Buzz is the guy that hired me there, and the person to whom I tendered my resignation when I came to Schwab. He is a neighbor of mine and has remained a trusted friend and advisor. Buzz's response to my question about retirement was short, "What are you going to tell Parker?" he said.

Not many of you know I have two sons. Parker, at 15, is the elder. He is also a learning differenced kid. Unlike me, and most if not all of you, school is for him a battle. . . . [Chuck's learning difference was not spoken of directly.] Very hard work . . . every day . . . and then there is homework . . . .

So, we work very hard to instill in him the value of hard work. That is the norm, not the exception. And I try to model that behavior. Given that, how could I suddenly sleep in, work on my golf game three or four days a week, and spend my afternoons in my workshop trying to perfect the American Cherry Highboy Chest of Drawers? Well, I couldn't. So retirement was out.

But while the decision not to retire was pretty easy, the process of deciding to stay here versus working elsewhere was not easy. It was, however, once again a chance to grow a little. And I am a growth junkie. Growth means change and adventure, and, of course, the phrase, "growing pains," was not coined without cause . . . growth is usually painful, and absolutely essential to life. This has been a hallmark of my career, and I believe of my personal life, for more than 45 years. And those ideas about growth were predominant in my thinking about staying or leaving Schwab. Here is just some of my thinking.

First: When we get to the point that we are in our chosen field . . . and this really goes for everyone in the room, we just simply have to learn to cope with what we might think of as career setbacks. I needed to not just understand, but really experience, the value of commitment and loyalty to the mission of the company and to all of you, and to see how far that commitment went beyond my own particular disappointment.

Now that might sound like B.S. but it isn't, at least not for me. Understand that I'm not saying that if the headhunters call, and they will, that I won't listen. I'm still working through whether or not I need to be president of a company. And if I decide that I do, I will leave. But I really believe at our level in the organization, we should be expected to carry the mission of the company inside of us . . . at a gut level . . . in fact, it should be part of the requirement to be an officer of the company.

Along with that responsibility comes the requirement to recruit peers who can compete with us, people who are really good . . . and who can be better than we are. I have always preached this and practiced it. But of course, this means that we have to face the inevitability that our subordinates will become our peers, and our peers will become our bosses. But there is a payoff. It also means that we can take pride in those people rising to be our peers in the organization—like Susanne [Susanne Lyons, enterprise president, retail investor specialized services], and Karen [Karen Chang, executive president, general investor services], or like Linnet [Linnett Deily, enterprise president, services for investment managers] has risen with John [Coghlan].

This is just part of the biology of a good organization, and I think it is part of the DNA of a good leader.

Both John and I had to really go through some questions and answer them truthfully. And the first question was, "What are the right questions?" Here were some of the others that each of us asked:

1. Do I believe in the mission of the company? Answer: of course.
2. How does the fact that you didn't get this job affect my commitment to the mission of the company? Answer: not at all.
3. Is there any place else in the world, other than starting your own company, where you could express that commitment? Answer: probably not.
4. Do I believe in the strategy? Answer: I helped fashion it.
5. Is there any group of people that you would rather be with, leading and following . . . with all of the foibles and all the successes? Can you imagine having the kind of long-standing and committed relationships in another environment? Answer: of course not.
6. Do you respect the new person you are going to be working for? The answer: absolutely.

So then, for me, the only reason to leave would be petulance . . . because I didn't get to play the position I wanted to play. [See page 200.] And then I asked, "How am I going to explain this to Jake, my 12-year-old son . . . who is a starting halfback on his middle school soccer team, but now wants to play center forward because there is more glory there? And who talks about quitting the team because the coach won't play him there . . . that I quit the team because I didn't get to be starting center forward? I had no answer to that . . . and I couldn't find one.

To have to answer the question years from now . . . to my son or to anyone else . . . when someone asked me why I left Schwab . . . to answer that it was because my ego was injured . . . that was totally unacceptable to me.

So I decided that I wanted to stay. But there was a final set of questions about whether I should stay. The moral issue about whether or not it was right to continue taking a paycheck from the shareholders. This was framed in stark relief when Bill Klipp [William Klipp, executive vice president, SchwabFunds] rolled into my office a couple of weeks ago and said he'd heard he was going to be working with me again. I asked how he felt about that and he answered with a question of his own: "Are you here or are you 'in transition'?" And, we all know what he meant. Was I excited? Did I have the energy? Or, would I just be going through the motions?

The answer was suggested by John McGonigle [executive vice president, mutual funds] who left a phone mail about whether or not he should refer to a phrase I coined back in 1992 regarding the mutual fund business. The slogan was "World Domination in Mutual Funds." Well, his question started me thinking . . . Gee, now I've got International as well as Mutual Funds. How about just plain 'World Domination'! So, the final question was answered right then and there.

As you can see, in the final analysis, the decision was really pretty easy. The hard part was really coming to grips with growing up as a leader, to decide not to pout and retreat, but to constructively go forward, to go on to the next challenge and continue to build on what we have here that is so very, very special.

So John and I are still playing, better than ever I hope, in the right industry, where we can actually provide something that people need, in the right company, where we are truly serving, not selling, and with the right group of people . . . all of you and the thousands who are not here. As Chuck said . . . it's nice to go to work every day feeling like you are doing something important . . . fundamentally to help people . . . with people you care about. And then, of course, there is the world domination part!

Truthfully, it doesn't get a whole lot better.

As it turned out, McCarthy lasted less than a year as president of Schwab. McCarthy declined to explain his reasons for leaving and Pottruck won't comment. The April 1998 news release announcing the resignation quoted McCarthy this way: "I've reached a time in my life where I can afford to take the plunge and become an entrepreneur." In corporate speak, this statement usually is translated to mean, "I've got enough money so, Mr. Boss, I don't have to put up with your nonsense." What we know is that admirers of McCarthy outside Schwab seduced him with $100 million he could play with in the Asian capital markets. Most likely, McCarthy resigned because the organization could not transcend his status as an outsider.

Pottruck calls Seip a "highly principled, thoughtful, and dedicated man," and insists that "Seip would've made a fine president, but we felt at the time there was a better choice." Fair enough. But when McCarthy resigned and Pottruck got another opportunity to choose, did he choose Seip? He did not. Pottruck declined to name Seip president when the office was once again available and he has not appointed a president of the company since. Another humiliation was too much. Tom Seip retired in June, 1998.

What hurt Pottruck most was that by 1997 Chuck seemed to be giving faint but discernible signals that he was finally ready to assume the mantle of chairman, giving Pottruck the CEO title so important to the man laboring in Chuck's shadow for so many years. Pottruck went into the executive management meetings half believing that the company would reorganize along these lines: Chuck (chairman), Pottruck (CEO), and Timothy McCarthy (president). Chuck didn't have the courage to face Pottruck with his decision. A stunned and visibly shaken Pottruck heard the news from the board of directors: the best Chuck would do was share the CEO role.

The problem is not the co-CEO structure per se. A number of such partnerships at Goldman Sachs and other financial services firms have demonstrated that the structure is not only viable, but offers a number of benefits. But the arrangement requires the partners to be equals. The most successful co-CEO partnerships in business history are just that, true 50–50 partnerships.

But let's be clear. Even the casual observer understands that the co-CEO arrangement at Schwab is not 50–50. Pottruck goes out of his way to acknowledge that Chuck is the senior member. So it's not 50–50. Is it 55–45? Or is it 51–49? It hardly matters. Whatever it is, it diminishes Pottruck without strengthening Chuck. The pretense of equality debilitates the organization.

It was an unequal co-CEO arrangement from the beginning. "Nothing really will change for me," Chuck told the *San Francisco Chronicle* a day after the announcement. "I don't think anybody who knows me personally thinks Chuck is going to be retiring anytime soon." This comment is the first and only instance of Chuck referring to himself in the third person. About the only tangible concession Chuck made to equality is that Pottruck's pay would be raised to be equal to his own. "If you're co-chief executives, you get paid the same," said Anthony Frank, former U.S. postmaster general and a Schwab director.

If Pottruck is frustrated with this arrangement, he is careful not to display it in public. While every heavyweight executive in Pottruck's class harbors a consuming desire to become No. 1, Pottruck says he is happy being No. 2. No one believes him. Although a decade younger than his 65-year-old boss, Pottruck resists every opportunity to express desire for the CEO spot. In public Pottruck says all the right things. "I would consider myself unrecruitable. I have too much sense of ownership. There's no position anyone could offer me, including a CEO position, which would make me leave," he said. Such statements are reminiscent of Civil War General William Tecumseh Sherman, who expressed similar disinterest in becoming president. "If nominated, I will not run, and if elected I will not serve," he said. What happened is that no one asked him. Meanwhile, Chuck digs in his heels and takes every opportunity to indicate he might stay around forever. "I don't have any plans to leave. I'm here, like the flag on top of the Bank of America building," he said.

But insiders know that Pottruck's public utterances are window dressing. According to some, tensions between the two men were so high at some points during Schwab's fat years (1997–2000) that Pottruck threatened to quit if Chuck didn't step back a bit. A recruitment probe from Fidelity expressing interest in Pottruck scared Chuck enough to give Pottruck more breathing room. While business was rosy, Chuck withdrew from day-to-day operations and concentrated on philanthropy and serious recreational projects: fly fishing in New Zealand, duck hunting on his Montana Ranch, and perfecting his already stellar golf game. But when the economy went south and the company started shrinking, Chuck came back and asserted his dominance, making himself much more active in the nuts-and-bolts of the business. After all, he has a legacy to protect and no single individual, not even Pottruck, can trump that.

The board of directors must have been nervous about the inevitable crisis that would expose the deep rift between the two men. Some members of the board secretly wish that Chuck would bump himself up to chairman and let Pottruck have not only the title of CEO but the authority that goes with it. Some members of the board are getting impatient with Chuck's apparent inability to relinquish the title and believe the co-CEO structure can't last. "The co-chief executive thing is a contraption; it keeps the trains running," says a confidential source close to the board. "Pottruck is obsessed with the title and Chuck is obsessed with not giving it up."

The toxic management environment fostered by Schwab's co-CEO arrangement claimed another victim when Steven L. Scheid, a vice chairman of the company and head of the retail investing division, resigned on February 15, 2002, after serving just 2 years. Scheid's public comments were unusually frank. In most cases, the announcement of a resignation at this level—Scheid was paid $2.15 million in salary and bonuses in 2000—is described with code such as "pursuing other opportunities" and "personal interests." So it is significant that Scheid went on record as quitting because of autonomy issues: Pottruck, in Scheid's view, insisted on exercising too much control over his division. Scheid wanted more control over daily decisions and tactical details of implementation. Scheid, forty-seven, a former chief financial officer of the company, told *Bloomberg News*, "I've been doing this business for 25 years, and I felt like I needed a bit more autonomy." In a companywide E-mail that went out on February 20, Pottruck said, "We had different views about the level of autonomy that was appropriate."

Scheid was the latest victim of power politics driven by Chuck's recent decision to be more involved in the company's operations and to take back autonomy from Pottruck. As Chuck withdraws autonomy from Pottruck, Pottruck responds by withdrawing autonomy from his lieutenants like Scheid. More experienced Schwab managers tried to warn him. "If you want to be Pottruck's assistant, he's a great boss to work for," says an executive who warned Scheid to back off from flexing his demands for autonomy.

Scheid joins an impressive roster of executives who have left Schwab. "The board feels helpless that the company develops people and moves them up and then Dave finds a way to knock them down," says an executive close to the board. Some board members were further irritated by Pottruck's announcement that Scheid's replacement would come from within Schwab's ranks. "Why did he have to announce that he would fill the slot internally?" a current director asks. "We should at least have considered outside candidates." In fact, Pottruck carved up Scheid's job and parceled it out to four senior executives. The most charitable view of this step is that Pottruck wants each member of the executive committee to get specific experience in retail, operations, and marketing to develop them for leadership. However, at least two members of the board believe that Pottruck is simply unwilling to delegate so much authority to a single individual who might eventually become a rival. "Had Chuck stepped aside and let Pottruck take the CEO role he needs, it is likely that Scheid would have received the autonomy and independence he not only deserved, but earned, in guiding the company's retail operations through the worst downturn in 20 years," says a former director.

Next to the succession issue, Schwab's other pieces of unfinished business almost pale in significance. The company has no lack of challenges, but four issues stand out as most pressing. All require Schwab to confront its deep-rooted precedents; all call for Schwab to enter into new relationships with its clients and partners; and all demand structural changes to the company.

The first challenge is to finally find a revenue stream that is not as cyclical as trading commissions. Schwab knows that the bulk of this revenue will come by serving the growing population of wealthy investors. And the only way to do that is with a robust advice offering. The company that said it would never tell customers what stocks to buy did just that in May 2002 when it announced Schwab Equity Ratings, a computer-assisted stock picking service. Schwab computers will select stocks—giving them letter grades of A through F, indicating whether Schwab expects the stocks to outperform or underperform the market. (See the Epilogue for more details on Schwab Equity Ratings and the company's responses to emerging challenges.)

The second challenge is international. It is not at all clear that the Schwab model is exportable. The intimate relationships he established with individual investors in the United States have eluded Chuck in his forays into England, Germany, Japan, Australia, and even Canada. The company must decide if it will make a serious push to reestablish itself in the markets it has recently abandoned. The board, with the exception of former Secretary of State George Schultz, is weak in international expertise and Chuck is clearly uncomfortable in foreign settings. Apart from the Latin American market it serves out of its Miami branch, Schwab's international presence in the next 5 years will not be significant.

The third challenge is integrating selected banking services into the Schwab portfolio as part of any overall investment/money management strategy. The company has applied for a national bank charter to serve online customers. If approved by federal regulators, the bank will be Federal Deposit Insurance Corp.-insured and will have all the services offered by most banks, including ATM cards, checking accounts, and overdraft protection. The impetus for this strategy is to provide a better overall experience to Schwab's affluent clients who need a more integrated offering of both brokerage and cash management services. Whatever happens, Schwab will be playing catch-up in the banking area.

The fourth challenge facing Schwab is the crisis of confidence confronting the entire financial services industry. Investors are spooked. The failures of the industry's compliance efforts suggest that the U.S. financial markets are deeply flawed. The watchdogs responsible for keeping the industry honest have lost all credibility themselves. Chuck has long railed at analysts who shape stock recommendations to woo investment-banking customers, auditors who bend the rules to curry favor with corporate clients, and government regulators too timid or politicized to keep track of the frenzy. His most pessimistic projections pale against the reality of Enron, Andersen Consulting, Global Crossing, and other companies that have systemically defrauded the investing public.

The future belongs to companies that have earned credibility. In this area Schwab shines. For all its problems, Schwab still retains the confidence of customers and investors. They believe not only that Schwab is a company whose accounting practices are safely within the bounds of the law, but that it is an organization where people look facts in the eye, speak plainly, and avoid promoting initiatives they haven't yet achieved. It's an organization that is constitutionally incapable of exaggerating. Schwab is a company, in short, that puts its credibility ahead of anything else. Awakening from a decade of mind-numbing credulity, investors are on a search-and-destroy mission against companies who display contempt for the principles of fiduciary responsibility and disclosure. The good news is that Schwab is well positioned to weather the storm and once again take its place as the moral center for the securities industry.

In 1998, Chuck made a video. The narrator asked Chuck what he wanted the business pundits to say about his company in two hundred years. His response was very uplifting. He said that this "little company on the West Coast" had started a revolution that allowed people who had never had access to financial markets to make a happier and more secure future for themselves, that we had demystified a vital part of the system for the majority of Americans." On that score, the little company that Chuck started, and to which tens of thousands of men and women have devoted their hearts and minds, is a success. Chuck's cause—"to build the most useful and ethical financial services company in the world"—is complete.

Schwab's final challenge loops back to the fundamental question of the company's unique value proposition and what it stands for. What are we? We're not deep discount; we're not full commission, Chuck must occasionally muse, acknowledging that it's easier for revolutionaries to define themselves by what they are not rather than what they are. Schwab's answer—"We're a category of one"—resolves one question, but begs another.

Who defines "a category of one"? For Charles Schwab & Co., continuing to occupy that category suits the company just fine. But it's an increasingly lonely place to be.

Schwab Account

Founded as a brokerage for the average investor, Charles Schwab & Co. prided itself on three standards: no advice, no cold calling, no commission-paid brokers. In its desire to recreate itself as a full-service brokerage, Schwab is systematically abandoning the principles on which it was established.

The first pillar to go: no advice. It died shamelessly in front of news cameras on May 16, 2002. The company that was founded on the principle that brokerages are incapable of delivering conflict-free advice formally buried the first of its founding values at a New York City press event. Ailing for many years, the no-advice principle survived for 28 years before it finally succumbed to market forces. Chuck Schwab and David Pottruck were among the pallbearers. There was no eulogy. "We will be reaching out to investors with more advice than we ever have before," Chuck told the financial reporters already itchy from reports that Merrill Lynch was about to accept a $100 million fine for giving investors the kind of tainted advice and research that Chuck harped against. There was no mention of Schwab's legacy of disdain for brokers offering advice.

So it was that Schwab announced Schwab Equity Ratings as its vehicle into the conflict-ridden world of full-service brokerages. Schwab Equity Ratings is a stock research and advice service that assigns a letter grade of A through F to each of the 3,000 U.S. equities that the firm will cover. "This is perhaps the most significant moment in the company's history," Chuck said. "We are moving from the edges of client's investment decisions to helping them make those decisions."

Note how Schwab Equity Ratings finesses the advice game as it meshes with the remnants of the company's fraying principles. First, it avoids the unappetizing spectacle of individual Schwab brokers actually touting stocks. By automating and objectifying the process, the service lets computers do the dirty work. Second, it allows all of Schwab's 3,000 or so brokers to speak with one voice on the ratings. Third, the program avoids camouflaging drab facts in trendy broker-speak: labeling a company a "transitional category underperformer" when the broker really means "a nest of dirtballs." Schwab Equity Ratings grades stocks the same way a student gets scored on a test—with A for outstanding and F for failures. Stocks rated A are expected to strongly outperform the market and F stocks are expected to strongly underperform the market. Stocks rated A and B are considered buy recommendations, while Ds and Fs are sell recommendations. Stocks rated C are neutral.

A gutsy and welcome part of this service is that the number of sell recommendations will be equal to the number of buy recommendations. In contrast to its Wall Street rivals—which almost always recommend buying, and almost never selling, stocks of their firm's clients—Schwab will give about 30 percent of stocks the equivalent of a buy rating and 30 percent a sell rating, with a neutral rating going to the rest. The computer-generated ratings also relieve Schwab of the need to hire an army of research analysts. The research comes courtesy of the system run by Chicago Investment Analytics, a company Schwab acquired in 2000. The Schwab rating system crunches twenty-four objective factors, including company fundamentals, historical stock movements, and the opinions of analysts at other firms, to predict how each stock will perform during the next 12 months.

Schwab insists that these ratings really give investors an edge. But if that's true, why doesn't Schwab simply close down its retail practice and make money trading stock? Of course, that observation is not a criticism solely of Schwab's financial management practices; it's applicable to the entire financial services industry. On the one hand, at least Schwab makes it relatively cheap for customers to churn themselves to death. On the other, people want relationships with people they trust, not computers.

It's not easy to offer conflict-free advice. The day after Schwab Equity Ratings was announced, arch-rival Merrill Lynch agreed to pay a $100 million fine, made a statement of contrition, and accepted significant structural reforms to settle charges that the firm's analysts misled investors with their stock advice so the company could win lucrative investment banking fees. Merrill Lynch was caught because internal E-mails disclosed that some brokers were publicly encouraging customers to buy stocks that the same brokers privately derided. Chuck was determined that Schwab's advice offering be hardened against any such hanky-panky.

Even as it rolls out Schwab Equity Ratings, the company will continue to offer its customers the views of other research groups. But what are customers to think when Schwab Equity Ratings contradicts the analysts at the Goldman Sachs Group, the investment bank whose research Schwab makes available to its best customers? As this book went to press, Schwab had assigned an F to the American Tower Corporation, one of Goldman's preferred stocks and prominently displayed on its list of investment banking clients. General Electric's stock was also on Goldman's recommended list, but earned a C rating from Schwab.

And what of Schwab's remaining founding values? The no-selling principle will be the next to go. Pottruck insists that Schwab brokers will never "cold call" customers. But market forces are forcing Schwab to encroach on this taboo, as well. The company is gearing up for an aggressive E-mail alert program that is in reality "warm calling" in disguise. Customers can expect to be bombarded by E-mails alerting them to a variety of conditions that Schwab believes can inspire a trade. For example, customers will get E-mails when a stock they own has been downgraded by Schwab's rating system, when the cash in their account exceeds a threshold, or when an account triggers a portfolio asset allocation recommendation. The question is, Will customers be any less distressed by such E-mails than they are by unsolicited telephone calls from their brokers? Schwab is very concerned about the privacy implications and is proceeding cautiously.

Another value—that of paying brokers by salary instead of by commission—continues to be respected. The conflicts of interest manifested by brokers compensated by commissions are so execrable that Schwab will never link employee compensation to commissions. The company's proxies and partners, however, are not bound by the standard, and Schwab will likely offload much of the sales burden to them. Moreover, linking Branchland bonuses to the assets an employee aggregates can also expose the company to unintended conflicts. For now, however, the no-commission standard remains an integral part of Schwab's commitment.

Finally, Schwab's transformation as a broker to the wealthy continues without a glance at the customers of modest means being left behind. The evidence is everywhere. Schwab no longer provides postage-paid envelopes for customers to use to mail in checks. While other brokerages are reducing trading fees, Schwab is raising them. Schwab, which battles with Merrill, UBS PaineWebber, and other rivals to get the nation's wealthiest investors, announced a private client group that features one-on-one services from a broker for a minimum annual fee of $1,500 plus 0.6 percent of their noncash holdings. This service is for customers with $500,000 to $5 million in assets. Schwab's super-wealthy clients are encouraged to go to U.S. Trust, where they have access to a full range of wealth management, financial planning, trust and estate planning, and private banking services. Schwab no longer welcomes customers with accounts of less than $50,000.

Inside Schwab, these changes do not go down easily. As much as Schwab people throughout the organization acknowledge the need for these changes, it is not easy to give up the practices and values that have defined the company. The company, desperate to re-create itself, is not being sensitive to the needs of employees to grieve for the precious values being lost. Thousands of employees have retired, preferring to cherish the noble causes that Schwab stood for rather than work to make rich people even richer.

Charles Schwab & Co. Timeline

1963 Charles Schwab and two other partners launch *Investment Indicators,* an investment advisory newsletter. At its height, the newsletter has 3,000 subscribers, each paying $84 per year to subscribe.

1971 Charles establishes First Commander Corp., a traditional brokerage, with $100,000 borrowed from his entrepreneurial uncle, Bill Schwab.

1973 Charles buys out his other partners, assuming all of the company's debt. He changes First Commander's name to Charles Schwab & Co., Inc.

1974 The SEC mandates a 13-month trial period for the deregulation of certain brokerage transactions. While many brokerages take the opportunity to raise commissions, Charles Schwab seizes the opportunity to create a new kind of brokerage, a discount broker and pitchman is born.

The information in this timeline is based on a similar presentation found on the Schwab Web site (www.schwab.com) and augumented with updated detail.

1975   On May 1, the SEC officially approves "negotiated" commissions, marking the birth of the discount brokerage industry. The Pacific Coast Stock Exchange approves Schwab's membership. Schwab opens a Sacramento office—its first branch outside of San Francisco.

1976   First ads feature Charles Schwab in shirt sleeves: The Schwab brand is born. Early foray into high-tech innovation: Bunker Ramo System 7, begins delivering stock quotes to customers. Options Clearing Corp. membership approved. Branch strategy stakes off with new offices in Seattle, Los Angeles, and Denver. Branches: 3.

1977   Schwab establishes telephone call center in Reno, Nevada. Branches: 7.

1979   Schwab risks $500,000—100 percent of its revenues—on a turnkey back-office settlement system, running on a used IBM 360 mainframe. Customers: 33,000. Branches: 15.

1980   Schwab introduces 24-hour weekday quote service. Adopts tagline: "America's largest discount brokerage." Larry Stupski joins Schwab. Company proposes and then withdraws its first IPO. Branches: 23.

1981   In first big merger among discounters, Schwab acquires Kingsley, Boye and Southwood. Also acquires Letterman Transaction Services and Ridgeway. Becomes member of the New York Stock Exchange. Announces intention to be acquired by Bank of America. Opens first office in Manhattan. Branches: 33.

1982   Schwab introduces the Schwab One Account, an innovative cash management account. Branches: 52.

1983   Bank of America officially acquires Schwab for $57 million. Company opens up 500,000th customer account. Branches: 69.

1984   Launches Mutual Fund MarketPlace with 140 no-load funds. Branches: 89.

1985   Introduces three new online products: The Equalizer—a DOS-based application that would point the way toward an online future; SchwabLink—a service for fee-based financial advisors; and the SchwabQuotes Touch-Tone quote system. Launches stand-alone Financial Independence software for managing personal finances on the PC. David Pottruck joins the firm as EVP of marketing and advertising. Branches: 88.

1986   Introduces No-Annual-Fee IRA. Abandons Financial Independence product for lack of fit with core brokerage business. Branches: 96.

1987   Completes management-led buyback from Bank of America for $280 million. In September, The Charles Schwab Corporation (the parent corporation) completes IPO of eight million shares at $16.50. In October, the stock market crashes, exposing Schwab to critical margin exposure. Company announces $22 million write-off to uncollected trading losses. Branches: 106.

1988   Advisor Source, referral service for fee-based independent financial investment advisors takes off. For early day traders: a 900-telephone number hawks news and tips to trading junkies. Branches: 111.

1989   October earthquake threatens Schwab computer system. TeleBroker replaces SchwabQuotes; introduces Touch-Tone trading and quote system. Branches: 111.

1990   Opens Indianapolis call center. Branches: 130.

1991   Acquires Mayer & Schweitzer, one of nation's premier over-the-counter market makers, now known as Schwab Capital Markets LP. Introduces Schwab 1000 Index Fund, along with Schwab U.S. Government Bond Fund. Opens call center in

Denver. Holds its first national conference for independent investment managers. Launches first network television advertising campaign. Branches: 158

1992   Larry Stupski felled by heart attack on January 10. Schwab introduces no-transaction fee Mutual Fund OneSource service. Adds Schwab California and National Tax-Free Bond Funds. Opens call center in Phoenix. The Charles Schwab Corporation establishes Charles Schwab Trust Company. Opens Latin American Center in Miami. Surpasses two million active investor accounts. Branches: 175.

1993   StreetSmart online trading system replaces Equalizer. Branches: 198.

1994   Schwab reaches $1 billion in revenues and $100 billion in customer assets. Decentralization of the company into nine customer enterprises. Larry Stupski steps down; David Pottruck becomes president. Branches: 208.

1995   Schwab commits to moving enterprise to Electronic Brokerage. Branches: 225.

1996   Internet trading launched. Company introduces eSchwab. Schwab pitches Select List, its top mutual fund picks. Branches: 235.

1997   eSchwab and Schwab retail merge back together. One price for Web trades. Opens one-millionth online account. Creates Charles Schwab Europe as well as subsidiaries in Hong Kong and Cayman Islands. SchwabLink available on the Web. First speech-recognition service for investors. Forms alliance with First Boston, J.P. Morgan and Chase H&Q to give Schwab customers access to IPOs. David Pottruck is named Co-CEO. Introduces Mutual Fund Report Cards and $29.95 commission for online equity trades up to 1,000 shares. Standard & Poor's promotes Schwab stock (SCH) to S&P 500 index, replacing Morgan Stanley Group. Branches: 272

1998 Launches Schwab.com. Schwab passes Merrill Lynch in total stock market capitalization. Schwab hits 1.8 million online accounts. Full-service firms play catch-up with me-too offerings. MoneyLink: Electronic funds transfer service. First U.S. website enabling order placement in Chinese. Schwab begins online investing service in Britain. Schwab enters Canadian market. Branches: 291.

1999 The former discounter goes upscale with intention to acquire U.S. Trust. Preaches asset allocation, diversification, and other investing. Reaches more than $700 billion in assets; almost $4 billion in revenues. Introduces After-Hours trading and Retirement Planner online. MySchwab launches. Branches: 349.

2000 Schwab reaches $1 trillion in assets. Acquires U.S. Trust for $2.7 billion. Acquires Cybercorp (later renamed Cyber-Trader). Enters into global financial services alliance with AOL Time Warner. Schwab and Barclays announce Internet-based foreign exchange service. Launches Stock Analyzer, offering third-party equity analyst recommendations and earnings projections. Branches: 384.

2001 Tech sector sell-off forces Schwab to lay off nearly one in four employees. Schwab abandons trading joint venture in Australia and Japan. Branches: 395.

2002 In January Schwab reports its first quarterly loss in 14 years. Further consolidation forces sale of Schwab Canada to Bank of Nova Scotia. Announces Schwab Equity Ratings advice service, Schwab Private Client, and Schwab Advisor Network. Branches: 430.

Charles R. Schwab's Employment Agreement

This Agreement is made and entered into as of March 31, 1995 by and between The Charles Schwab Corporation, a Delaware Corporation (hereinafter referred to as the "Company"), and Charles R. Schwab, an individual (hereinafter referred to as the "Executive") effective March 31, 1995.

WITNESSETH:

WHEREAS, the Company desires to reward the Executive for his continuing contribution to the Company and provide additional security for the Executive and to provide an inducement to the Executive to remain with the Company and not to engage in competition with it.

NOW THEREFORE, in consideration of the mutual obligations herein contained, the parties hereto, intending to be legally bound hereby, covenant and agree as follows:

1. EMPLOYMENT

(a) The Company hereby employs the Executive to render services to the Company in the positions of Chairman of the Board and Chief Executive Officer, in the capacity defined in the By-laws of the Company, as may be amended from time to time. The Executive shall perform such duties commensurate with his position and shall have full authority and responsibility, subject to the control of the Board of Directors, for the overall strategic direction, management, and leadership of the Company.

(b) Throughout the term of this Agreement, the Executive shall devote his full business time and undivided attention to the business and affairs of the Company and its subsidiaries, except for reasonable vacations and except for illness or incapacity, but nothing in the Agreement shall preclude the Executive from devoting reasonable periods required for serving, as appropriate, on Boards of Directors of other companies, and from engaging in charitable and public service activities provided such activities do not materially interfere with the performance of his duties and responsibilities under this Agreement.

2. TERM

This Agreement shall commence on March 31, 1995, and shall continue through March 31, 2000, subject to the terms and conditions herein set forth. Beginning on March 31, 1996, and on each subsequent anniversary of this date, one year shall be added to the term of the Agreement, unless, prior to such anniversary, the Company or the Executive has notified the other party hereto that such extension will not become effective.

3. COMPENSATION

For services rendered by the Executive during the term of this Agreement, and for his performance of all additional obligations of employment, the Company agrees to pay the Executive and the Executive agrees to accept the following salary, other compensation, and benefits:

(a) Base Salary.   During the term of this Agreement, the Company shall pay the Executive in periodic install-ments, a base salary at the annual rate of $800,000, such base salary to be reviewed on March 31, 1996, and on each subsequent anniversary, taking into account, among other things, individual performance, competitive prac-tice, and general business conditions.

(b) Annual Incentive.   In addition to the base salary pro-vided in Section 3(a) above, the Executive shall be eligi-ble to receive an annual incentive award based upon the Company's attainment of pre-established performance targets relative to specified performance standards. The performance standards upon which annual incen-tive payments will be earned shall be defined to include consolidated pretax profit margin (defined as net in-come before taxes, divided by net revenue) and annual net revenue percentage growth of the Company.

  For each fiscal year during the term of this Agree-ment, the Executive's incentive opportunity shall be com-puted as the amount of total cash compensation earned pursuant to the formula-based matrix, which shall be adopted each year by the Compensation Committee of the Board of Directors of the Company, minus the Ex-ecutive's actual base salary paid during that year. For the 1995 fiscal year, the target total annual cash com-pensation amount (including base salary) is $3,500,000; therefore, the incentive target is $2,700,000 for achiev-ing specified pretax profit margin and revenue growth objectives.

  The formula-based matrix, as amended at the sole discretion of the Board of Directors, shall be the sole basis for determining the Executive's annual incentive award. For each calendar year for which this Agreement is in effect, beginning with the calendar year 1996, the interior values in the formula-based matrix shall be in-creased by a fraction, based on the U.S. Consumer Price

Index (for all consumers, as published by the Bureau of Labor Statistics); provided that no interior value shall be increased above $12 million. The fractional increase shall be the CPI for that year divided by the CPI for calendar year 1995. The Compensation Committee of the Board shall annually review and approve the performance standards and targets with respect to the Executive's incentive opportunity, which review and approval shall be completed no later than the 90th day of the Company's fiscal year for which such incentive opportunity may be earned.

(c) Long-Term Incentive.   The Executive will be considered for stock options in accordance with the Company's 1992 Stock Incentive Plan, as amended, or any successor thereto ("Stock Option Program") and any other long-term incentives offered to other executives of the Company from time to time during the term of this Agreement.

(d) Benefits.   The Executive shall be entitled to participate, as long as he is an employee of the Company, in any and all of the Company's present or future employee benefit plans, including without limitation pension plans, thrift and savings plans, insurance plans, and other benefits that are generally applicable to the Company's executives; provided, however, that the accrual and/or receipt by the Executive of benefits under and pursuant to any such present or future employee benefit plan shall be determined by the provisions of such plan.

(e) Perquisites.   The Executive will be provided such additional perquisites as are customary for senior level executives of the Company provided that each perquisite is approved by the Board of Directors.

(f) Business Expenses.   The Executive will be reimbursed for all reasonable expenses incurred in connection with

the conduct of the Company's business upon presentation of evidence of such expenditures, including but not
limited to travel expenses incurred by the Executive in
the performance of his duties, security for the Executive,
his family, and principal residence, professional organization dues, and club initiation fees, dues and expenses.

(g) Any annual incentive award earned by Executive under
this Section 3 shall be paid as soon as reasonably practical
after the end of the Company's fiscal year end; provided,
however, that if any such payment would be nondeductible to the Company under Internal Revenue Code
Section 162(m), then any nondeductible amounts shall
be deferred from year to year until the payment of such
amounts is deductible by the Company.

4. TERMINATION OF EMPLOYMENT

(a) Resignation.   Notwithstanding Section 2 hereof, this
Agreement may be terminated by the Executive at any
time upon six (6) months written notice of resignation by
the Executive to the Company, and in such event any payments pursuant to Section 3 and 4 of this Agreement
shall automatically terminate (except for the Company's
obligations relative to voluntary termination under its
compensation and benefit plans, as specified in the various plan documents and the Executive's obligations set
forth in Section 5). Subsequent payments may be made
to the Executive as provided pursuant to Section 6 of this
Agreement.

(b) Termination by the Company Other Than for Cause.
Termination of the Executive by the Company other
than for Cause, as defined in Section 4(c) below, shall
cause the Company to make payments to the Executive
hereunder pursuant to the provisions of this Section
4(b). Such a termination shall require at least sixty (60)
business days' prior notice and must be signed by at least

three-fourths (3/4) of all the non-employee members of the Board of Directors.

Notwithstanding anything to the contrary contained in Stock Option Program or any agreement or document related thereto, the Executive's total outstanding and unvested shares and/or options under the Stock Option Plan shall at the date of termination be deemed to be 100% vested. No further grants of stock or options shall be made under the Plan after such termination.

With respect to base salary and annual incentive compensation, the Company's obligation shall be to pay the Executive, according to the terms of this Agreement and for a period of thirty-six (36) months, an amount equal to the annual salary and incentive paid to the Executive [at the bonus level for the year prior to which such termination occurs unless performance of the Company as defined in the matrix referenced in Section 3(b) is better in the year of termination, in which event such bonus shall be based on the matrix calculation as described in Section 3(b)], such annual amounts to be paid in equal monthly installments.

During the 36-month severance payment period, the Executive shall be entitled to all payments, benefits and perquisites as provided for in this Agreement, and office space and secretarial support comparable to that provided to the Executive during his employment by the Company. The Executive shall be entitled to all payments and benefits as provided for in this Section for a period of thirty-six (36) months.

If the Board of Directors fails to reelect the Executive to a position comparable to that described in Section 1(a) of this Agreement or, without terminating the Executive's employment, removes the Executive from his position for reasons other than Cause, substantively reduces the Executive's duties and responsibilities, reduces his pay and/or benefits, forces relocation, or requires excessive travel, then the Executive may, by notice to the Company, treat such action or removal as a termination of the Executive by the Company pursuant to this Section 4(b).

In the event of the Executive's death before the completion of the payments pursuant to this Section 4(b), the remaining payments hereunder shall be made to the beneficiary or beneficiaries designated by the Executive to the Company in writing or, absent such a designation, to his estate.

(c) Termination by the Company for Cause.   The Company may terminate the Executive's employment for Cause if the Executive has committed a felonious act, or the Executive, in carrying out his duties hereunder has been willfully and grossly negligent or has committed willful and gross misconduct resulting, in either case, in material harm to the Company. An act or omission shall be deemed "willful" only if done, or omitted to be done, in bad faith and without reasonable belief that it was in the best interest of the Company. In the event of termination of the Executive by the Company for Cause, the Executive shall no longer be entitled to receive any payments or any other rights or benefits under this Agreement.

(d) Disability.   In the event the Executive's employment terminates due to total and permanent disability (for the purposes of this Agreement "disability" shall have the same meaning as applies under the Company's Long-Term Disability Plan), he will continue to receive the same base salary and benefits which he was receiving prior to such disability for 36 months, offset by payments under the Company's Long-Term Disability Plan. In addition, he shall receive a pro-rated annual incentive payment for the year in which his employment is terminated, based on the formula described in Section 3(b).

(e) Death.   In the event of the death of the Executive during the term of this Agreement, the rights and benefits under employee benefit plans and programs of the

Company, including life insurance, will be determined in accordance with the terms and conditions of such plans and programs as in effect on his date of death. In such event, the Company shall pay in a lump sum to the Executive's estate an amount equal to five times the then current rate of the Executive's base salary, and no further payments shall be required pursuant to this Agreement.

(f) Change in Control.   In the event of a change in control of the Company, as set forth below, the Executive may at any time and in his complete discretion during a 24-month period following a change in control, elect to terminate his employment with the Company. For purposes of this Agreement, a "change in control" shall mean a change in ownership of the Company that would be required to be reported in response to Item 1(a) of a Current Report on Form 8-K pursuant to the Securities and Exchange Act of 1934 ("Exchange Act"), as in effect on the date hereof, except that any merger, consolidation or corporate reorganization in which the owners of the capital stock entitled to vote in the election of directors of the Employer or the Company ("Voting Stock") prior to said combination, own 75% or more of the resulting entity's Voting Stock shall not be considered a change in control for the purposes of this Agreement; provided that, without limitation, such a change in control shall be deemed to have occurred if (i) any "person" (as that term is used in Sections 13(d) and 14(d)(2) of the Exchange Act), other than a trustee or other fiduciary holding securities under an employee benefit plan of the Company is or becomes the beneficial owner (as that term is used in Section 13(d) of the Exchange Act), directly or indirectly, or 30% or more of the Voting Stock of the Company or its successor; or (ii) during any period of two consecutive years, individuals who at the beginning of such period constitute the Board of Directors of the Company ("Incumbent Board") cease for any reason to constitute at least a majority thereof; provided, however, that any person becoming a director of the Company after the beginning of the period whose election was approved by a vote of at least three-quarters of the directors comprising the incumbent Board shall, for the purposes hereof, be considered as though he were a member of the incumbent Board; or (iii) there shall occur the sale of all or substantially all of the assets of the Company. Notwithstanding anything in the foregoing to the contrary, no change in control of the Company shall be deemed to have occurred for purposes of this Agreement by virtue of any transaction which results in the Executive, or a group of persons which includes the Executive, acquiring, directly or indirectly, more than 30% of the combined voting power of the Company's outstanding securities. If any of the events constituting a change in control shall have occurred during the term hereof, the Executive shall be entitled to the privilege provided in subparagraph (f) herein to terminate his employment.

Any termination by the Executive pursuant to this Section shall be communicated by a written "Notice of Termination."

If, following a change in control, the Executive shall for any reason voluntarily terminate his employment during the 24-month period following a change in control, then the Company shall pay base salary up to the date of termination and a prorated annual incentive award based on the calculated bonus for the year in which termination occurred, as defined in Section 3(b), in a lump sum on the thirtieth (30th) day following the Date of Termination.

5. COVENANT NOT TO COMPETE

(a) As a material inducement to the Company's entering into this Agreement, the Executive agrees that during the term of this Agreement, he will not become associated with, render service to or engage in any other business competitive with any existing or contemplated business of the Company or its subsidiaries, except that the Executive may serve as a member of the board of directors of other companies or organizations, provided that he provides written notice to the Board of each significant activity, and that he will do nothing inconsistent with his duties and responsibilities to the Company.

(b) If the Executive voluntarily resigns from the employ of the Company prior to the expiration of the term of this Agreement, he specifically agrees that for a period of five (5) years commencing with the date of his voluntary resignation he will not engage in or perform any services either on a full-time or a part-time or on a consulting or advisory basis for any business organization that is in competition with the Company at the time such services are being performed by Executive, with the exception that this Section 5(b) shall not apply in the event the Executive resigns voluntarily following a change in control of the Company as defined in Section 4(f).

(c) The Executive will not at any time, whether while employed by the Company or after voluntary or involuntary termination or after retirement, reveal to any person, firm or entity any trade or business secrets or confidential, secret, or privileged information about the business of the Company or its subsidiaries or affiliates except as shall be required in the proper conduct of the Company's business.

6. CONSULTING ARRANGEMENT

Following a voluntary termination of employment pursuant to Section 4(a) and 4(f), or an involuntary termination subsequent to a change in control of the Company, for any reason but during a 24-month period following a change in control as defined in Section 4(f), after the Executive ceases to render services as the Chief Executive Officer, he may in his sole discretion elect to act as a consultant to the Company for a period of five (5) years. During this period of consulting services, the Executive shall, at reasonable times and places, taking into account any other employment or activities he may then have, hold himself available to consult with and advise the officers, directors, and other representatives of the Company. As compensation thereof, the Executive shall be entitled to receive, and Company shall pay, an annual amount equal to seventy-five percent (75%) of his annual base salary rate in effect immediately prior to his termination of employment, but in no event an annual amount to exceed $1,000,000, for each year of such period, payable in equal monthly installments.

7. WITHHOLDING

All amounts payable hereunder which are or may become subject to withholding under pertinent provisions of law or regulation shall be reduced for applicable income and/or employment taxes required to be withheld.

8. MISCELLANEOUS

   (a) This Agreement supersedes any prior agreements or understandings, oral or written, with respect to employment of the Executive and constitutes the entire Agreement with respect thereto; provided, however, that nothing contained herein shall supercede that certain Assignment and License Agreement entered into as of March 31, 1987, as amended. This Agreement cannot be altered or terminated orally and may be amended only by a subsequent written agreement executed by both of the parties hereto or their legal representatives, and any material amendment must be approved by a majority of the voting shareholders of the Company.

   (b) This Agreement shall be governed by and construed in accordance with the laws of the State of California.

(c) This Agreement shall be binding upon and shall inure to the benefit of the Company and its successors and assigns. In that this constitutes a personal service agreement, it may not be assigned by the Executive and any attempted assignment by the Executive in violation of this covenant shall be null and void.

(d) For the purpose of this Agreement, the phrase "designated beneficiary or beneficiaries" shall include the estates of such beneficiaries in the event of their death before the receipt of all payments under this Agreement and shall also include any alternate or successor beneficiaries designated in writing to the Company by the Executive.

(e) The invalidity or unenforceability of any provision of this Agreement shall not affect the validity or enforceability of any other provisions, which shall remain in full force and effect.

(f) The Section and Paragraph headings contained herein are for reference purposes only and shall not in any way affect the meanings or interpretation of this Agreement.

(g) Any dispute or controversy arising under or in connection with this Agreement shall be settled exclusively by arbitration, conducted before a panel of arbitrators in accordance with the rules of the American Arbitration Association then in effect. Judgment may be entered on the arbitrator's award in any court having jurisdiction. The expense of such arbitration shall be borne by the Company.

(h) Any notices, requests or other communications provided for by this Agreement shall be sufficient if in writing and if sent by registered or certified mail to the Executive at the last address he has filed in writing with the Company or, in the case of the Company, at its principal offices.

IN WITNESS WHEREOF, the parties have executed this Agreement on the day and year first above written.

Company:
THE CHARLES SCHWAB
ATTEST   CORPORATION
By: /s/ Mary B. Templeton   By: /s/ Luis E. Valencia

Corporate Secretary   Title: Executive Vice
President—Human Resources
Executive: /s/ Charles R. Schwab

Charles R. Schwab

The majority of direct quotations in this book reference former Schwab employees who agreed to be interviewed and named for the record. Charles Schwab & Co. did not make current employees available for interviews for this book. It did not, however, discourage former employees from speaking with me and I subsequently interviewed more than two hundred people who were at one time associated with the company. Interviewees ranged from three former presidents of the company to managers and associates in every department. The combined length of their service exceeds 1,500 years and represents every period of the company's history. In addition, I interviewed more than one hundred analysts, financial advisors, financial journalists, and Schwab partners, consultants, and competitors. Unless otherwise noted, all direct statements are derived from personal interviews conducted with the individuals in question. In rare instances, individuals have asked that their identities not be disclosed. I have honored those requests. In reconstructing conversations, I have relied on one or more of the persons present. In some cases, sources shared contemporaneous records of meetings to support their memories of events.

Some of the statements attributed to Charles R. Schwab are drawn from his first book, *How to Be Your Own Stockbroker* (1984), especially the early autobiographical chapters. Some of the statements attributed to David Pottruck are drawn from his book, *Clicks and Mortar* (2000). In addition, both executives have been quoted extensively in thousands of magazine articles, newspaper stories, speeches, videos, radio interviews, and television appearances. Additional valuable information was derived from Joseph Nocera's *A Piece of the Action: How the Middle Class Joined the Money Class* (1994), which features a rich analysis of Schwab's contribution to the financial empowerment of the middle class. Statements attributed to Schwab or Pottruck that are not otherwise referenced have been independently verified by two or more former colleagues who do not wish to be identified.

Chapter 1, May Day

Page 14 " . . . *the median annual household income in 1965 was $6,597.*" In contrast, in 1999, the figure was $38,885. From the U.S. Department of Commerce, *Statistical Abstract of the United States.*

Page 14 "*He called the fund Investment Indicators and it soon became the largest mutual fund in California. . . .*" From Charles Schwab, *How to Be Your Own Stockbroker* (New York: Macmillan, 1984), p. 14.

Page 15 "'*Let's begin with the first step for a lot of investors'. . . .*" Arthur Levitt's final speech as SEC Chairman, Philadelphia, January 2001. Quoted in Tracy Price Stoneman and Douglas J. Schulz, *Brokerage Fraud: What Wall Street Doesn't Want You to Know* (Chicago: Dearborn Trade Publishing, 2002).

Page 16 "'*May Day is a great holiday in Russia'. . . .*" From Benjamin Mark Cole, *The Pied Pipers of Wall Street: How Analysts Sell You Down the River* (Princeton, NJ: Bloomberg Press, 2001), p. 49.

Page 17 "*The Securities Acts of 1933 and 1934, which in addition to requiring brokerages to be licensed by the SEC, officially sanctioned the NYSE's price fixing. . . .*" Ibid., p. 47.

Page 17 "*In a typical year, such as 1967. . . .*" Ibid., p. 48.

Page 18 "'*I can't believe this. Suddenly you've got $29.95 trades, and you're empowered'. . . .*" From David Colbert, *Eyewitness to Wall Street: Four Hundred Years of Dreamers, Schemers, Busts and Booms* (New York: Broadway Books, 2001), pp. 348–349.

Page 19   *"'I'm reminded of an eager-beaver stock salesman I knew in Florida'. . . ."* From Schwab, *Your Own Stockbroker*, pp. 1–2.

Page 24   *"According to data put together by Zaks Investment Research. . . ."* From Cole, *Pied Pipers of Wall Street*, p. 97. There were an additional 224 recommendations, or 0.7 percent, that could be interpreted as sells, such as ratings with such tepid language as "market underperformer."

Page 24   ". . . Dave Barry lampooned the analysts who covered the stock. . . ." *The Miami Herald*, February 3, 2002.

Page 25   *"Executives at Bear Stearns. . . ."* From Colbert, *Eyewitness to Wall Street*, p. 206.

Page 25   ". . . *most brokers had cut their fees 25–35 percent.* . . ." Ibid., p. 204.

Chapter 2, Opening Investment

Page 29   *"'Although my father's life. . . .'"* From Charles Schwab, *How to Be Your Own Strockbroker* (New York: Macmillan, 1984), p. 16.

Page 30   *" 'Some other kids thought I was a little crazy,. . . .'"* Ibid., p 16.

Page 30   *"'I sold the eggs; . . . ."* Ibid., p. 17.

Page 33   *"'I bluffed my way through much of it, I'm sure,. . . .'"* Theresa Johnston, "Charles Schwab's Secret Struggle," *Stanford Magazine*, March/April 1999.

Page 33   *" 'When I read, I can feel myself converting the written code into sounds. . . .'"* Ibid. Like millions of other often distinguished people around the world, Chuck copes with dyslexia. The condition first known as "word blindness" is characterized by unusual difficulty sounding out letters and distinguishing words that sound similar. Dyslexia is by far the most common language-related learning disability.

Page 35   *"Annual income in 1961 topped $61 billion . . . ."* Ibid., p. 56.

Page 35   *" 'I was the guy with the slide rule,'. . . ."* Ibid., p. 56.

Page 36   *" 'Very hot stuff.' "* From Schwab, *Your Own Stockbroker*, p. 19.

Page 36   ". . . *Investment Indicators.* . . ." Features in the newsletter included an analysis of stock market cycles. "We were predicting the beginning of a new 'up' cycle," Chuck wrote in *How to Be Your Own Stockbroker.* "Our technique was to predict future movements of the market by evaluating a series of market indicators. The stock market is in many ways a living organism, with a past history that contains the seeds of upcoming growths, ages, and declines."

Page 36   *"In physics, they called it chaos theory."* See *The Age of Unreason* by Charles Handy (Cambridge: Harvard Business School Press, 1989), page 9, for a discussion of discontinuous change.

Page 37   *". . . $20 million in assets."* From Joseph Nocera, *A Piece of the Action: How the Middle Class Joined the Money Class* (New York: Simon and Schuster, 1994), p. 111.

Page 37   *" 'That's an ugly word, '. . . ."* From Schwab, *Your Own Stockbroker*, p. 14.

Page 38   *". . . blamed the regulators, ..."* From Schwab, *Your Own Stockbroker*, pp. 14–15.

Page 39   *"He lost his investment team's. . . ."* From Lisa R. Sheeran, "Sadder but Wiser; Discount Broker Charles Schwab Is Doing All Right—but He Knows How It Feels When an Investment Goes Sour," *Inc.*, Oct. 1985, v. 70, p. 139.

Page 40   *" 'Chuck, there's room for a new kind of business, '. . . ."* From Johnston, "Schwab's Secret Struggle," p. 101.

Chapter 3, Building the Brand

Page 47   *"In 1977, Chuck became the first person to have his photograph in the Wall Street Journal."* Even today, the WSJ relies on line art to depict individuals. Chuck's photograph was the first to appear in the newspaper by virtue of appearing in an advertisement.

Page 51   *"In its 28-year history. . . ."* Pearson (1975–1985) was the first, Larry Stupski (1985–1998), whom Pearson recruited, the second, and David Pottruck (1984 through the present) the third.

Page 52   *"He left about $300 million. . . ."* By the time Pearson quit in 1985, he had built some of the most advanced business information systems in the world and set the technical foundations for the company's future growth. But the daily

grind of trying to keep the systems running burned him
out. One day he walked into Larry Stupski's office and
said, "I can't do it anymore." The company went public 2
years later. Had he stayed and cashed out at the top of the
market, the value of the options and shares to which he
would have been entitled would have been . . . well, no
sense obsessing about it. Pearson had no regrets then and
has none now.

Page 54   " *'People warned him he'd have all those weird technical people
working for him,'. . . .*" From Clinton Wilder, "Leaders of
the Net Era," *InformationWeek*, November 27, 2000.

Page 56   " *'I could not for the life of me'. . . .*" From Paul J. Bother, *Presidential Anecdotes* (New York: Penguin Books, 1981), p. 129.

Page 58   " *'Suddenly, the impressive-looking offices'. . . .*" From Benjamin Mark Cole, *The Pied Pipers of Wall Street: How Analysts
Sell You Down the River* (Princeton, NJ: Bloomberg Press,
2001),p. 51.

Page 59   " *'The major firms employed the rankest discrimination'. . . .*"
From Charles Schwab, *How to Be Your Own Stockbroker*
(New York: Macmillan, 1984), p. 7.

Page 60   " *In September 1975, the Philadelphia Stock Exchange. . . ,*"
Schwab Registration Statement filed with the SEC, May 9,
1980, p. 29.

Page 61   " *'You couldn't be accused of'. . . .*" From Joseph Nocera, *A
Piece of the Action: How the Middle Class Joined the Money
Class* (New York: Simon and Schuster, 1994), p. 120.

Chapter 4, Innovation

Page 71   " *'The first principles of generating engagement,. . . .'* " From
David S. Pottruck and Terry Pearce, *Clicks and Mortar:
Passion-Driven Growth in an Internet-Driven World* (New York:
John Wiley & Sons, 2001), p. 199.

Page 72   " *'We learned a lot about innovation during this period'. . . .*"
Ibid., p. 146.

Page 72   "*Jeff Lyons, currently executive vice president. . . .*" The firm at
that time had two people named Jeff Lyons. The Lyons
referenced here is currently executive vice president, asset
management products and services, and is married to

Schwab executive Susanne Lyons. The other Jeff Lyons managed the disaster recovery plan in use during the San Francisco earthquake. He was a very successful fund raiser for the San Francisco AIDS walk and is now deceased.

Page 73 *" 'Then we could look each other in the eye and ask'. . . ."* Pottruck, p.151.

Page 74 *" 'This is a case where incumbency could have kept us'. . . ."* Ibid, p. 149.

Chapter 5, Branchland

Page 76 *"But Sacramento?. . . ."* In 1975, Sacramento had a population of 260,000 people. The economy of the city was centered around the state capital. Per capita income was less than $13,000. From Sacramento Area Council of Governments available at http://www.cityofsacramento.org/planning/geoarea/phdata/pop_cpa.htm

Page 79 *Over the next two decades,. . . ."* From Schwab prospectus statements, 1980 and 1987, and its annual reports, 1987–present.

Page 90 *" 'The card alone was a remarkable creature,'. . . ."* From Joseph Nocera, *A Piece of the Action: How the Middle Class Joined the Money Class* (New York: Simon and Schuster, 1994), p. 156.

Chapter 6, Advice and Advisors

Page 100 *"Not goals, but standards. . . ."* In 1961, President John F. Kennedy set a goal for reaching the Moon, but once the goal was attained in 1969, the country soon lost most of its interest in the space program and, without public support, the program was scaled back.

Page 107 *" 'Schwab's relationship with independent fee-based advisors'. . . ."* From Sanjeev Dewan and Haim Mendelson, Schwab.com, Case number EC-18, Graduate School of Business, Stanford University, March 2001.

Page 107 *" 'We don't compete with the discounters,'. . . ."* *Institutional Advisor*, April 1996.

Chapter 7, Forsaken IPO

Page 115   *"There was never anything smooth about any of it'. . . ."* From Joseph Nocera, *A Piece of the Action: How the Middle Class Joined the Money Class* (New York: Simon and Schuster, 1994), p. 263.

Page 118   *"The average error rate for NYSE. . . ."* The company's own prospectus blamed the error rate on the new computerized order processing system that broke down frequently under the heavy trading volumes of the first quarter of 1980. However, the prospectus itself suggests that the back-office foul-ups should be considered business as usual. Its error rate was typically higher than average: 3.4 percent in 1978, 5.4 percent in 1979, and more than 10 percent in 1980.

Page 120   *"'In registering the deal with the SEC'. . . ."* From "A Big Setback for Discount Brokers," *Business Week*, August 18, 1980, pp. 94–95.

Page 121   *" 'Many observers think'. . . ."* From *Business Week*, August 18, 1990, p. 94.

Page 122   *"The company's cash needs were met. . . ."* First Nationwide Savings, the country's seventh largest savings and loan, bought 20 percent of the company, anticipating a move by Bank of America, which would also see in Schwab an opportunity to expand into the securities industry. First Nationwide's chairman, Anthony M. Frank, later became postmaster general during the first Bush administration and in 1993 joined the Schwab board of directors.

Chapter 8, Birthright

Page 126   *"'No Schwab will ever work for the Bank of America again!'"* The story is almost certainly apocryphal. Archivists at The Bank of America could not confirm it. According to Gary Hector, the Bank of Italy name disappeared on November 3, 1930, when it merged with Bank of America of California to become Bank of American National Trust and Savings Association. From Gary Hector, *Breaking the Bank: The Decline of BankAmerica* (Boston: Little, Brown and Company, 1988), p. 50.

Page 131   "'*Cultural incompatibility is a fact of life*' . . . ." In fact, the same dynamic happened when Schwab acquired Cyber-Corp in March 2000 and founder Philip R. Berber bolted because he couldn't tolerate the bigger company's oversight.

Page 132   "*McLin was through fencing with Moss. . . .* " From Hector, *Breaking the Bank*, p. 156.

Page 133   " '*After all the struggling we've done*'. . . ." From Joseph Nocera, *A Piece of the Action: How the Middle Class Joined the Money Class* (New York: Simon and Schuster, 1994), p. 269.

Page 133   "*However, Anthony Frank,. . . .*" From Moira Johnston, *Roller Coaster: The Bank of America and the Future of American Banking* (New York: Ticknor & Fields, 1990), p. 149.

Page 134   " '*We're doing that 20,000 times per day*'. . . ." Maybe on a very, very good day. Most days Schwab's volume was much less. McLin remembers a decidedly low-tech blackboard at Schwab that kept track of the number of trades. When the tally hit 1,000, people cheered. It didn't happen often. "If the daily tally hit 1,000, it was a huge day," he says.

Page 135   "*A company that had never made as much as. . . .*" From Nocera, *A Piece of the Action*, pp. 271–272.

Page 135   "*When Chuck rebuffed him. . . .*" From Nocera, *A Piece of the Action*, p. 272. It is a mark of Chuck's generosity that years after firing Moss, he invited him to participate in the profits of taking the company private again.

Page 138   " '*In this case, we redefined the problem*'. . . ." From David S. Pottruck and Terry Pearce, *Clicks and Mortar: Passion-Driven Growth in an Internet-Driven World* (New York: John Wiley & Sons, 2001), p. 145.

Page 139   "*The results were far worse than anyone expected. . . .*" From Nocera, *A Piece of the Action*, p. 326.

Page 140   " '*What a naïve, dumb guy I was*'. . . ." From Johnston, *Roller Coaster*, p. 250.

Page 141   " '*It was a great liberating thing*'. . . ." Ibid., p. 310.

Page 141   " '*I could go across the street*'. . . ." Ibid., p. 151.

Page 142   "*Milken was, Quackenbush says,. . . .*" The italics are Quackenbush's. Ibid, p. 328.

Chapter 9, Market Crash

Page 144 *"From the prospectus filed with the SEC. . . ."* Registration number 16192, Form S-1 Registration Statement filed July 31, 1987.

Page 147 *"'Better [Chuck and his executives] had taken cash instead'. . . ."* From "How Schwab's Hierarchy will Profit on Stock Sale," *San Francisco Chronicle*, August 20, 1987, A:30.

Page 152 *"'There were times that day when stock traders'. . . ."* From Joseph Nocera, *A Piece of the Action: How the Middle Class Joined the Money Class* (New York: Simon and Schuster, 1994), p. 355.

Page 154 *"And selling naked index puts was a risky, even reckless form of stock speculation."* Options are bets on the future price of a stock, or on the direction of the market itself. Put options oblige the investor to buy or sell an underlying stock, or set of stocks, at a future date. When you sell index puts, the partner who buys them from you has the right to sell you the value of an index at a certain price. If the market goes down, the seller has to pay that certain price for something that now has little or no value. What makes options so attractive also makes them so dangerous. Options traders put up very little of the purchase price at the time they buy their option. The ante is small or—in the case of a "naked" or uncovered option, nonexistent—and if the bet pays off, the winnings can be enormous. But the reverse is just as true. Should the market suddenly turn against them, investors must then deliver the stock underlying the option. The result is a margin call. If the investor is unable to meet his obligations, then the brokerage firm that sold the option is responsible.

Page 157 *"'We could talk for a long time. . . .'"* From David S. Pottruck and Terry Pearce, *Clicks and Mortar: Passion-Driven Growth in an Internet-Driven World* (New York: John Wiley & Sons, 2001), p. 41.

Chapter 10, Margin Call

Page 161 *"The* New York Times *had no such reticence. . . ."* *New York Times*, November 3, 1987, IV 26:4.

Page 161   " *'No one knew he was going around'. . . .*" "Looking to the Long Term," *Nation's Business,* December 1998, p. 43.

Page 167   "*Rosseau quickly put a stop to that.*" From Joseph Nocera, *A Piece of the Action: How the Middle Class Joined the Money Class* (New York: Simon and Schuster, 1994), p. 364.

Chapter 12, OneSource

Page 185   " *'In the days before supermarkets'. . . .*" Tim Ferguson, "Do it Yourself: Charles Schwab Has Ridden the Bull Market to a Splendid Present, but Its Future Is in Boomer Retirements," *Forbes,* April 22, 1996, p. 70.

Page 185   "*'In the past, anyone who wanted a diversified portfolio'. . . .*" David Whitford, "The Mutual Fund Revolution: Is it Good for You?," *Fortune,* February, 1997.

Page 188   "*'Oh, this will be easy.'. . . .*" From David S. Pottruck and Terry Pearce, *Clicks and Mortar: Passion-Driven Growth in an Internet-Driven World* (New York: John Wiley & Sons, 2001), p. 99.

Page 189   " *'To take advantage of Schwab's marketing and distribution'. . . .*" From Adrian J. Slywotzky, *Value Migration,* (Cambridge: Harvard Business Bulletin, 2001), p. 221.

Page 189   " *'To gain access to Schwab's distribution network'. . . .*" Ibid., p. 222.

Chapter 13, Heart Attack

Page 184   " *'My law school training heightened an already unhealthy sense of perfectionism,'. . . .*" From "Growing (with) a Company: Lessons in Leadership Learned at Yale Law School," *Yale Symposium on Law and Technology, 2000.* Available at http://lawtech.law.yale.edu/symposium/00/speech_stupski.htm.

Page 197   "*Stupski turned him down in favor of Bernell V. Flath, . . .*" Bernie Flath was a senior vice president responsible for branch expansion—identifying markets for new branches and supervising the real estate and facilities details involved. With his deep background in all aspects of the securities business, he was a resource of first choice for hundreds of Schwab executives. "He was the first guy I'd go to at Schwab when I needed advice about how to handle a situation from an operational or risk perspective," Anne Hennegar says. When he retired in 1993, the company had 208 branches.

Page 207   " *'How many of you went to the same place on vacation more than once,' . . . .*" From David S. Pottruck and Terry Pearce, *Clicks and Mortar: Passion-Driven Growth in an Internet-Driven World* (New York: John Wiley & Sons, 2001), p. 143.

Chapter 14, eSchwab

Page 212   " *'Schwab's instincts, honed through years of competition' . . . .*" From Adrian J. Slywotzky and David J. Morrison, *How Digital Is Your Business?* (New York: Crown Business, 2000), p. 121.

Page 215   " *'Back in 1994, when the Net first gave inconspicuous signals' . . . .*" From David Stauffer, *Dinosaur to Dynamo: How 20 Established Companies Are Winning in the New Economy* (Oxford, U.K.: Capstone, 2001), p. 101.

Page 216   " *'But if we hadn't stumbled around with it for 10 years,' . . . .*" From Clinton Wilder, "Leaders of the Net Era," *Information Week*, November 27, 2000.

Page 217   " *'The new enterprise was going to use a' . . . .*" From David S. Pottruck and Terry Pearce, *Clicks and Mortar: Passion-Driven Growth in an Internet-Driven World* (New York: John Wiley & Sons, 2001), p. 158.

Page 217   " *'Breakneck change and a raft of Internet upstarts' . . . .*" From Jerry Useem, "Internet Defense Strategy: Cannibalize Yourself," *Fortune*, September 6, 1999.

Page 221   " *Even Pottruck himself wasn't quite sure of what he was doing. . . .*" Ibid.

Page 221   " *Based on a number of contemporaneous sources, the conversation went like this. . . .*" See Schonfeld, Erick, "Schwab Puts it All Online," *Fortune*, December, 1998; Perkins, Tony, "The Red Eye: The Year of Clicks and Mortar," *Red Herring*, April 11, 2000; "Hearts and Souls: an Interview with David Pottruck and Terry Pearce," *Context*, December 2001.

Chapter 15, Balance of Power

Page 228 *"'By no stretch of the imagination' . . . ."* From David S. Pottruck and Terry Pearce, *Clicks and Mortar: Passion-Driven Growth in an Internet-Driven World* (New York: John Wiley & Sons, 2001), p. 77.

Page 229 *"'I had worked for some great companies' . . . ."* Ibid., p. 8.

Page 231 *"'Larry, how can a leader be too persuasive?'"* This exchange has been reconstructed from interviews with one of the principles and supplemented by accounts of the conversation as described in Pottruck and Pearce's *Clicks and Mortar*, page 35, and Joe Nocera, "A Mug Only 20,000 Employees Could Love..." *eCompany*, June 2000. Available at http://www.business2.com/articles/mag/0,1640,6584,00.html.

Page 232 *"'I needed to examine the extent to which' . . . ."* From Joe Nocera, "A Mug Only 20,000 Employees Could Love," *eCompany*, June 2000.

Page 233 *"'He out-trained and out-worked everybody' . . . ."* Ibid.

Page 233 *"'It was like being on the inside' . . . ."* Ibid.

Page 234 *"'What I came to learn was that I didn't have a wife selection problem. I had a husband behavior problem,' . . . ."* From Pottruck and Pearce, *Clicks and Mortar*, pp. 113–114.

Page 235 *"'Later, when I thought over Chuck's message,' . . . ."* Ibid., p. 95.

Page 236 *"'My staff and I would rehearse the answers' . . . ."* Ibid., p. 117.

Page 237 *"'These changes did nothing to alter' . . . ."* From Terry Pearce, *Leading Out Loud: The Authentic Speaker The Credible Leader* (New York: Jossey-Bass, 1995), pp. 6–7.

Page 241 *"The company announced that Chuck's second in command, ..."* The other officers of the company included Timothy McCarthy, president and chief operating officer of the brokerage division. Seven executive vice presidents were given the more prestigious title of enterprise president: Karen Change, in charge of general investor services; Susanne Lyons, in charge of active trader and affluent customer services; Linnet Deily, services for investment managers; Lon Gorman, capital markets and trading; Gideon Sasson, electronic brokerage; John Coghlan, retirement plan services; and Tom Seip, international and mutual funds. Within four years, McCarthy, Deily, Lyons, and Seip would be gone.

Chapter 17, Unfinished Business

Page 255   *"Pottruck thought Seip's speech so remarkable . . . ."* From David S. Pottruck and Terry Pearce, *Clicks and Mortar: Passion-Driven Growth in an Internet-Driven World* (New York: John Wiley & Sons, 2001), pp. 22–25. It is instructive to compare the full text of the speech with the edited version in *Clicks and Mortar*. Pottruck used the speech as an example of Schwab culture in action, and that it is. But the speech is also a revealing gloss on how an employee internalizes that culture. Pottruck omits most of Seip's personal reflections and all of his references to Schwab colleagues.

Page 261   *"Pottruck calls Seip a 'highly principled, thoughtful, and dedicated man,' . . ."* Ibid., p. 22.

Page 262   *"'Nothing really will change for me,' . . . ."* Arthur M. Louis, "Schwab Gives Its President Co-CEO Title, *San Francisco Chronicle*, December 2, 1997. In 2000, Chuck and Pottruck were each paid a salary of $800,004 and a bonus of $8,101,000. In 2001, to reflect the poor performance of the company, they reduced their salaries to $650,000 each and, like the other executives, received no bonus.

Page 262   *"I would consider myself unrecruitable . . . . I don't have any plans to leave.' . . ."* Arthur M. Louis, "Schwab's No. 2 Carries the Weight: Broker's COO Keeps the Wheels Turning Smoothly," *San Francisco Chronicle*, February 12, 1996.

Page 263   *"'I've been doing this business for 25 years,' . . . ."* Christian Berthelsen, "Schwab Senior Exec Resigns: Retail Investment Chief Wanted More Autonomy," *San Francisco Chronicle*, February 21, 2002.

BIBLIOGRAPHY

Aaker, David A., and Erich Joachimsthaler. *Brand Leadership*. New York: The Free Press, 2000.

Arbel, Avner, and Albert E. Kaff. *Crash: Ten Days in October . . . Will It Strike Again?* Longman Financial Services Publishing, 1989.

Bell, Chip R., and Oren Hari. *Beep! Beep! Competing in the Age of the Road Runner*. New York: Warner Business Books, 2001.

Bernstein, Peter L. *Against the Gods: The Remarkable Story of Risk*. New York: John Wiley & Sons, 1996.

Boulton, Richard E. S., Barry D. Libert, and Steve M. Samek. *Cracking the Value Code: How Successful Businesses Are Creating Wealth in the New Economy*. New York: HarperBusiness, 2000.

Bowen, John, and Daniel C. Goldie. *The Prudent Investor's Guide to Beating Wall Street at Its Own Game*. New York: McGraw-Hill, 1998.

Brandenburder, Adam M., and Barry J. Nalebuff. *Co-optition*. New York: Doubleday, 1996.

Brouwer, Kurt, and Stephen Janachowski. *Mutual Fund Mastery: Wealth-Building Secrets from America's Investment Pros*. New York: Times Business, 1997.

Burke, Dan, and Alan Morrison. *Business @ the Speed of Stupid: Building Smarter Companies After the Technology Shakeout*. Cambridge, MA: Perseus Publishing, 2001.

Cassidy, John. *Dot.con: The Greatest Story Ever Told*. New York: Harper Collins, 2002.

Christensen, Clayton M. *The Innovator's Dilemma.* New York: Harberbusiness, 2000.

Cohan, Peter S. *Net Profit: How to Invest and Compete in the Wild World of Internet Business.* San Francisco: Jossey-Bass, 2001.

Colbert, David. *Eyewitness to Wall Street: Four Hundred Years of Dreamers, Schemers, Busts and Booms.* New York: Broadway Books, 2001.

Cole, Benjamin Mark. *The Pied Pipers of Wall Street: How Analysts Sell You Down the River.* Princeton, NJ: Bloomberg Press, 2001.

Collins, Jim. *Good to Great: Why Some Companies Make the Leap . . . and Others Don't.* New York: Harper Collins, 2001

Cousineau, Phil. *The Once and Future Myth.* Berkeley: Conari Press, 2001.

Cronin, Mary J. *Unchained Value: The New Logic of Digital Business.* Boston: Harvard Business School Press, 2000.

Dauphinias, G. William, Grady Means, and Colin Price. *Wisdom of the CEO: 29 Global Leaders Tackle Today's Most Pressing Business Challenges.* New York: John Wiley & Sons, 2000.

Dauten, Dale. *The Gifted Boss.* New York: William Morrow, 1999.

Davis, Bob. *Speed Is Life: Street Smart Lessons from the Front Lines of Business.* New York: Currency, 2001.

Deal, Terrence E., and Allan A. Kennedy. *The New Corporate Cultures: Revitalizing the Workplace after Downsizing, Mergers, and Reengineering.* Cambridge, MA: Perseus, 1999.

Downes, Larry, and Chunka Mui. *Unleashing the Killer App: Digital Strategies for Market Dominance.* Boston: Harvard Business School Press, 1998.

Doz, Yves L., and Gary Hamel. *Alliance Advantage: The Art of Creating Value through Partnering.* Boston: Harvard Business School Press, 2001.

Evensky, Harold. *Wealth Management: The Financial Advisor's Guide to Investing and Managing Your Client's Assets.* New York: McGraw-Hill, 1996.

Farrell, Paul B. *Mutual Funds on the Net: Making Money Online.* New York: John Wiley & Sons, 1997.

Fradkin, Philip L. *Magnitude 8: Earthquakes and Life Along the San Andreas Fault.* New York: Henry Holt, 1998.

Garten, Jeffrey E. *The Mind of the C.E.O.* New York: Basic Books, 2001.

Godin, Seth. *If You're Clueless About Mutual Funds and Want to Know More*. Chicago: Dearborn Publishing, 1997.

Goldenberg, Susan. *Trading: Inside the World's Leading Stock Exchanges*. New York: Harcourt Brace Jovanovich, 1986.

Hamel, Gary. *Leading the Revolution*. Boston: Harvard Business School Press, 2000.

Handy, Charles. *The Age of Unreason*. Cambridge: Harvard Business School Press, 1989.

Hartman, Amir, John Sifonis, and John Kador. *Net Ready: Strategies for Success in the E-conomy*. New York: McGraw-Hill, 2000.

Hector, Gary. *Breaking the Bank: The Decline of BankAmerica*. Boston: Little, Brown and Company, 1988.

Hoover, Gary. *Hoover's Vision: Original Thinking for Business Success*. New York: Trexere, 2001.

Jennings, Jason, and Lawrence Houghton. *It's Not the Big That Eat the Small, It's the Fast That Eat the Slow*. New York: HarperCollins, 2001.

Johnston, Moira. *Roller Coaster: The Bank of America and the Future of American Banking*. New York: Ticknor & Fields, 1990.

Judson, Bruce. *HyperWars: 11 Essential Strategies for Survival and Profit in the Era of Online Business*. New York: Touchstone, 1999.

Kanter, Rosabeth Moss. *eVolve!: Succeeding in the Digital Culture of Tomorrow*. Boston: Harvard Business School Press, 2001.

Kazanjian, Kirk. *Wizards of Wall Street: Marketing-Beating Insights and Strategies for the World's Top-Performing Mutual Fund Managers*. New York: New York Institute of Finance, 2000.

Keywell, Brad. *Biz Dev 3.0: Changing Business As We Know It*. New York: ALM Publishing, 2001

Klebanoff, Arthur. *The Agent: Personalities, Politics & Publishing*. New York: Texere Publishing, 2001.

Levine, Rick, Christopher Locke, Doc Searls, and David Weinberger. *The Cluetrain Manifesto*. Cambridge, MA: Perseus Books, 2000.

Martin, Chuck. *New Future: The Seven Cybertrends That Will Drive Your Business, Create New Wealth, and Define Your Future*. New York: McGraw-Hill, 2000.

Maxwell, John C. *The 21 Irrefutable Laws of Leadership: Follow Them Well and People will Follow You*. Nashville: Thomas Nelson, 1998.

Mayer, Martin. *Markets: Who Plays, Who Risks, Who Gains, Who Loses?* New York: W.W. Norton & Company, 1988

Mayer, Martin. *The Bankers: The Next Generation. The New World of Money, Credit and Banking in an Electronic Age.* New York: Truman Talley Books, 1997.

McGehee, Tom. *Swoosh. Business in the Fast Lane: Unleashing the Power of a Creation Company.* Cambridge, MA: Perseus Publishing, 2001.

Metz, Tim. *Black Monday: The Catastrophe of October 19, 1987 and Beyond.* New York: William Morrow, 1988.

Mitchell, Lawrence E. *Corporate Irresponsibility.* New Haven: Yale University Press, 2001.

Morrison, Ian. *The Second Curve: How to Command New Technologies, and New Consumers, and New Markets.* New York: Ballantine Books, 2001.

Naisbitt, John. *Megatrends 2000.* New York: Avon, 1991.

Neff, Thomas J., and James M. Citrin. *Lessons from the Top: The 50 Most Successful Business Leaders in America—and What You Can Learn From Them.* New York: Currency Doubleday, 1999.

Nocera, Joseph. *A Piece of the Action: How the Middle Class Joined the Money Class.* New York: Simon and Schuster, 1994.

Nolan, Richard. *Dot Vertigo: Doing Business in a Permeable World.* New York: John Wiley & Sons, 2001.

Pearce, Terry. *Leading Out Loud: The Authentic Speaker, the Credible Leader.* New York: Josey-Bass, 1995.

Pottruck, David S., and Terry Pearce. *Clicks and Mortar: Passion-Driven Growth in an Internet Driven World.* New York: John Wiley & Sons, 2001.

Ragas, Matthew W. *Lessons from the Efront: 50 Top Business Leaders Reveal Their Hard-Won Wisdom on Building a Successful High-Tech Enterprise.* Roseville, CA: Prima Venture, 2001.

Rayport Jeffrey F., and Bernard J. Jaworski. *e-Commerce,* McGraw-Hill/ Irwin, 2001.

Reich, Robert B. *The Future of Success.* New York: Knopf, 2001.

Rothchild, John. *A Fool and His Money: The Odyssey of an Average Investor.* New York: Viking, 1988.

Sawi, Beth. *Coming Up for Air: How to Build a Balanced Life in a Workaholic World.* New York: Hyperion Books, 2000.

Schwab, Charles. *How to Be Your Own Stockbroker.* New York: Macmillan Publishing, 1984.

Schwab, Charles. *Charles Schwab's Guide to Financial Independence: Simple Solutions for Busy People.* New York: Crown, 1988.

Schwartz, Evan I. *Digital Darwinism: 7 Breakthrough Business Strategies for Surviving the Cutthroat Web Economy.* New York: Broadway Books, 1999.

Siebel, Thomas M. *Cyber Rules: Strategies for Excelling at E-Business.* New York: Currency/Doubleday, 1999.

Slywotzky, Adrian J., and David J. Morrison. *How Digital Is Your Business?* New York: Crown Business, 2000.

Slywotzky, Adrian. J. *Value Migration.* Cambridge: Harvard Business Books, 2001.

Smith, B. Mark. *Toward Rational Exuberance: The Evolution of the Modern Stock Market.* New York: Farrar, Straus and Giroux, 2001.

Stauffer, David. *Dinosaur to Dynamo: How 20 Established Companies Are Winning in the New Economy.* Oxford, U.K.: Capstone, 2001.

Stern, Carl W., and George Stalk Jr., editors. *Perspectives on Strategy from the Boston Consulting Group.* New York: John Wiley & Sons, 1998.

Stewart, Thomas A. *The Wealth of Knowledge: Intellectual Capital and the Twenty-First Century Organization.* New York: Currency, 2001.

Stoneman, Tracy Pride, and Douglas J. Schulz. *Brokerage Fraud: What Wall Street Doesn't Want You to Know.* Chicago: Dearborn Trade Publishing, 2002.

Tapscott, Don, David Ticoll, and Alex Lowy. *Digital Capital: Harnessing the Power of Business Webs.* Boston: Harvard Business School Press, 2000.

Treacy, Michael, and Fred Wiersema. *The Discipline of Market Leaders: Choose Your Customers, Narrow Your Focus, Dominate Your Market.* Reading, MA: Addison-Wesley, 1995.

Trout, Jack. *Differentiate or Die: Survival in Our Era of Killer Competition.* New York: John Wiley & Sons, 2000.

Wang, Charles. *TechnoVision: The Executive's Guide for Understanding and Managing Technology.* New York: McGraw-Hill, 1994.

Wasserstein, Bruce. *Big Deal: Mergers and Acquisitions in the Digital Age.* New York: Warner Business, 2001.

Accounting Today, 99
Acquisitions, 100, 274–275
Advertising campaigns, 42–43, 47, 80,
  158, 235–236, 274, 276
Advice, core values and, 2, 6–7, 42,
  57–58
AdvisorSource program, 105–110,
  241, 275
After-Hours trading, 277
Agee, William, 81
Agnos, Art, 176
Ahmajan, Barbara L. (later Wolfe),
  119
Alliances, 276
Ameritrade, 79, 91, 211, 216
Andersen Consulting, 266
Andrews, Rhet, 102, 153–154, 158
A Piece of the Action (Nocera), 115, 294
Armacost, Samuel H., 129–131,
  133–135, 137, 139–141
Arnold, Richard W., 43, 120, 140,
  142–143, 148, 196, 201
Asset management, 99–100

Back office
  management, 48–51
  settlement system, 54–55, 274
Baily, Tom, 187
Baker, James, Treasury Secretary, 150
Baldwin, Mike, 53

BankAmerica Corporation, *see* Bank
  of America
Banking services, future directions in,
  265–266, 272
Bank of America
  acquisition of Charles Schwab &
    Co., Inc., 129–132, 136
  Armacost, Samuel H., as CEO,
    129–131, 133–135, 137, 139–141
  ATM network, 63
  BASH (Bank of America and
    Schwab), 138
  Black Monday, impact on, 152
  board of directors, 139
  branches, growth of, 125
  establishment of, 124–125
  leveraged buyout (LBO) from,
    141–147, 275
  losses, 140
  sale to, 7, 56–57, 63, 76, 123–127,
    133–135, 274
  stock decline, 135–136, 147–148
  success of, 124
Bank of Italy, 125
Barmann, Mark, 175, 201, 208,
  231–232
BASH (Bank of America and
  Schwab), 138
Batten, William, 81
Bear Stearns, 25, 105

Bentham, Jeremy, 223
Bernstein, Peter, 21
BETA (Brokerage Execution and
     Transaction Analysis) system,
     54–55, 119, 211
Biggs, Barton, 187
Black Monday, 7, 149–152
Bloodgood, William G., 119
Bloomberg News, 263
Bonus program, 92, 272
Booker, Katrina, 17–18
Bowen, John, 73, 99, 110
Branch offices
    advice rules/principles, changes in,
        102–103
    asset gathering, 92
    in Bank of America, 137
    Black Monday, impact on, 153
    bricks-and-mortar, 222
    compensation structure, 92–94, 272
    competition in, 93, 95–96
    broker description of, 93–94, 96
    customer need for, 77–78
    eSchwab and, 219–220
    establishment of, 41, 75–77, 274
    lease problems, 59–60
    list of, 78–80
    Loma Prieta earthquake, impact
        on, 179–181, 275
    management, 96–97
    marketing of, 78
    products offered, 81–82
    Schwab.com and, 223
    success of, 76–77
    success factors, 82–83
    value of, 91–92
    Welcome Representative program,
        94–97
    workload, 96
Brandin, Mark, 201
*Breaking the Bank: The Decline of Bank
    America* (Hector), 132
Broker(s), generally
    full-commission, 17–18, 21
    salaried, 42, 89, 272
    as salespeople, 14–15, 57, 101, 250

selection factors, 15
Series 7 license, 48
Brokerage industry, *see also* Financial
     services industry
    confidence crisis, 9–10
    corruption in, 5–6
    gender discrimination, 86
    monopoly in, 17–20
    trading rate deregulation, 19,
        24–25, 40, 42–43, 273–274
Broker–investor relationship, 58, 60,
     81–83, 88
Burke, Dan, 105
Business cycles, 29, 32, 35
Business Week, 120–121

Caen, Herb, 142
California
    earthquake, impact of, 171–181,
        275
    San Francisco location, benefits of,
        21–22, 40, 246
Call center reps, 87–89. *See also*
     Customer service telephone
     centers
Capital requirements, 56, 114
Capital resources, *see* Financial
     resources
Cardinal, Bruce, 65–66, 71
Carter, President Jimmy, 61
Casey, William, 81
Cash Management Account (CMA),
     84, 89–90, 274
CEG Worldwide, 73
Chang, Karen, 258
Chaos management
    employee descriptions of, 48–51,
        115–117
    journalist perspectives, 121
Chaos theory, 36
Charles Schwab & Co., Inc., generally
    assets, 2, 214, 240
    board of directors, 149, 251–252,
        261, 263
    core values, *see* Core values
    daily average trades, 44

development/establishment of, 13, 15, 40

as discount brokerage, 40–44, 128–129

expansion strategies, 114–115

financial resources, *see* Financial resources

future directions for, 264–267

growth of, 47–48, 113, 115, 122, 135

market capitalization, 224, 248, 277

monthly statements, 45

120 Montgomery Street, 49–51

NYSE membership, 113, 274

order volume, 55–56

performance of, 12, 135, 140, 172, 214

profitability/success of, 113–115

sale price, 136, 142

San Francisco location, 21–22, 40, 246

Schwab.com, impact of, 223–224

traditional brokerages compared with, 85–87

Charles Schwab Corporation, The, 104, 208, 275–276

Charles Schwab Europe, 276

Charles Schwab Investment Management, Inc., 198

Charles Schwab's Guide to Financial Independence: Simple Solutions for Busy People (Schwab), 241

Charles Schwab Trust Company, 276

Chase H&Q, 276

Checking account, 90

Chief executive officers (CEOs), *see* McCarthy, Timothy F.; Pottruck, David; Schwab, Charles R.

Chief financial officer (CFO), *see* Gambs, A. John

Chief operating officers (COOs), *see* Pearson, Bill; Stupski, Lawrence J.

Chinese Wall, 24

Christensen, Clayton, 73

Clark, Dennis, 109–110

Clausen, Tom, 129, 141–143

Clicks and Mortar: Passion Driven Growth in an Internet Driven World (Pottruck), 69, 71, 207, 229–230, 234, 255, 293

Clicks and mortar strategy, 8, 222

Co-chief-executive structure, 9, 241, 253, 261–263

Coaching, 202–203, 208, 232–235

Coghlan, John, 99, 104, 187, 254–255, 258, 260

Cold calling, 35, 41, 57, 93, 271

Cole, Benjamin Mark, 17, 58

Coming Up for Air: How to Build a Balanced Life in a Workaholic World (Sawi), 206

Commander Corporation, 39

Commissions
  core values and, 2, 101
  deregulation of, 5–6, 13, 15–16, 19, 40, 42–43, 273–274
  earning strategies, 14–15
  fixed, 15–17, 20, 132
  NYSE and, 16–17, 20–21
  one-price-trading scheme, 221–223
  structure, 15

Commitment, importance of, 202, 237, 259

Compensation structure, 92–94, 157

Competency, importance of, 106, 217

Competition, *see also specific corporations*
  online trading, 215–216
  financial advisors and, 104
  obstacles from, 59–60

Compliance issues, 85, 103–104

Computer Associates International, "Simply Money," 69–70

Computer technology, importance of, 52, 62, 213–214

Conflict-of-interest-free trading, 2, 42, 44, 57, 81, 98, 101, 250, 272

Congoland, USA, 38–39

Consumer behavior, impact of, 61

Consumer Price Index (CPI), 61

Controller, *see* Moss, Peter

Core values
  in branch offices, 82
  cause, creation of, 3
  importance of, 202, 269
  legends and, 248–249
  types of, 2, 202
Creating Equity: How to Build a Hugely Successful Asset Management Business (Bowen), 99
Credit department, risk management, 157
Crisis management
  California earthquake, 171–181, 275
  employee descriptions of, 48–51, 115–116
  during growth, 115–116
  initial public offering, *see* Initial public offerings (IPOs)
  journalist perspectives, 121
  margin calls, 159–170
  stock market crash of 1987, 150–158, 182–183, 275
  Stupski, Larry, heart attack, 191–208, 256, 276
Crocker Bank, 76
CS/First Boston, 276
Culture, power of, 3–4
Customer loyalty, 58, 70, 83
Customer profiles, 104
Customer relationship management, 83–84, 88, 265
Customer retention, 104–105
Customer segmentation, 105
Customer service
  as core value, 2, 42, 82
  importance of, 182–183
  post-Bank of America merger, 138–139
  post-Black Monday, illustration of, 152–156
  traffic light signal system, 48
  world class, 202
Customer service telephone centers
  on Black Monday, 152
  call volume, 87–88

establishment of, 59, 68, 274–276
  importance of, 87–88
  integrated voice response (IVR) system, 88
  Market Storm, 88
  purpose of, 59, 87
  taped transactions, 102
Cutcliffe, Joe, 199–201, 202–203, 238–240
Cyclicality, 29, 31

Day traders, 50, 275
Debit cards, 90
Decision-making process, 5
Deep-discount brokerages, 216
Deily, Linnett, 258
Delegators, 105
Diener, Alan, 179–180
Dinosaur to Dynamo: How 20 Established Companies Are Winning in the New Economy (Stauffer), 215
Disaster recovery, 181
Discount brokerage, establishment of, 40–42, 128–129
Discounting, 20, 132
Dong, Ken, 50
Dongieux, Gene, 99
Dow Jones Industrial Average, 145, 149–150, 152
Dow Jones News Service, 67, 180
Drexel Burnham Lambert, 161
Dreyfus, 90, 151
Dryden, Phyllis Kay, 149

Edward Jones, 91
EF Hutton, 22, 40
800 toll-free telephone services, 59
Electric.Dave (D. Pottruck's e-mail address), 215
Electronic Brokerage, 276
Electronic trading, development of, 3, 210–211. *See also* eSchwab; Schwab.com
E-mail, 214–215, 271–272
Employee(s)
  Bank of America merger, 137

chaos management descriptions, 48–51, 115–117
dedication of, 115, 158, 178–179
earthquake, impact on, 173–175, 178–179
eSchwab, 220–221
hiring of, interviews, 21, 51
layoffs, 277
number of, 113
telephone call centers, 87–89, 102–103
treatment of, 86–87, 158
Empowerment, customer, 2, 42, 58, 212
End-around trading, 20
Enron, 24, 266
Equalizer, The, 68–69, 211, 213, 215, 275–276
eSchwab
commissions, 219–220
customer service, 219–220
development of, 8, 209–216
employees, 220–221
launch of, 219, 276
leadership, 218–220
one-price-trading scheme, 221–222
revenues, 217, 221
staffing, 218
Ethics, 86–87. *See also* Core values
E*Trade, 65, 79, 91, 117, 211–212, 216, 219
Evensky, Harold, 99–100, 107, 110

Farson, Doug, 142
Federal Reserve, 134–135
Fidelity Investments, 66, 72, 90,104,151, 184–185
Financial advisors
fee-based, 106–107
as free agents, 103
investment management criteria, 106–107
Financial crises, 75–76, 122, 124–126
Financial Independence software, 69–70, 275

Financial resources
personal funds, 127
private placement, 122
remortgages, 114
Schwab, William, 15, 39–40, 75–76
Financial services industry, investor confidence and, 266
First Boston Corporation, The, 146
First Commander Corporation, 14–15, 39–40, 273
Fisher, Donald G., 149
Fivis, Robert W., 148
Flath, Bernell V., 197
FOCUS (Financial and Operational Combined Uniform Securities) report, 56
Forbes, 168, 185
Ford, President Gerald, 61
Fortune, 17, 185
Foster Investment Services, 35–36
Franchising, 197
Frank, Anthony M., 133, 147, 262
Friedman, Elliott D., 77
Friedman, Milton, Dr., 67
Front-end load funds, 15
Full-service brokerages
commissions and, 23
discount, 41
Fuller, Jim, 53, 77, 80–81, 84, 89–90, 117
Fundamental analysis, 24
Fund management, 186–188

Galbraith, John Kenneth, 38
Gambs, A. John, 21, 150–152, 157–159, 168, 174–175, 180, 201
Gates, Bill, 41, 244
Giannini, Amadeo Peter, 124–126
Gillis, William F., 64–69, 71, 211
Give-ups, 20
Glass-Steagall Act, 128–129
Global Crossing, 266
Go-Go Years, 14, 44
Gold and Company, 120
Goldman Sachs Group, 271
Great Depression, 149

Greed, impact of, 19–20
Grosskopf, Robert, 88–89
Growth/expansion phase, 114–115, 122, 215
Growth objectives, 202

Hackley, Jim, 255
Handy, Charles, 36
Harvey, James R., 149
Hector, Gary, 132
Heinrich, Barbara, 173, 230, 235
Hennegar, Anne, 44, 210
Hobbs, Woodson M., 148
Hoffman, Claire, 126
How Digital Is Your Business?, 212
How to Be Your Own Stockbroker
 (Schwab), 19, 29, 293
Human resource management, *see*
 Wheeler, Kevin; Wiggett, Jim

Inc., 39
Index mutual fund, defined, 58
Individual investor, importance of, 42, 202. *See also* Core values;
 Customer service
Individual retirement accounts (IRAs)
 legislation, 72
 No-Annual-Fee IRA, 3, 72–74, 184, 220, 275
Inflation, impact of, 61–62
Information Technology (IT), 71, 181, 209–210, 213
Infraction penalties, 60
Initial public offering (IPO)
 as capital resource, 114–115
 failure of, 118–122, 126
 on New York Stock Exchange, 144–145
 prospectus, 117–120, 147
 Schwab Technologies, 70–71
 success of, 145–146, 275
 underwriters, 118, 146
 withdrawal of, 118–119, 274
Innovation, 70, 72, 86. *See also* Product
 development; Schwab
 Technology Services

Innovator's Dilemma, The
 (Christensen), 73
Inside Information, 108
Integrity, importance of, 202
International market, 265, 277
Internet
 impact of, 64, 70, 211, 217–218
 trading, *see* eSchwab; Schwab.com
Investment Indicators, 14, 36, 273
Investment Indicators fund, 37, 39
Investment management criteria, 106
Investment reports, 23–24
Investment research, 18–19
Investor confidence, 9–10

James, Henry, 5
Jobs, Steve, 244
Johnson, Ned, 114
Johnston, Moira, 35
J.P. Morgan, 276

Kahr, Andrew, 89–91
Keen, Sam, 247
King, Mark, 87, 153
Kingsley, Boyd and Southwood, 274
Klipp, William, 260

Latin American Center, 276
Leading Out Loud (Pearce), 236
Leemon, Dan, 220
Legislation
 Glass-Steagall Act, 128–129
 Securities Act of 1933, 17
 Securities Act of 1934, 17
Lepore, Dawn, 213, 218
Letterman Transaction Services, 274
Leveraged buyout (LBO), from Bank
 of America, 141–147, 275
Levinson, Kathy, 115–117, 152–153, 157, 174, 181, 198, 208, 212
Levitt, Arthur, 15
Liability
 margin call, 159–170
 undisclosed contingent, 38

Loma Prieta earthquake
  descriptions of, 173–175
  101 Montgomery Street, building
    inspection, 177–178
  recovery strategies, 175–181
Los Angeles Times, 34
Losi, James, 154–155
Lyons, Jeffrey, 72–73
Lyons, Susanne, 222–223, 258

McCarthy, Timothy F., 253–256,
    260–261
McGonigle, John, 260
MacKillop, Scott, 99, 110
McLin, Stephen T., 127–134, 149
McNealy, Scott, 41
Management mind-set, 47. *See also*
    Top management
Margin account(s)
  cash management account, 89–90
  stock market crash of 1987, impact
    on, 150–156, 159–170
Margin calls, 7–8, 160–170
Margin debt, 152–156
Margin department, risk
    management, 157
Margin securities, 55–56, 60
Market capitalization, 224, 248, 277
Market Storm, 88, 249
Markups, 15
Marshall, Kathy, 181
May Day, 6, 13, 15, 21, 25–26, 43, 45,
    49, 274
Mayer & Schweitzer, 275
Meahan, Melinda, 49–50
MegaTrends 2000 (Naisbitt), 81
Merger, with Bank of America, *see*
    Bank of America
Meritocracy, 202
Merrill Lynch, 4, 17–18, 21–23, 25, 40,
    44, 58, 84, 91, 104–105, 107, 127,
    151, 185, 215, 224, 248, 269,
    271–272, 277
Micromanagement, 204
Microsoft, 41
Milken, Michael, 142

Mission, reframed, 105. *See also*
    Vision
Mistakes
  dealing with, 4–5, 115, 117,
    120–121
  Noble Failures, 216
Mitchell, Desmond, 36
Mitchell, Morse & Schwab, 36–37
Money market account, 90
Money market funds, 61–62
Monthly statements, 45, 107
Morgan Stanley & Co., 146
Morse, John, 36
Moss, Peter H., 59, 119, 128, 131–136,
    148, 201
Moszkowski, Guy, 189–190
Music Expo 1972, 39
Mutual Fund MarketPlace, 184, 188,
    220, 275
Mutual Fund OneSource
  benefits of, 186
  development of, 7, 103, 182–185,
    276
  fund families, 186
  risk management, 186–187
  StreetSmart Software, 185
  success of, 188–190
  trade execution, 185
  Version 1.0, 184–185
Mutual Fund Report Cards, 276
Mutual funds, *see also specific funds*
  development of, 7
  front-end loads, 15
  Investment Indicators, 14, 37
  Mutual Fund MarketPlace, 184,
    188, 220, 275
  OneSource, *see* Mutual Fund
    OneSource
  market outperformance, 14
  Select List, 276
Mythology
  creation of, 249–250
  in organizational culture, 243–244
  Schwab, Charles, 244–247
  underdog stories, 247–250
  us-against-them legend, 246–247

Naisbitt, John, 81
National Association of Securities
    Dealers, 60
National Tax-Free Bond Fund, 276
Newsletters
    development of, 14, 36
    Inside Information, 108
    Investment Indicators, 14, 36, 273
New York Stock Exchange (NYSE)
    capital requirements, 56, 114
    fixed commissions, 15–17, 20–21
    initial public offering on, 144
    inquiries from, 60
    membership in, 113, 274
    mutual funds volume, 184–185
    paperless transactions, 55
New York Times, 25, 72, 161
Nixon, President Richard M., 19–20
No-advice policy/rule
    change in, 98–110. *See also* Schwab
        Equity Ratings
    importance of, 2, 6–7, 42, 57–58,
        60–61, 82, 85, 100–101
No-Annual-Fee IRA, 2, 72–74, 184,
    220, 275
Noble Failures, 216
Nocera, Joseph, 115, 152, 294

Obstacles, overcoming
    branch office leases, 59–60
    telephone call center, 59
Old-boy networking, 18–19
O'Neill, Joseph I., 147
Online trading, 211
Options, 53
Options Clearing Corp., 274
Order tickets, 52–53
Organizational development theory,
    200, 203, 238–239
Oshman, M., Kenneth, 149
Ownership structure, in prospectus,
    120, 147

Pacific Coast Stock Exchange, 60, 274
PaineWebber, 84
Paper trails, 52–53

Pearce, Terry, 232, 234, 236–237
Pearson, Bill (Schwab COO), 43,
    50–53, 60, 118–120
Pearson, William, eSchwab
    development, 210–214
Perry, Earlene, 137–139, 173–175
Personal investment management, *see*
    AdvisorSource
Philadelphia Stock Exchange,
    Uniform Net Capital rule, 60, 76
*Pied Pipers of Wall Street: How Analysts
    Sell You Down the River, The*
    (Cole), 58
PocketTerm, 69
Porter, Bill, 65, 211
Portfolio diversification, 107
Pottruck, David
    accomplishments of, 241
    on advice/advisors, 105, 108–109
    AdvisorSource program, 241
    Bank of America merger, 137
    Bank of America, leveraged buyout,
        148
    as branch manager, 230
    as Charles Schwab Corp. president,
        208
    childhood, 228
    Clicks and Mortar, 69–71, 229–230,
        234, 255
    coaching, 208, 232–235
    as co-CEO, 116, 240–241, 262–264,
        276
    customer relationships, 96–99
    earthquake recovery, 175, 181
    educational background, 228–229
    as Electric.Dave, 215
    Equalizer, The, 216
    eSchwab, 213–214, 216–217,
        219–222
    family background, 227–228
    leadership skills, development of,
        233–234
    marriages, 232, 234
    managerial style, 74, 229–232
    market crash recovery, 155, 157, 169
    in marketing, 275

McCarthy, Timothy, relationship with, 253–254, 261

Mutual Fund OneSource program, 187–188

personality characteristics, 201, 228

professional experience, 227–229

responsibilities of, 9, 148, 183, 201

Schwab.com, 223–224

Schwab Equity Ratings, 269

succession planning, 208, 238–240, 251–267

workaholism, 207–208

working relationships, 238

Pottruck, Emily Scott, 234–235

Price fixing, 15–17, 20, 25–26

Private placement, 122

Product development, 63, 65, 70. *See also* Schwab Technologies; Technological advances

Prospectuses, 117–120

Prudent Investors Guide to Beating Wall Street at Its Own Game, The (Bowen), 99

Prudential, 104

Prussia, Leland, 129

Public relations, 44, 162–163

Pull business, 32, 58

Push business model, 32, 58

Quackenbush, Hugo, 40, 44, 77, 90, 119–120, 142, 149, 201

Rammer Duck, 53

Readmond, Ronald, 201

Reagan, President Ronald, 61–62, 80

Recommendations
  core values and, 2
  securities analysts', 24

Reconciliations, 51

Record-keeping, 107

Recruitment
  board of directors, 149
  employee interviews, 21, 51, 122
  investment management criteria, 106

Stupski, Larry, 195–196

Reed, John, 114, 229

Regan, Don, Treasury Secretary, 114

Reinvention strategies, 5–6, 9

Rescission, 37–38

Retirement planning, 277

Ridgeway, 274

Risk management, 60, 151, 157–159, 186–187, 253

Roame, Charles "Chip," 45

Roberts, Mr. and Mrs., 153–156

Rodden, Ed, 210

Rosenwald, E. John, Jr., 25

Rosseau, Robert H., 149, 163–169

Sales, core values and, 2, 250

Sales-oriented management, 109

S&P 500 index, 276

San Francisco Chronicle, 142, 147, 262

Sasson, Gideon, 218

Sawi, Elizabeth (Beth) Gibson, 149, 206, 218–220, 223

Scheid, Steven L., 263–264

Schulte, Buzz, 257

Schwab, Barbara M., 120

Schwab, Carrie, 38

Schwab, Charles, Jr. (Sandy), 34, 38, 102–103

Schwab, Charles R.
  adolescent years, 30–33
  Armacost, Samuel H., relationship with, 129–131, 139–141
  Bank of America, holdings and sale of, 134–135, 140, 147–148
  on Bank of America board of directors, 126, 141
  birth of, 1, 13, 28–29
  business lessons, in early years, 30–32
  charisma, 252
  chicken business, 30–31
  childhood, 29–30
  Charles Schwab & Co., Inc., establishment of, *see* Charles Schwab & Co., Inc.
  as co-CEO, 253–267

Schwab, Charles R. (*cont.*)
Congoland, USA, 38–39
dyslexia, dealing with, 27, 32–34
educational background, 31, 33–35
employment agreement, 141–142,
279–291
family background, 29–30
at Foster Investment Services, 35–36
golf, 32, 62
How to Be Your Own Stockbroker, 19,
29, 293
Investment Indicators fund, 37, 39
management style, 47–48
marriages, 38
Mitchell, Morse & Schwab, 36–37
Music Expo 1972, 39
nut enterprise, 30
personality characteristics, 27–28,
87
philanthropy, 34
privacy of, 28–29
professional experience, 34–37
prospectus description, 119–120,
147
rejection, dealing with, 30
responsibilities of, 148
Schwab, William, relationship with,
39–40, 75–76
succession planning, 199, 208
Texas lawsuit, 37–38
as visionary, 43, 183–184, 238
Schwab, Helen (daughter), 38
Schwab, Helen (wife), 34, 38, 56, 62,
114, 120, 126–127, 140
Schwab, Michael, 38
Schwab, Robert, 29
Schwab, Susan, 38
Schwab, Virginia, 38
Schwab, William, 15, 39–40, 75–76
Schwab Advisor Network, 277
Schwab California Bond Fund, 276
Schwab Capital Markets LP, 275
Schwab.com, 222–224, 277
Schwab Equity Ratings, 265, 269–272,
277
Schwab 500 accounts, 153

Schwab Foundation for Learning, 34,
240
SchwabFunds, 253, 260
Schwab Institutional, 104, 108
SchwabLine, 69, 211, 213
SchwabLink, 106–107, 275–276
Schwab One Account, 62, 81–82,
90–91, 274
Schwab 1000 Index Fund, 275
Schwab Private Client, 277
Schwab Profit Sharing Plan, 147
SchwabQuotes, 66–68, 274–275
Schwab Services for Investment
Managers (SIM), 98, 108–110
Schwab Technologies
Equalizer, The, 68–69, 275–276
establishment of, 64–65
Financial Independence, 69–70,
275
initial public offering (IPO), 70
PocketTerm, 69
product development, 65–69
SchwabLine, 69
SchwabLink, 275
SchwabQuotes, 66–68, 274–275. *See
also* Telebroker
Schwab Technology Services, 64
Schwab U.S. Government Bond Fund,
275
Securities Act of 1933, 17
Securities Act of 1934, 17
Securities analysts, functions of, 23–24
Securities and Exchange Commission
(SEC) regulation
capital requirements, 114
commissions deregulation, 15–16,
19–20, 38, 273–274
disclosure filings, 136
excess margin securities, 60
know-your-customer rule, 60–61
operations inquiries from, 60
prospectus registration, 120–121,
147
SEC FOCUS (Financial and
Operational Combined Uniform
Securities) report, 56

Securities Industry Association, 19
Seip, Tom, 91, 108, 174, 178,
    187–188, 195, 197–198, 210, 213,
    254–261
Self-directed investing, 2, 6–7, 42, 44,
    57–58, 83, 104–105
Series 7 broker's trading license, 48
Settlement system, automated, 54–55
Shaw, Art, 210
Shearson, 104
Sheeran, Lisa, 39
Silicon Valley, 22
Skinner, Jim, 84–85, 102, 180
Slywotzky, Adrian, 189
Smith Barney, 104
Snowbarger, Barry G., 149
Solomon Smith Barney, 189–190
Spaugh, Patricia, 44–45, 53
Stauffer, David, 215
Stockbrokers, *see* Broker(s)
Stock market crash of 1987, *see also*
    Black Monday
    customer service, illustration of,
        152–156
    impact of, 7, 150–152, 157, 160,
        162, 170, 182–183, 275
    market recovery, 157–158
Stock quotes, automated, 66, 274
Strategic planning, 59
StreetSmart software, 185, 210, 213,
    216, 276
Stupski, Joyce, 205
Stupski, Lawrence J. (Larry)
    Bank of America merger, 124, 126,
        136–137
    as branch manager, 70, 73, 197, 274
    as chief operating officer (COO),
        122, 198–199, 201
    childhood, 193
    coaching of, 202–204, 238
    description of, 8, 192–193
    earthquake recovery, 175, 181
    educational background, 193–194
    family background, 175
    heart attack, 191–192, 204,
        206–207, 238, 256, 276

Pottruck, David, evaluation of,
    231–232
    professional experience, 193–195
    recruitment to Schwab, 116,
        195–196
    stock market recovery, 147–148,
        165
    Type A personality, 193–194,
        206–207
    as vice chairman, 239–240
Succession planning, 238–240,
    251–267
Sun America, 88
Sun Microsystems, 41

Taggart, Tom, 174–175, 207
Taylor, David, 60
Technological advances
    BETA (Brokerage Execution and
        Transaction Analysis) system,
        54–55, 119, 211
    disconnection, between
        technologists and
        businesspeople, 71
    Equalizer, 211, 213, 215–216
    eSchwab, 212–224
    SchwabLine, 211, 213
    significance of, 52, 54–57, 62, 64
    StreetSmart software, 210, 213, 216
    TechnoVision (Wang), 71
Telebroker, 68, 184, 275
Telephones, traffic light signal system,
    48
Texas, rescission litigation, 37–38
Thatcher, Margaret, 150–151
Thompson, Mark, 180
Tiburon Strategic Advisors, 45
Tinker, Grant, 4
Top management
    coaching, 202–203
    goal-setting, 202
    management styles, 199
    principles of, 202
    responsibilities of, 148–149,
        201–202
    workaholism, 206–207

Trade execution
  commissions and, 17, 223
  price of, 18–19
  trading rate, 6, 19
TradePlus, 65
Trading volume, implications of, 6,
  120–121, 152
Trustees, in prospectus, 120
21 Irrefutable Laws of Leadership, The
  (Maxwell), 252

UBS PaineWebber, 272
Umbay, Awk, 178
Unbundling services, 41
Uniform Net Capital rule, 60, 76, 118
U.S. Department of Justice, 19
Us-against-them legend, 246–247
U.S. Trust, acquisition of, 100, 277

Validators, defined, 105
Value Migration (Slywotzky), 189
Value-added business, characteristics
  of, 41, 71, 107–108, 212
Values-driven management
  benefits of, generally, 1
  core values, implications of, 2
Vanguard, 151
Venture capital, 122
Veres, Robert, 108
Vision, 43, 183–184
VisionQuest, 249

Wall Street Journal, 25, 42, 47, 62, 104,
  158, 180
Walther, Roger O., 149
Wang, Charles, 71, 244
Wang, Nina, 165–168
Wang, Teh-huei "Teddy," 161–170
Warm sales calls, 93, 271–272
Warrants, 148
Watson, Thomas J., 168
Wealth Management (Evensky), 99
Web-based services, 8, 89
Web dividend, 224
Welcome Representative program,
  94–97
Wheeler, Kevin, 22–23, 91–92
White, Donald K., 147
Wiggett, Jim, 33, 149, 175, 192, 199,
  204–205, 232
Wilshire Associates, 150
Wolfe, Barbara A. (Ahmajan), 148,
  201, 240, 256
Workaholism, 206–207
Wriston, Walter, 114, 229

Yee, Sherm, 221
Young President's Organization
  (YPO), 81

Zacks Investment Research, 24
Zakaria, Mansoor, 65, 68–71